'Reality is the page. Life is the word.'

David Mitchell , *number9dream*

GYLPHI CONTEMPORARY WRITERS: CRITICAL ESSAYS

Series Editor: Sarah Dillon

Gylphi Contemporary Writers: Critical Essays presents a new approach to the academic study of living authors. The titles in this series are devoted to contemporary British, Irish and American authors whose work is popularly and critically valued but on whom a significant body of academic work has yet to be established. Each of the titles in this series is developed out of the best contributions to an international conference on its author; represents the most intelligent and provocative material in current thinking about that author's work; and, suggests future avenues of thought, comparison and analysis. With each title prefaced by an author foreword, this series embraces the challenges of writing on living authors and provides the foundation stones for future critical work on significant contemporary writers.

Series Titles

David Mitchell: Critical Essays (2011)
Edited by Sarah Dillon. Foreword by David Mitchell.

Maggie Gee: Critical Essays (2013)
Edited by Sarah Dillon and Caroline Edwards. Foreword by Maggie Gee.

David Mitchell
Critical Essays

Edited by

Sarah Dillon

TWENTIETH CENTURY

Gylphi
ARTS &
HUMANITIES
PUBLISHER

AND BEYOND

A *Gylphi Limited* Book

First published in Great Britain in 2011
by Gylphi Limited

Copyright © Gylphi Limited, 2011

A CIP catalogue record for this book is available from the British Library.

ISBN 978-1-78024-002-2 (hbk)
ISBN 978-1-78024-003-9 (pbk)
ISBN 978-1-78024-004-6 (eBk)

Printed and bound in the UK by the
MPG Books Group, Bodmin and King's Lynn

Thanks are due to Kai and Sunny and Sceptre Books for allowing the cover to echo colours used on the cover of *number 9dream*.

Gylphi Limited
PO Box 993
Canterbury CT1 9EP
UK

For Isaac

Acknowledgements

I would like to thank Anthony Levings at Gylphi and the School of English, University of St Andrews, for their support in running the David Mitchell Conference. I would also like to thank all the paper-givers and attendees at the conference for making the event such a success – papers delivered there but not included here, as well as the discussion they prompted, have informed this collection. Finally, I would like to thank David Mitchell for attending the event, giving his support to this collection and creating the fictional world in which we all take such delight.

List of Abbreviations

Abbreviations of works cited by David Mitchell:

G   Mitchell, David (1999) *Ghostwritten*. London: Sceptre.

n9d   Mitchell, David (2001) *number9dream*. London: Sceptre.

CA   Mitchell, David (2004) *Cloud Atlas*. London: Sceptre.

BSG   Mitchell, David (2006) *Black Swan Green*. London: Sceptre.

TA   Mitchell, David (2010) *The Thousand Autumns of Jacob de Zoet*. London: Sceptre.

Contents

Contents

FOREWORD

David Mitchell

One danger of the question 'What was it like to attend a conference on your fiction?' is that your answer can inadvertently suggest an ego-trip of Saturn-V rocket-launcher proportions. Another difficulty is that you feel not one but many things, as I found during my three days as a guest of the University of St Andrews in September 2009, when the papers in this book were presented. First up was a sense of strangeness: the strangeness of being spoken about in the third person. This privilege is usually reserved for politicians, celebrities, criminals, eavesdroppers and ghosts, but not, on the whole, novelists. Maybe it was dicey for the academics, too – what if the notorious contrarian started heckling from the back row? To cope with this awkwardness we evolved an unspoken *modus operandi*: simply to pretend that the David Mitchell who wrote the books under discussion was not quite the same David Mitchell in the room, but rather a sort of dodgy twin. After the strangeness came trepidation, as it sunk in that over a hundred international academics had convened to discuss various aspects of my not-fat oeuvre of four novels. All those air-miles ... all those kilowatts of mind-energy expended by brains more methodical, cerebral and erudite than mine. What if I opened my mouth and pure drivel came gushing forth? (It's happened before, God knows, and it'll happen again.) Would all these bright people not feel hoodwinked if they found out that Derrida did my head in? Would the Literature Police kick down the bedroom door of my B&B and arrest me for imposture?

Luckily, I remained free to attend the first academic conference I'd ever been to, on writing in general and my writing in particular; and thereon in the dominant sensation was intellectual curiosity, well-fed.

The range of papers was diverse and stimulating. Sessions on Japan were followed by sessions on science fiction, on language, on postmodernism, the anatomy of narrative, and a wide raft of other topics integral to what and how I write. As is true for all attendees of all conferences, some papers spoke to me more than others, but even where I disagreed, I learnt. The participants had too much class to ask me 'Am I right?' or 'Did you mean ... ?' but the beauty of literary studies is that just because an author didn't consciously put something into the text, that doesn't mean it isn't there. A year has passed since the conference, but what remains is a sense of gratitude and privilege that those three days in St Andrews took place and that I could be there. So thank you to Sarah Dillon for all her hard work in making the conference happen, to St Andrews for hosting the event, to Gylphi for publishing this book, and to all participants at the conference for their insights, friendliness and humour. It was a great honour that I'll remember for the rest of my life.

September 2010

1

Introducing David Mitchell's Universe
A Twenty-First Century House of Fiction

Sarah Dillon

I

On 3–4 September 2009, the first David Mitchell Conference took place at the University of St Andrews, bringing together in intellectual dialogue and exchange scholars working on David Mitchell's writing. The aim of the conference was to consolidate and advance academic work currently underway on Mitchell's writing; the outcome is this collection of critical essays. Focusing on Mitchell's first three novels – *Ghostwritten* (1999), *number9dream* (2001) and *Cloud Atlas* (2004) – this volume represents the first sustained analysis of Mitchell's complex narrative techniques and the literary, political and cultural implications of his early work.[1] The essays collected here cover topics such as narrative structure, genre, the *Bildungsroman*, representations of Japan, postmodernism, the construction of identity, utopia, science fiction and postcolonialism. Their scope, however, is in no way exhaustive. Rather, this volume serves as a foundation stone for future critical work on Mitchell's continually expanding oeuvre: the detailed analyses and arguments of the essays represent the most intelligent and provocative material in current thinking about Mitchell's texts; in their footnotes can be found a breadcrumb trail of suggestions for future avenues of thought, comparison and analysis.

In order to complement the volume's focus on Mitchell's first three novels, this introduction will map the terrain of Mitchell's fiction, and the volume's engagement with it, using Mitchell's two most recent works as its compass – *Black Swan Green* (2006) and *The Thousand Autumns of Jacob de Zoet* (2010). This is illuminating, not least, because of the structural dissimilarity of these works to Mitchell's earlier and more experimental fiction. *Ghostwritten* consists of nine interconnected short stories, each narrated by a different character and set in a different geographical location; *number9dream*'s main *Bildungsroman* narrative is interrupted by fantasies, video games, a fabulist's children's stories, memories, flashbacks, excerpts from a wartime journal and dreams; and, *Cloud Atlas* comprises six generically and temporally distinct narratives each of which is interrupted by the next until the sixth undivided narrative after which each of the previous five stories is completed in turn.[2] In contrast to such generic and structural inventiveness, *Black Swan Green* and *The Thousand Autumns of Jacob de Zoet* appear more traditional: the former is a semi-autobiographical *Bildungsroman* that, as Mitchell himself observes, is 'carefully structured – like all halfway decent books – but simply structured too, with one story per month for thirteen months' (Begley, 2010); the latter, Mitchell's first sustained use of third-person narrative, is a historical novel set in the late eighteenth century on the man-made island of Dejima in Nagasaki bay, cat flap to the otherwise closed Shogun Empire of Japan.

Despite their seemingly simpler and less experimental structures, Mitchell's two most recent texts share a basic design principle with his earlier works, that of the 'compounded short story'. In interview with Robert Birnbaum (2006), Mitchell explains this formal principle: 'I think all novels are actually compounded short stories. It's just the borders get so porous and so squished up that you no longer see them, but I think they are there. And I do structure my novels in that way'. While this technique is clearly in evidence in Mitchell's first four works, the borders are perhaps most porous in *The Thousand Autumns of Jacob de Zoet*. The separate stories, despite this, can still easily be found – comprising Jacob's experiences on Dejima, Orito's incarceration at the mountain shrine, Uzaemon's mission to rescue her, and Captain Penhaligon's attack on Dejima – and Mitchell also states that he wrote the novel in this way. Mitchell employs the method in order to take advantage of the condensed intensity of the short story form, but at a novelistic level, in order to suggest a larger fictional world around and beyond that of the specific story he is at that point telling. 'Short stories', he explains, 'have a background white noise that creates the illusion that the world is much bigger than the mere 10 or 15 pages, and I wanted to see if I could sync up the white noise of the background of short stories' (Birnbaum, 2006).

Mitchell's ambition goes even further than this. In his writing, Mitchell is creating a fictional universe of which one mere four- or five-hundred page novel is just a fractional part. As he reveals to Wyatt Mason:

> I've come to realize … that I'm bringing into being a fictional universe with its own cast, and that each of my books is one chapter in a sort of sprawling macronovel. That's my life's work, for however long my life lasts. Of course, it's important that each of the books works as a stand-alone, so that readers don't have to read everything else I've written to make sense of the novel in their hands. But I write each novel with an eye on the bigger picture, and how the parts fit into the whole. (Mason, 2010)

In his novels, Mitchell offers various models for understanding the parallel relationship between the stories in his novels and the novel as a whole, and a specific novel and the macronovel that is his life's work. These include that of an atlas of clouds (a phrase which repeats across texts)[3] and the postcards that Jason Taylor buys at the tourist shop in *Black Swan Green*: 'a series of thirteen dinosaur postcards. Each one's got a different dinosaur, but if you put them end to end in order, the background landscape joins up and forms a frieze' (*BSG*, 212-3).[4] Critical work on Mitchell is beginning to suggest additional models for this, such as Gilles Deleuze's concept of the rhizome and theoretical biology's autopoietic and allopoietic systems.[5] I would like here to suggest a model based on Mitchell's recent work writing the libretto for the Dutch Nationale Reisopera, to commemorate the Vuurwerkramp disaster in the city of Enschede in the east of the Netherlands in 2000, in which a firework depot exploded killing 23 people and injuring 947. In a piece for the *Guardian*, Mitchell explains how he and the composer, Klaas de Vries, initially conceived of the opera:

> Klaas, Gerrie and I agreed that one way to honour the commission without transgressing laws of taste could be to stage nine stories in

nine rooms, on an ordinary evening in an unnamed city. Nine stories would unfold simultaneously: eventful stories, quiet ones, sad ones, comic ones, thoughtful ones, brash ones. The nine occupants of the 3x3 grid of rooms would sing four lines each when the 'spotlight' visited his or her room. There are just three rounds, so each singer has only 12 lines to convey character and plot, but when the spotlight is elsewhere, the stories in each room continue to develop, like nine silent movies showing simultaneously. Different members of the audience would follow those storylines that won their attention. After the third round, a sonic representation of a disaster (not the disaster) would occur, finishing the main act with a suggestion that the occupiers of the nine rooms would also cease to exist. (Mitchell, 2010a)

Mitchell's oeuvre, especially given his repeated attraction to the figure nine, can be understood in precisely this way, with each novel, both those written and those yet to be written, constituting a room in the house of fiction that he is constructing. Very different to Henry James's nineteenth-century house of fiction at the windows of which different authors stand, viewing in their own way the 'real' world, Mitchell's twenty-first-century house of fiction stands alone, a universe unto itself, inhabited not by the author but by his cast of characters who move from room to room, unencumbered by divisions in time and space.[6]

On the BBC World Book Club, Mitchell referred to the reappearance of characters across his novels as 'reality concreteness' (Gilbert, 2010). In interview with Adam Begley he expands on this idea, explaining that:

I grow fond of these characters I bring into being. In my adult life I have spent more weeks in the company of people such as Timothy Cavendish or Jacob de Zoet than I have with my own flesh-and-blood parents or brother. Letting them dissolve into nothingness feels too much like abandoning an inconvenient cat by a reservoir. There's a practical reason as well – the example I use is Falstaff, though it works just as well for a character like Captain Jack Sparrow: because Falstaff exists in the history plays, our perception of him in *The Merry Wives of Windsor* is different and enriched. We invested emotions in him during his time with young Hal, and these emotions are still there in

Windsor. Belief in a character and his milieu is retentive and transferable. This is why sequels exist. (Begley, 2010)

Much fun has been had in reviews, interviews and previous critical work tracing the characters that reappear across Mitchell's first three novels, and I will not reiterate these transmigrations here. I would just add that this character migration across texts continues in Mitchell's recent work and in work drafted and envisaged. In *Black Swan Green*, the reader finds the reappearance of Eva van Outryve Crommelynck, the wilful young daughter of Vyvyan Ayrs in *Cloud Atlas*'s 'Letters from Zedelghem'; and we meet the young Neal Brose, whose fate we have already encountered in *Ghostwritten*. *Black Swan Green* also includes a minor character, Clive Pike, 'SKM's mathematical brainbox' (*BSG*, 250) who is to become a significant character in Mitchell's next novel.[7] In *The Thousand Autumns of Jacob de Zoet*, we find Boerhaave, the young midshipman aboard the *Prophetess*, who we have previously encountered in *Ghostwritten* as the first mate of that same ship, and, towards the end of the novel, we discover that Con Twomey – whose 'true name is Fiacre Muntevary' (*TA*, 395) – is a distant ancestor of Mo Muntevary from *Ghostwritten*. Perhaps most intriguing in Mitchell's latest work is the cantankerous but charismatic Dr Marinus about whom Mitchell has enjoyed creating a certain mystery both within the text and without. In interview with Begley, Mitchell confides that 'readers of this book don't know it, but in *Thousand Autumns* he's on his twenty-eighth lifetime' (Begley, 2010) and to John Self he elaborates that 'there's much more than meets the eye with Marinus in particular. He will appear in my next novel, set around now. In the book after that he'll be the main character' (Self, 2010). These extra-textual shared secrets of Dr Marinus's immortality highlight the intra-textual hints to that effect. Explicitly anticipating and recalling H. G. Wells's *The Sleeper Awakes* (1899), in his discourse on the becoming-sentient of science Dr Marinus speculates:

> Had a man fallen asleep two centuries ago ... and awoken this morning, he should recognise his world unchanged in essence. Ships are still wooden, disease is still rampant. No man may travel faster than a galloping horse, and no man may kill another out of eyesight. But were

David Mitchell: Critical Essays

the same fellow to fall asleep tonight and sleep for a hundred years, or eighty, or even sixty, on waking he shall not recognise the planet for the transformations wrought upon it by Science. (*TA*, 207)

In response to Yoshida's question – 'when the doctor's imagined Sleeper awakens in the year 1899, shall the world most closely resemble Paradise or the Inferno?' (*TA*, 207), Marinus's mysterious response points towards his immortality: 'I shan't know until I see it, Mr Yoshida' (*TA*, 207). All these hints combined, when Orito observes at the end of the novel, on discussing Marinus's death with Jacob, that 'a great teacher attains immortality' (*TA*, 459), it is easy to take this remark literally, despite her ensuing modification, 'in his students' (*TA*, 459).[8]

Appealingly confirming the oxymoronic universal domesticity of the house of fiction image, throughout this house stalks a 'moon-grey cat', paradigm of the 'transdimensional' (*n9d*, 44) nature of all Mitchell's characters. In *number9dream*, Eiji observes that 'cats seem too transdimensional to get hit by traffic, but it happens all the time' (*n9d*, 44) and, later, 'cat bids me good morning and slips away to her own dimension' (*n9d*, 342). According to Eiji, 'cats know the secret of life and death' (*n9d*, 59), and such indeed is the case for Orito in *The Thousand Autumns of Jacob de Zoet* to whom Mitchell's cat reveals the means to escape her imprisonment. This same cat appears to Uzaemon later in the novel – 'a moon-grey cat, padding along the wall, catches Uzaemon's eye' (*TA*, 283) and stalks repeatedly across Jason's world in *Black Swan Green* (*BSG*, 46, 174, 291, 357). Given Mitchell's early avoidance of third-person narrative, and his use of it in *The Thousand Autumns of Jacob de Zoet* only via the limiting device of allowing the supposed omniscient narrator access to only one character's thoughts in each chapter, Mitchell's work has sometimes been criticized for lacking an authorial presence or voice. Rather than expecting Mitchell's writing to conform to such a traditional demand – instead of looking for the author at the window of the house of fiction observing the 'real' world – it might be more productive to understand Mitchell as the magical cat, himself an inhabitant of this fictional universe, an observer of it from within. He is as fabricated by it as the rest of its inhabitants are – as John Lennon says of his music in fictional exchange with Eiji in *number9dream*, 'it wrote me!' (*n9d*, 398).

II

Just as models for Mitchell's fiction apply both to the relation between the short stories and the novels of which they are a part, and to the novels and the macronovel of which they are a part, so too do textual interconnections occur at the micro and the macro levels, ranging from the microscopic repetition of motifs and phrases to the macroscopic repetition and intersection of characters, plots and themes. As Mo notes in *Ghostwritten*, however, 'nowhere does the microscopic world stop and the macroscopic world begin' (*G*, 373). Rather than a clear division between the two, then, Mitchell's oeuvre creates more of a *mise-en-abyme* effect in which the reader moves deeper and deeper into Mitchell's fictional universe, each time finding therein models for the structure and themes he is exploring. To extend the house of fiction metaphor, on the wall of each room is a picture of that room, which itself contains a picture of the room, and so on. As the *noncorpum* of *Ghostwritten* observes: 'how do I know that there aren't noncorpi living in me, controlling my actions? Like a virus within a bacteria?' (*G*, 191), or, as Caroline Edwards articulates it in her contribution to this collection: 'Mitchell's thematic preoccupation with networking between globally and historically dispersed characters *becomes* the aesthetic form he uses to structure his narratives'. Recalling the imagery of *The Thousand Autumns of Jacob de Zoet*, we might say that Mitchell's oeuvre, novels, short stories, paragraphs, sentences, words are pregnant with explanations of each other, mining an infinite literary fertility:

> The Goddess is disrobed for the Annunciation of Engifting: her exposed breasts are ample with milk; and her belly, devoid of a navel, is swollen with a female foetus so fertile, according to Abbess Izu, that the foetus's own tiny womb encloses a still smaller female foetus, which is, in turn, impregnated with a still smaller daughter ... and so on, to infinity. (*TA*, 208)

As this suggests, the examples here are endless. Just one might be Will McMorran's observation that although *The Thousand Autumns of Jacob de Zoet* eschews the globe-trotting nature of *Ghostwritten* and *Cloud Atlas* for a specific place and time, one of the most striking things about it is the way in which it similarly collects such a multitude of stories. It does so, not by travelling, but by choosing a location populated by travellers who each have their own story to tell, their own pregnant world to take us into, characters that Tzvetan Todorov (1971) describes as 'les hommes récits'.[9] Another might be Adam Begley's observation of *Cloud Atlas* that 'the first chapter – the first half of Ewing's narrative – is itself cut in half by the narrative of the savage Autua ... so that the first chapter mirrors the shape of the book as a whole'. Even more than this, the shape of the book is here mirrored at the level of a single word – the name 'Autua' – which in its palindromic structure offers another model for understanding the shape of *Cloud Atlas*.

Using *Black Swan Green* and *The Thousand Autumns of Jacob de Zoet* to limit, to some extent, this infinite literary fertility, I would like here to briefly enumerate just a few of Mitchell's central themes, thematic 'indestructible whack-a-moles' as he so brilliantly describes them: 'A writer only has a relatively small family of themes', he tells Begley (2010), 'and however hard you try to write about something else, they reemerge like indestructible whack-a-moles'. Perhaps the most significant of these is predacity and its associated concerns of colonialism, abusive exploitation, slavery and rampant consumerism. While this theme is most powerfully explored across global space and time in *Cloud Atlas*, it is nevertheless also a chief concern within the 'galaxy squashed flat' (*BSG*, 319) that is Jason's world in *Black Swan Green*. The politics of power, standing, rank and exploitation of the weak all structure Jason's boyhood world. In the very first chapter, the kids are waiting to be picked for a game of British Bulldogs 'like slaves in a slave market' (*BSG*, 6): 'Games and sports aren't about taking part or even about winning', Jason explains, 'Games and sports're really about humiliating your enemies' (*BSG*, 7). The children are divided into 'servants' (*BSG*, 9), 'middle-rank kids' (*BSG*, 9) and the powerful popular children, such as Tom Yew, whom the others seek to impress and whose opinions they adopt unthinkingly: 'Tom Yew started saying he'd seen *The Great Escape* and everyone agreed everything else'd been crap compared to *The Great Escape* … But then Tom Yew said he thought it'd gone on a bit long and everyone agreed that though the film was classic it'd dragged on for ages' (*BSG*, 9). Just like the wars between tribes on Zachry's island home, in Jason's scaled down world tribes and wars also exist: 'sometimes all the Welland and the Castlemorton lot come over on their bikes and then the games are more like battles' (*BSG*, 87). And just like Unanimity's sinister manipulation of Sonmi's ascension in *Cloud Atlas* in order 'to make every last pure-blood in Nea So Copros mistrustful of every last fabricant' (*CA*, 364), so too Jacob observes that 'all leaders can sense what people're afraid of and turn that fear into bows and arrows and muskets and grenades and nukes to use however they want. That's power' (*BSG*, 289).

Jason stands out in this corrupt world as a lone individual brave and strong enough to resist the way in which 'mass gang-ups … have a will of their own that swallows up resistance' (*BSG*, 257). Jason forfeits his much coveted place in the legendary gang Spooks in order to check that his friend Dean Morran has survived his fall through Mr Blake's greenhouse (*BSG*, 178). The novel ends with a narrative of hope as Jason rises up against the bullies, who get their comeuppance, and as the tables are turned on one of the ring leaders: 'Philip Phelps crashed round the bend, just twenty paces after Grant Burch. Not any Philip Phelps, *I've* ever seen, mind. *This* Philip Phelps was cracked and crimson with pure rage that'd only be calmed by Grant Burch's broken body limp in its claws' (*BSG*, 367). In the same way, the unassuming but moral and independent Jacob de Zoet, betrayed by his the absorption of his mentors into the corruption he has been sent to eradicate, faces a bleak imprisonment as the persecuted underdog on Dejima. This is his future until a surprising turn of events renders him the respected leader of the remaining men and secures his comfortable inhabitance there forthwith. As the reader learns in all the stories of *Cloud Atlas*, and as Grote articulates in *The Thousand Autumns of Jacob de Zoet*: 'Loyalty looks simple … but it ain't' (*TA*, 106).

11

Mitchell's most recent novel, therefore, continues his exploration of this theme with the unchecked greed of the Dejima inhabitants and the Japanese; its discourses on slavery and its insight into the machinations of power even as they function at the level of the family: 'Mother wasted no time, Uzaemon registers, in sending her spy along' (TA, 230). Its prevailing theme, however, another of Mitchell's thematic whack-a-moles, is incarceration and, in opposition to the cannibalism of predacity, the sustenance of stories that make imprisonment tolerable. The world of The Thousand Autumns of Jacob de Zoet is colonized by different levels of imprisonment: Jacob and his fellow men are imprisoned on Dejima, unable to leave unless a ship is departing, forbidden to step on Japanese soil; Orito and the other sisters are imprisoned in Enomoto's mountain shrine; the Japanese are themselves imprisoned within their Empire, forbidden to visit the outside world. Orito's imprisonment and the enforced prostitution of the Sisters recalls that of Kozue Yamaya in number9dream whose pimp, like Master Suzaku in The Thousand Autumns of Jacob de Zoet, personally dispenses drugs to numb the women's minds and, it might be supposed, suppress any thoughts of rebellion or escape (n9d, 335; TA, 184). Like the Soap-drugged clones in Sonmi's underground prison, the Sisters are comforted by the idea of future release – while the clones who have fulfilled their quota of twelve years will ascend to Xultation, the Sisters will descend to the world below when their term is served. In both instances this is a hollow promise: the used clones are recycled into the Soap fed to the the fabricants; the Sisters are simply killed; and, Yamaya's fellow whores are killed and also recycled, their body parts supplying the Yakuza black market for organ transplants.

These sinister drugged incarcerations recall the more darkly comic enforced imprisonment of Timothy Cavendish in Cloud Atlas. Like Orito, Cavendish realizes he must plot his escape by pretending to acquiesce to the will of his captors, not by fierce resistance (CA, 183; TA, 196). Also, like Orito, he realizes that it is stories that provide escape. Cavendish observes that:

> Mother used to say escape is never further than the nearest book.
> Well, Mumsy, no, not really. Your beloved large-print sagas of rags,

riches and heartbreak were no camouflage against the miseries trained on you by the tennis-ball launcher of life, were they? But, yes, Mum, there again, you have a point. Books don't offer real escape but they can stop a mind scratching itself raw. (*CA*, 373)

Similarly, Orito observes that, '*an ink-brush ... is a skeleton key for a prisoner's mind*' (*TA*, 192). Rather than the drugs, it is the forged New Year letters from the Sister's Gifts that enable them to endure their captivity: '*The belly craves food ... the tongue craves water, the heart craves love and the mind craves stories*. It is stories, she believes, that make life in the House of Sisters tolerable, stories in all their forms' (*TA*, 238). Combining these themes of predacity and incarceration, the remarkable internal monologue of Fischer's slave in *The Thousand Autumns of Jacob de Zoet* shows how, in his own gesture of fictional world-making, he creates 'a mind like an island' (*TA*, 316) on which he is 'as free as any Dutchman' – since he can neither read nor write, this is his version of the stories that make imprisonment tolerable and represent some form of escape.

There are many other repeated themes in Mitchell's fictional universe – a sense of apocalypse and the end of the world; hope that the actions of individuals can quell the tide of human predacity; the role of memory and story in creating identity; cultural dislocation; language and miscommunication; reincarnation; fate and causality – all of which, and more, are addressed in the essays in this collection. Suffice it to say here, that the recurrence of these themes across novels points to Mitchell's one most persistent and powerful theme – that of interconnection. As Steven Poole (2001) summarizes: 'His guiding thesis is a comfortingly simple one: everything is somehow interconnected, even if we don't know why'. While this may seem a simple thesis, Mitchell's simultaneous exploration and performance of it in and across his novels makes for an endlessly complex and uncannily vital fictional universe.

III

The essays in this collection immerse themselves in that universe with both scholarly precision and readerly delight. In 'The Novels in

Nine Parts', Peter Childs and James Green develop Childs's plenary address at the conference into a sweeping introduction to Mitchell's fictional world. Echoing Mitchell's attraction to the nine-part structural form, they consider nine aspects of Mitchell's first three novels: the Planetary novel; *noncorpum* identity; narrative form; meronymy; history; cloud/ocean; looking for connections; fiction/fabulation; and, the storyteller. Connecting their discussion and analysis in these sections is the belief that Mitchell's novels neither insist on the self-containment of their separate parts, nor collapse the distinctiveness of their fictional building blocks into a totalling vision of architectural wholeness. Instead, they present the multiple effect of networked narratives, histories and subjectivities incessantly cutting across and filtering into each other. Childs and Green conclude their discussion with a coda that maintains that there is an ethics of fiction in the assertion of human possibility in the novels, but also that Mitchell's experimentation with structure parallels a wider aesthetic and cultural condition, and that the new stylistic directions in the novels express contemporary life through their multidimensional terrain of transmigratory dreamscapes.

Bringing this broad introduction to Mitchell's work into more specific focus, Kathryn Simpson's essay, '"Or something like that": Coming of Age in *number9dream*', explores the tension between Mitchell's choice of the traditional *Bildungsroman* genre, with its centralized narrative structure committed to the notion of progress, and the postmodern qualities of the novel (which include self-conscious fictionality, an emphasis on dreams, memories and the telling of tales, as well as recurrent twinning and substitution [of characters, narrative events and linguistic play]). Simpson reads *number9dream* as a postmodern *Bildungsroman* that questions the viability of the conventional coming-of-age quest for self-knowledge in a postmodern, late capitalist context while simultaneously tantalizing the reader with this possibility. Continuing the collection's opening attention to *number9dream*, Baryon Tensor Posadas's 'Remediations of "Japan" in *number9dream*' takes a different approach to this text, foregrounding its engagement with the politics of cultural translation. Posadas pays particular attention to two of Mitchell's narrative strategies in *number9dream*:

the embedding and remediation of the motifs of cyberpunk, a genre through which 'Japan' is produced and circulated as an image-commodity; and, the novel's extensive quotations from and allusions to the fictions of Murakami Haruki. He does so in order to suggest that *number9dream* recognizes the impossibility of locating a 'Japan' not already mediated and subsumed under the logics of global modernity. In doing so, Posadas argues that the text opens up a productive space to articulate a politics of cultural translation that is attentive to the unevenness of the immaterial labour of fantasy production.

Moving the discussion on to *Cloud Atlas*, Courtney Hopf's 'The Stories We Tell: Discursive Identity Through Narrative Form in *Cloud Atlas*' examines the prevalence of storytellers and storytelling in Mitchell's works in order to consider the effects of narrative form on reader subjectivity. Hopf argues that both the diegetic readers within the novels and the external readers *of* the novels are led to experience a conflation of life and narrative, calling into question the heretofore strict distinction between the two. Hopf details how this conflation occurs through a variety of discursive techniques: the moments of recognition incited by recurring characters, themes, images and ideas across all of Mitchell's works; remediation, the representation of one medium within another; and metalepsis, the transgression across narrative levels. Hopf concludes that these techniques reveal Mitchell's emphasis on stories and storytelling as ways of not just understanding our identities, but of forming them. Continuing this focus on *Cloud Atlas*, Hélène Machinal's '*Cloud Atlas*: From Postmodernity to the Posthuman' sees the novel as exemplifying an evolution from postmodern writing towards a reflection on humanity through the introduction of the posthuman. Although, Machinal argues, *Cloud Atlas* undeniably belongs to postmodernity with its generic hybridity, fragmented structure, interrupted narratives, and emphasis on illusion and simulacrum, its two central speculative fictions imagine a posthuman world characterized by the annihilation of human identity, a subjection of the human through technology, and a reduction of human beings to mere commodities. Machinal concludes that through an elaboration of the social, political and environmental facets of this posthuman world Mitchell asserts the necessity of pondering the future of humanity and explores what it means to be human.

In 'Cloud Atlas and If on a winter's night a traveller: Fragmentation and Integrity in the Postmodern Novel', McMorran continues this interest in the postmodern by juxtaposing Cloud Atlas to the text that Mitchell has repeatedly cited as its structural inspiration: Italo Calvino's If on a winter's night a traveller. McMorran observes that while the two texts would seem to offer evidence of the mistrust of grand narratives that Jean-François Lyotard famously identified as part of the postmodern condition, both If on winter's night a traveller and Cloud Atlas are clearly rooted in a classical aesthetic tradition that continues to prize continuity and formal integrity: Calvino's fragments are housed in a teleological frame narrative that leads inexorably from first encounter to happy ever after for its two reader-protagonists; and, Cloud Atlas weaves an intertextual web of connecting topoi and characters between its various sections. McMorran explores the similarities and differences between the structural approaches of Calvino and Mitchell in order to suggest a more complex relationship between narrative and metanarrative than Lyotard has allowed for postmodern fiction.

Bringing Ghostwritten into the discussion, Caroline Edwards's '"Strange Transactions": Utopia, Transmigration and Time in Ghostwritten and Cloud Atlas' argues that Ghostwritten and Cloud Atlas are two examples of an emerging trend in contemporary British fiction demonstrating utopian 'moments of possibility' that network between various geographical spaces and historical times. Drawing on recent developments in theories of 'processual' or 'minor' utopianism, as well as post-Marxist theories of collective agency, Edwards outlines what she calls the 'microtopian' impulses at work within Mitchell's texts through an analysis of his use of sequential novella-style chapters, transmigratory metamorphoses of narrative voice through different historical moments, and the ways in which coincidence connects seemingly disparate, geographically dispersed characters. Edwards's exploration of these 'minor' utopian possibilities foregrounds the ways in which contemporary novelists like David Mitchell are rejuvenating speculative fiction and using emerging cosmopolitan identities to reveal the possibilities and impossibilities of utopian writing in the twenty-first century. Continuing this interest in speculative fiction, in 'Speculative Fiction as Postcolonial Critique in *Ghostwritten* and *Cloud Atlas*', Nicholas Dunlop discusses the tropes of speculative fiction in the two novels in order to explore the often-overlooked political element of Mitchell's work. Dunlop argues that while Mitchell's undoubted technical achievement and its postmodern implications are indeed a central part of any discussion of his fiction, such a unilateral perspective runs the risk of sidelining Mitchell's imaginative dialogue with the politics of postcoloniality by overlooking the oppositional politicized engagement that his technique enables. In particular, Dunlop posits that the extrapolative potential of SF in all its forms is uniquely configured to negotiate discourses of 'otherness' and difference, to propose alternative modes of interpreting the world, and to imaginatively trace the potential consequences of monolithic, myopic and exploitative hegemonic practices. Dunlop explores the ways in which Mitchell uses these three strategies in order to embed postcolonial critiques in his fiction and to articulate a persuasively subversive reading of the history and projected future of colonialism and its associated ideologies.

This attention to the speculative aspects of Mitchell's writing continues in the final essay in the collection, '"Moonlight bright as a UFO abduction": Science Fiction, Present-Future Alienation and Cognitive Mapping', in which William Stephenson explores how *Cloud Atlas*, *Ghostwritten* and *number9dream* articulate on a symbolic level a future that appears paradoxically already to be here, due to the pace of technological change and the increasingly estranged basis of everyday experience. Stephenson argues that in Mitchell's writing, however, this sense of the presence of the future does not lead to a threatened, reactionary response, but instead causes a sense of estrangement brought about by the paradoxical coexistence of accepted present-time data along with objects (or tropes or events) that seem rightly to belong to an imagined or foreseen future. Stephenson argues that Mitchell's fictions update the estranging strategies of previous SF, for example those of Philip K. Dick, and force the reader into a new and exhilarating form of cognitive cartography, a re-territorialization of the plural, decentred, estranging present and the already emerging future that is reality in the early twenty-first century.

From these summaries, it is evident that many of the essays in this collection address the question of postmodernism, and, more specifically, the question of whether Mitchell is writing postmodern fiction.[10] The point on which all the essays seem to agree is that the answer is both yes and no. While Mitchell undoubtedly and unashamedly employs techniques that have come to be understood as postmodern – but which, as Will McMorran helpfully demonstrates, have their origin as far back as early modern literature, not least in Cervantes's *Don Quixote* – there is always something in Mitchell's texts that, as Jose Borghino (2010) writes, 'keep[s] the worst excesses of po-mo at bay'. For Borghino (2010) these are Mitchell's 'clarity of language, a strong narrative momentum and his humane, anti-miserablist vision'. Here, for Childs and Green it is the changing world conditions to which Mitchell's fictions are responding, conditions that are no longer those of the Cold War relations to which postmodernism was a specific response; for Simpson, it is the retention of the *Bildungsroman* genre with its commitment, even if it is a compromised one, to a teleological narrative of coming-of-age; for Machinal, it is the inclusion of speculative fiction with its delineation of a posthuman vision that transcends postmodernism by introducing a philosophical dimension that goes beyond the individual level to a more collective one; for McMorran it is the rootedness of the playful techniques of postmodernism in the classical literature of the early modern period; for Dunlop, it is Mitchell's imaginative dialogue with the politics of postcoloniality.

The consensus seems to be that while Mitchell employs postmodern literary techniques, he does not adhere to the apolitical and antisocial nihilism of postmodernity with its ironic take on modern life and its paradoxical insistence on the inadequacy of narrative, language and literature. On the contrary, Mitchell's use of every literary device available to him is part of his delight in the continuing power and affect of literature. While Mitchell might repeatedly indulge the self-referentiality characteristic of postmodern fiction, this self-referentiality is in fact always about the fertility, power and sustenance of fiction, not its exhaustion: 'Ink, thinks Jacob, you most fecund of liquids' (*TA*, 13); "'The printed word is food," says Marinus, "and you look hungry, Domburger'" (*TA*, 140).[11] Contemporary readers are always hungry; Mitchell provides us with a feast.

IV

Unsurprisingly, given his work's popular success and critical acclaim, the holding of an academic conference on David Mitchell's work attracted attention in the global media. In a blog on the *Los Angeles Times* website, Carolyn Kellogg's attention is caught because, unlike many on the academic calendar, this conference was devoted to a still living author and one who 'might even be said to still be in the early phase of his career' (Kelllogg, 2009). She described the titles of the papers at the conference as 'charmingly arcane', and thought their discussions would be 'silly and removed ... from the job of writing and the joys of reading!'.[12] The pages of this volume demonstrate the opposite, since the topics of discussion at the conference, as evidenced by the essays collected here, were directly related to the job of writing and the joys of reading, as well as being academically and scholarly informed – these two things are in no way mutually exclusive: when we love someone, we want to know them better, we want to break them down to all their component parts, to see how they fit together, to see how they make up this spectacular mystifying compelling individual who revitalizes and reinvigorates our lives. At the same time we know, implicitly or explicitly, that each person is their own gestalt, that the whole is greater than the sum of their parts, that no categorization, taxonomy or analysis can in the end account adequately for their power and the effect they have on us. The same applies to the texts that we love, the great works of literature that have seduced and captured us. We may work very hard – with all of the literary, theoretical and philosophical means available to us – to account for their profound power and affect. At the same time, we know and welcome the fact that they exceed us and our ability to explain, analyse and critique them. They would not have caught our attention in the first place if this were not so. It is, therefore, possible to both love and analyse, to delight and dissect – each activity fuels the other, but neither

19

exceeds nor exhausts the text that has prompted such attention in the first place.

Kellogg concludes her blog by asking 'Are these really the kinds of discussions a novelist should be aware of? Ask Mitchell. The sprightly young novelist is scheduled to appear at the conference in person'. Kellogg did indeed ask Mitchell in a subsequent interview if he attended the conference. Mitchell responded:

> I did. It sounds self-aggrandizing, but I just wanted to relish the weirdness of it. I was invited, and it seemed gracious to accept. I went, and as I expected, it was very strange to hear one referred to as 'Mitchell' in sentences like, 'In this passage, Mitchell clearly means…' when I'm actually in the room. It was odd for me; it was probably even stranger for people reading their papers out. I like to think we all enjoyed the strangeness of it together. (Kellogg, 2010)

We did. The presence of the author at all the papers and the curious and uncanny dialogue this created between reader and writer was a new and productive experience for both parties, both of whom learnt much from each other. Rather than breathing a sigh of relief that our great authors are dead and gone, this conference, and this collection, delights in the fact that at least some are still alive and looks forward to more such provocative engagements between contemporary writers and readers in the future.

Notes

1 Existing published critical work in English on Mitchell's writing includes: Philip Griffiths's '"On the Fringe of Becoming" – David Mitchell's *Ghostwritten*' (2004); Chapter 3 of Berthold Schoene's *The Cosmopolitan Novel* – 'The World Begins Its Turn with You or How David Mitchell's Novels Think' (2009); and, Sarah Dillon's 'Chaotic Narrative: Complexity, Causality, Time and Autopoiesis in David Mitchell's *Ghostwritten*' (2010).

2 See the essays here collected for a multitude of ways of describing *Cloud Atlas*'s narrative structure and accounting for its readerly and political effect.

3 It can be found prior to *Cloud Atlas* in *number9dream* – 'The cloud atlas turns its pages over' (*n9d*, 374), and afterwards, in *The Thousand Autumns*

of Jacob de Zoet – 'West to east, the sky unrolls and rolls its atlas of clouds' (*TA*, 340).

4 Mitchell explains to Birnbaum (2006) that he indulges himself by 'trying to sneak into all of my books' a model for each of them.

5 See, respectively, Peter Childs and James Green's contribution to this collection, and my essay on *Ghostwritten* (Dillon, 2010).

6 Henry James describes his idea of the house of fiction in the 1908 preface to the New York Edition of *The Portrait of a Lady*.

7 Clive makes his reappearance in Mitchell's excerpt from the new novel, which appeared in the *Guardian* in August 2010 entitled 'Muggins Here'. The reason for his fragile psychiatric state, 'the Fact' that plagues him and is connected with his former head teacher from *Black Swan Green*, Mr Nixon, is revealed in another short from the new novel, 'All Souls Day'. (My thanks to David Mitchell for sharing with me an early draft of this as yet unpublished chapter.)

8 In addition to the resurfacing of actual characters across Mitchell's fictional world, character types also reappear. Otane, the old lady who lives on the mountain in *The Thousand Autumns of Jacob de Zoet* is a clear double of the tea shack lady from *Ghostwritten*. Both share the same reluctance to winter in the valley, despite their relatives's insistence.

9 I am grateful to Will McMorran for sharing these thoughts on *The Thousand Autumns of Jacob de Zoet* in email correspondence with me.

10 Interestingly, the publication of *The Thousand Autumns of Jacob de Zoet*, with its more traditional choice of the historical novel genre and its constrained structural experimentation, has reignited this same debate within the media. See James Wood (2010) and Dave Eggers (2010) for opposing sides of the debate.

11 Continuing the foody imagery, Mitchell himself explains in interview with John Mullan that 'even with what we now call postmodern novels, experimental novels, if they last and if we like them, it's not the jiggery pokery that we really liked ... it is actually the old fashioned meat and potatoes plot and character development, in all of them' (Mullan, 2010).

12 Note that the conference prompted a similar discussion on the *Guardian* website in the UK (Flood, 2009).

Works Cited

Begley, Adam (2010) 'David Mitchell, The Art of Fiction No 24', *The Paris Review*, URL (consulted October 2010): http://www.theparisreview. org/interviews/6034/the-art-of-fiction-no-204-david-mitchell

Birnbaum, Robert (2006) 'David Mitchell', *The Morning News*, 11 May, URL (consulted October 2010): http:/www.themorningnews.org/archives/ birnbaum_v/david_mitchell.php

Borghino, Jose (2010) 'History and Narrative Gloriously Entwined', *The Australian*, 29 May, URL (consulted October 2010): http://www.theaustralian.com.au/news/arts/history-and-narrative-gloriously-entwined/ story-e6frg8nf-1225871180750

Dillon, Sarah (2010) 'Chaotic Narrative: Complexity, Causality, Time and Autopoiesis in David Mitchell's *Ghostwritten*', *Critique: Studies in Contemporary Fiction* 52(2): 1–28.

Eggers, Dave (2010) 'Empire of Desire', *The New York Times, Sunday Book Review*, 1 July, URL (consulted October 2010): http://www.nytimes. com/2010/07/04/books/review/Eggers-t.html

Flood, Alison (2009) 'Which Authors are Worth a Whole Conference?', *guardian.co.uk, Books Blog*, 9 September, URL (consulted October 2010): http://www.guardian.co.uk/books/booksblog/2009/sep/09/georgette- heyer-author-conferences

Gilbert, Harriett (2010), 'David Mitchell', BBC World Bookclub, 4 June, URL (consulted August 2010): http://www.bbc.co.uk/worldservice/ arts/2010/06/100604_wbc_david_mitchell.shtml

Griffiths, Philip (2004) '"On the Fringe of Becoming" – David Mitchell's *Ghostwritten*', in Stefan Glomb and Stefan Horlacher (eds) *Beyond Extremes: Repräsentation und Reflexion von Modernisierungsprozessen im zeitgenössischen britischen Roman*, pp. 79–99. Narr: Tübingen.

Kellogg, Carolyn (2009) 'Getting Academic about David Mitchell', *Los Angeles Times, Jacket Copy*, 2 September, URL (consulted October 2010): http://latimesblogs.latimes.com/jacketcopy/2009/09/david-mitchell. html

Kellogg, Carolyn (2010) 'David Mitchell', *Goodreads*, July, URL (consulted October 2010): http://www.goodreads.com/interviews/show/537.David_Mitchell

Mason, Wyatt (2010) 'David Mitchell, the Experimentalist', *The New York Times Magazine*, 25 June, URL (consulted October 2010): http://www. nytimes.com/2010/06/27/magazine/27mitchell-t.html

Mitchell, David (2010a) 'Adventures in Opera', *Guardian*, 8 May, URL (consulted October 2010): http://www.guardian.co.uk/culture/2010/may/08/david-mitchell-opera-wake

Mitchell, David (2010b) 'Muggins Here', *Guardian*, 14 August, URL (consulted October 2010): http://www.guardian.co.uk/books/2010/aug/14/david-mitchell-summer-short-story

Mullan, John (2010) '*Guardian* Book Club: John Mullan Meets David Mitchell', *Guardian*, 28 June, URL (consulted August 2010): http://www.guardian.co.uk/books/audio/2010/jun/16/david-mitchell-guardian-book-club

Poole, Steven (2001) 'I Think I'm Turning Japanese', *Guardian*, 10 March, URL (consulted October 2010): http://www.guardian.co.uk/books/2001/mar/10/fiction.davidmitchell

Self, John (2010) 'David Mitchell Interview', 24 May, URL (consulted October 2010): http://theasylum.wordpress.com/2010/05/24/david-mitchell-interview/

Schoene, Berthold (2009) *The Cosmopolitan Novel*. Edinburgh: Edinburgh University Press.

Todorov, Tzvetan (1971) 'Les hommes récits', in *Poétique de la prose*, pp. 78–9. Paris: Seuil. (*The Poetics of Prose*, trans. Richard Howard. Ithaca, NY: Cornell University Press.)

Wood, James (2010) 'The Floating Library: What can't the novelist David Mitchell do?', *The New Yorker*, 5 July, URL (consulted October 2010): http://www.newyorker.com/arts/critics/atlarge/2010/07/05/100705crat_atlarge_wood?currentPage=all

2

THE NOVELS IN NINE PARTS

Peter Childs and James Green

Three of David Mitchell's novels to date were conceived in nine parts, and yet none is actually so. His first book *Ghostwritten* (1999) is described as 'a novel in nine parts' but has a named coda and thus lists ten parts. His second novel *number9dream* (2001) is divided into eight sections, with a blank ninth. Finally, *Cloud Atlas* (2004) was to have nine stories but for reasons of length ended up as six.[1] Echoing Mitchell's toying with the number nine, this essay takes a related structural form.

1. Planetary Novel

In a *Time* review of *Black Swan Green*, Pico Iyer (2006) describes *Ghostwritten* as a 'planetary novel'. Later, in a profile of Mitchell for *Time*'s list of the top 100 people who are transforming the world – Mitchell is ranked at number 16 – Iyer (2007) argues that with *Ghostwritten* Mitchell 'created the 21st century novel'. We would like to review what these claims might mean. To begin with, they contrast with the verdict of Richard Bradford in *The Novel Now* (2007). In his survey of the British novel, Bradford includes Mitchell along with a selection of writers that he names the 'new postmodernists'; writers who are united by a range of techniques, devices and effects manifested in their work. Bradford seems to suggest that in the production and consumption of fiction in the current 'aesthetic supermarket', as David Lodge (1996: 11) labels it, Mitchell marries experimentation with consumer friendliness, dense textuality with rich storytelling.

We would argue that this misconceives, or at the very least underestimates, Mitchell's fiction. Mitchell's novels do not merely rehearse the stylistic inflections of a domesticated postmodernism, as Bradford terms it, but rather articulate a complex response to the current material conditions of the world (Bradford, 2007: 62–8). Postmodernism emerged against a backdrop of Cold War relations that in many ways wound down in 1989. Perceptions of the world have been transformed dramatically in the twenty years since then, such that the discourses of postmodernism and postcolonialism arguably offer rather limited perspectives on present circumstances. While postmodernism and postcolonialism challenge forms of power that impose relatively stable hierarchical structures, they seem increasingly unsatisfactory to describe the flows of mediated identity, the global reach of capital, the possibilities of new political paradigms, and the modulating networks of the world market. This is a contemporary reality that is, however, addressed in Mitchell's first three novels. *Ghostwritten, number9dream* and *Cloud Atlas* are palimpsests of competing voices and styles that cycle through disparate but always interlinked temporal and spatial settings.[2] As globalization forges new patterns of human interaction, interconnectedness and awareness, the nested layers of stories within stories in these novels, and their mixing of different modes of reality, articulate the fluidity and multiplicity of contemporary relations and subjectivities.

For example, the subtitle of *Ghostwritten* presents the book as 'a Novel in Nine Parts', its formal arrangement comprising nine discrete first-person narratives that trace an imaginative passage from East to West, encircling the globe's northern hemisphere. Though the narrative does come to pass through the more familiar 'centres' of the global cultural economy such as London and New York, much of the novel concentrates on places that have been perceived as alien and mysterious by the western cultural imagination: Japan, Hong Kong, China and Mongolia have all found themselves refracted through a prism of Eurocentric discourse that has world history radiating outwards from its 'over-developed' centres. *Ghostwritten*'s trajectory is not a *reversal* of this, as in the familiar postcolonial trope of the former empire 'writing back' to the centre,[3] but rather seems to be an alternative recognition of planetary con-temporality and dynamic synchronicity where people and places are inextricably linked regardless of distance. The novel does not just show events happening around the world at the same time for purposes of comparison, it animates an entire circuitry of global interaction and interdependence.

Against readings of globalization that frame it as a process of integration and assimilation homogenizing cultural difference, all of Mitchell's first three novels suggest that the site of the local is crisscrossed by innumerable paths of movement with varying speeds and directions. Encounters on these planetary trajectories are better seen as confluences in webs of relations. These entangle, however minimally, the wider world, where most people faced with the rhetoric of a 'war on terror' may have asked the opening question of Mitchell's first novel: 'Who was blowing on the nape of my neck?' (G, 3). *Ghostwritten*, like *number9dream* and *Cloud Atlas*, neither insists on the self-containment of its separate parts, nor collapses the distinctiveness of its fictional building blocks into a totalizing vision of architectural wholeness. Rather, it presents instead the multiplex effect of networked narratives, histories and subjectivities incessantly cutting across and filtering into each other.

2. *Noncorpum* Identity

> We live nowhere, and we are strangers everywhere. We drift, often on a whim, searching for something to search for ... My incredulous Chinese hosts who saw the first backpackers regarded them as quite alien entities. Which is exactly how humans would regard me. All minds pulse in a unique way, just as every lighthouse in the world has a unique signature. (G, 160)

Jules Verne's *Around the World in 80 Days* (1873) has a 'passage' in which the Englishman Phileas Fogg sojourns aboard the steamer *Mongolia* on his way to India, sailing from Brindisi to Bombay. He has of course set out to circumnavigate the globe. Fogg's journey is arranged in eight legs and has nine departure and arrival points: London, Suez, Bombay, Calcutta, Hong Kong, Yokohama, San Francisco, New York, and London again. As he circles the world, Fogg remains the archetypal travelling colonial Englishman, maintaining at all times his re-serve, dignity, and assurance. Published over one-hundred years later, *Ghostwritten* has a similar scope and number of key locations. Like Mitchell's succeeding novels, it is energized by the mutability of iden-tity created by mass migration and communications – 'contemporary nomadism' in Iain Chambers's (1994: 50) phrase. The novel's mac-rocosmic journey through disparate worlds brought together in its 'global village' of interconnected lives finds parallels in the peripatetic narrative of the 'Mongolia' chapter, which portrays the wanderings of a dis/embodied nomad, drifting between different mental terrains as the travellers it rides move across geo-national boundaries.

The *noncorpum*'s sense of freedom is vertiginous. It compares the experience of transmigration to 'a trapeze artist, spinning in empti-ness' or 'a snooker ball lurching round the table' (*G*, 165). At the same time, this freedom is accompanied by profound loneliness – having never encountered another of its kind, the *noncorpum* wanders be-tween minds looking for traces of the story that is its earliest memory and whose source seems tied to the mystery of its being. Like Eiji's search for identity in *number9dream*, this is a quest for home within storytelling that is also linked to the origins of individual existence: 'the story I was born with' (*G*, 172). Just as the *noncorpum* finds mem-ories and stories, imaginings and experiences, blurring together in the consciousnesses of its hosts, Mitchell's fiction constantly returns to such fundamental concerns: how our individual narratives are com-posed and re-composed; how these stories are interwoven and feed into the larger movements of human history that always threatens to consume them; the tension between writing and being written that inheres in the title of the novel.

'Mongolia' ends with the Borgesian *noncorpum* tracing a non-ge-netic family genealogy and weighing up whether to exchange the free-dom of disembodied levity, endlessly mindhopping between 'presi-dents, astronauts, messiahs' (*G*, 202), for the vicissitudes of mortality.[4] The *noncorpum* has an existence defined by mediation. Its identity is cycled through a potentially endless process of transit, transformation and translation. Isolated in an atomized world, though, its yearning for both kinship and self-identity compels the self-declared humanist to contemplate a more circumscribed existence bounded by the contingencies of a single mortal life. Though a representative of the Mongolian nomads of the Central Asian steppes and a contemporary example of ancient theories of metempsychosis, the *noncorpum* also seems a potent symbol for the advent of a historically unprecedented mode of planetary subjectivity constituted by constant mediation.

With its string of hosts, the *noncorpum* also provides a metafictional analogy for the larger design of the novel, and places the reader at once within and yet supplementary to the thoughts of the different narrators. But if this section of the novel hints at the notion of the reader as a *noncorpum* within the text, it also reflects on the narrative technique of the fiction. This similarly inhabits a range of voices, styles, and idioms while crossing thresholds of history, language and ontology. Just as the disembodied narrator of 'Mongolia' is fascinated by the plurality of the species – 'all minds pulse in a unique way, just as every lighthouse in the world has a unique signature' (*G*, 160) – Mitchell's texts describe both human variety and commonality. Indeed, beyond a traditional liberal-humanist accommodation with multiculturalism, Mitchell writes a world where humanity lives in difference on an unprecedented scale, bearing witness to the contingencies of the parallel locations of its narrators without permitting these differences to become fixed and immutable. This is also a world where no single perspective can encompass the multifaceted realties of human life, and vision emerges in the shifting interfaces of histories and cultures.

3. Narrative Form

Or is it not a question of cause and effect, but a question of wholeness? (*G*, 108)

The title of *Ghostwritten* seems to allude to the spectral ventriloquism of its first-person narrative, which transmigrates between multiple voices and spaces without properly belonging anywhere. This rootlessness mimics the contemporary dislocation of identities buffeted by the turbulent currents of globalization. Like the voice trace of the author, which roams from narrator to narrator and inhabits them fully but invisibly, the intangible presence of the *noncorpum* is an inflection of the 'ghostwriter', a term that can be applied to just about all authors of first-person narrative fiction. It also introduces important questions of autonomy and agency, because the *noncorpum* is not passive within the mind of its hosts but is able to access their memories and manipulate their thoughts and behaviour. As this ethereal narrator acknowledges, the very fact of its existence shadows the notion of subjectivity with the possibility of an ontological *mise en abyme* that is profoundly disturbing: 'how do I know that there aren't noncorpi living in me, controlling my actions? Like a virus within a bacteria?' (*G*, 191). In a comparable way, the extent to which existence is itself a form of biographical ghostwriting – scripted by forces beyond influence and understanding – is an issue that is repeatedly raised by *Ghostwritten*, *number9dream* and *Cloud Atlas*. It is appropriate here to recall that *Ghostwritten*'s epigraph is taken from Thornton Wilder's *The Bridge of San Luis Rey* (1927) – a text in which the disastrous collapse of a Peruvian bridge is the stimulus for a metaphysical investigation into the possibilities of celestial design and individual will. Like Wilder's fictional work, Mitchell's novel meditates on the mysteries of causality, culpability, and subjective experience, culminating in its own ethical debate over the possible destruction of a bridge, which features in the 'Night Train' section of *Ghostwritten* and is echoed in the story of the revived Luisa Rey in *Cloud Atlas*.

Mitchell's almost total eschewal of third-person narrative prior to *The Thousand Autumns of Jacob de Zoet* (2010) implies more than merely an aesthetic distrust of narratorial omniscience. Indeed, it suggests a resistance to all pretensions towards objectivity – in *Ghostwritten*, the unshakeable certainty in his own rectitude voiced by the millennial cultist Quasar, whose story bookends *Ghostwritten*, is forcefully undercut by the novel's kaleidoscopic form and the viral infiltration of one story into another. Rather than offering any kind of privileged answer, *Ghostwritten* functions as a neural hub of the thoughts and ideas of characters, each of which has its preferred suggestions for the right grand narrative: for Quasar, the holy work of separating the pure believers from the 'unclean' is the necessary precursor to the apocalyptic coming of the 'New Earth' prophesied by his Guru; living on the 'prayer wheel of time' (*G*, 113), the unnamed tea-shack owner in 'Holy Mountain' continues to affirm her spiritual beliefs as she is caught in the violent machinery of the Cultural Revolution; Mo Muntervary finds paradoxical structure in the 'syntax of uncertainty' (*G*, 373) articulated by the subatomic universe of quantum physics; Zookeeper, the sentient AI created by Muntervary, seeks to create a new world order based on his hard-coded ethical logic; while Marco, the musician and ghostwriter who narrates 'London', stakes his existence on the beneficence of chance.

The chains of cause and effect that run through the text may remain largely invisible to the local actors, but *Ghostwritten* suggests agency is everywhere immanent in the shared lives and narratives that trace a common world horizon differently traversed by the *noncorpum*, Zookeeper and the reader, as well as by travellers, criminals, officials, agents, migrants and so on. We will return later to how this might be conceptualized, but now we would like to note how, as opposed to providing any single plot, *Ghostwritten* works through a process of largely unforeseen contiguity and connection.

The formal segmentation of the text may suggest a world held still in cross-section, but as the storyline transmigrates between parallel lives there emerges a strong sense of human congruity, an interconnectedness and interdependency that undercuts tribal boundaries. The slices of the world that the novel depicts are less a series of internally coherent and bounded spaces than nodal points of a globally extended network made up of interactions that stretch from the infinitesimal to the immeasurable. The Deleuzian figure of the rhizome seems apposite here, as the novel spreads through a kind of textual diffusion whereby individual narratives continuously exceed their boundaries and flow into other stories.[5] The network woven by these slender lines of association is less a globe-spanning tapestry than an ephemeral web – characters from one story appear in another, sending ripples along the surface of the narrative as events in one chapter generate unforeseeable consequences elsewhere. As Eiji says near the end of *number9dream*: 'visible consequences are iceberg tips: most results of most actions are invisible to the doer' (*n9d*, 390).

31

4. Meronymy

Images and reasons for this rippling effect are expressed in many ways in the novels. For example, Meronym is the name of the prescient who builds a relationship with Zachry in the middle story of *Cloud Atlas*. Appropriately, a meronym in linguistics denotes a constituent part of a whole. In Mitchell's fiction everything seems to be demonstrably a part of the larger whole. Each character is a meronym of the web of relations entangling all the others. This explains, for example, the domino effect within *Ghostwritten* of Neal Brose's shady dealings and his death, but also their antecedents and perhaps provenance in *Black Swan Green*, where a young Brose attends the same school as the narrator, Jason Taylor.

The syntactic relation denoted by meronymy additionally seems to operate at the level of language: the minds of narrators are unconsciously in counterpoint across temporal and spatial distances; there are also a range of subtle repeated motifs that recur and mutate provocatively in new contexts. In *Ghostwritten*, these are metaphorical references to tunnels and catacombs, walls and barriers, bats and comets, cherry blossom and camphor trees, the theological figures of Buddha and Gabriel, as well as ghosts in a number of guises. At the level of the text these act as a rhythmic pulse that holds together each of the solo performances, involving characters in a choreography of intuitive meanings. Although they seldom become aware of their interconnections with myriad others, these dispersed characters are shown to be situated at points in one intricate circuit of dependency. The organizing principles used to explain this vary across the chapters. One is Mo Muntervary's subatomic version:

> Take any two electrons ... that originate from a common source, measure and combine their spins, and you will get zero. However far away they are: between John and me, between Okinawa and Clear Island, or between the Milky Way and Andromeda: if one of the particles is spinning down, then you know that the other is spinning up ... Phenomena are interconnected regardless of distance, in a holistic ocean more voodoo than Newton. The future is reset by the tilt of a

pair of polarised sunglasses. 'The simultaneity of the ocean ... ' (*G*, 375)

As the pun on 'polarised' indicates, there is a sense of a world in balance, psychically as much as ecologically, but which can be upset at any point.[6] Whether it is Zen Buddhism or the music of chance, the sense of 'an infinite tether' (*G*, 298), in the name of Dwight Silverwind's book, pervades the novel.

5. History

Of catastrophe and equanimity, catastrophe looms larger since a sense of apocalypse hangs over the novels. And because, as Zookeeper finds, there are no universally effective rules for action, the novels also intimate pivotal links between creation and destruction, Apollo and Dionysus, intention and accident, and so forth: *Cloud Atlas* draws out the insidious links between civilization and barbarism; *number9dream* suggests a symbiotic relationship between them, figured in the daylight capitalism of a limitless city and the nightmares of its underbelly. The repressed underside of the social imaginary of modernity finds particular expression in 'Reclaimed Land' as Eiji is pulled down into the submerged world of the Yakuza who control Tokyo's lawless hinterlands. The rampant consumerism in contemporary Japanese life is evident throughout the novel – crowds swirl at 'a thousand faces a minute' (*n9d*, 3) through shopping malls, bars and pachinko parlours like lubricant in a voracious machine. The revelation that the profits of the crime syndicate come chiefly from selling the bodily organs of its victims takes this commodification to a logical extreme. This is a buried terrain, uncolonized by modern rationality, a social order stripped down to a savage doctrine, later domesticated in the Nero pizza kitchen, 'the weak are meat, the strong eat' (*n9d*, 341).

In *Cloud Atlas*, the journal of Adam Ewing, who is exposed to the reality of similar predation, bookends a dramatized series of mailshots from the story of civilization's fall. It offers itself as a template for the embedded episodes as the narrative shells progressively fall away. Berthed on the suggestively-named *Prophetess*, Ewing is a modern-day Melville or Marlow who struggles to square his faith in the beneficent aspects of colonialism with what he sees before him on the Chatham Islands, 'that casual brutality lighter races show the darker' (CA, 31). He learns of the archipelago's history, specifically the fate of the indigenous Moriori people. This race were destroyed first by settlers and then by the invasion of British-backed Maori tribes who claimed Moriori land for their own, enslaving those who survived their slaughter in ways that directly anticipate Zachry's story at the centre of *Cloud Atlas*.

From Adam to Zachry, the recurring pattern of abusive exploitation is played out in miniature in Ewing's onboard narrative with his own secret sharers. Like an employee trained in the Nero kitchen, Ewing's travel companion Henry Goose cynically enacts his belief that the notions of progress, civil society and divine sovereignty that underpin the colonial project are necessarily fatuous mystifications of the immutable law that the strong prey on the weak; they are intellectual fig-leaves deployed to legitimize enslavement. In contrast to Goose's predatory relationship with Ewing – who he slowly poisons under the guise of treatment – the bond Ewing develops with a stowaway, Autua, opens his eyes to the possibility of a different future. His compassion in saving the Moriori tribesman from an almost certain death is repaid to him in kind when Autua rescues Ewing from his sickbed, and Goose, on the *Prophetess*. The possibility of sympathetic reciprocity, which acknowledges co-dependency, is glimpsed throughout the second-half of *Cloud Atlas* as an alternative social principle that could deflect a predatory world from consuming itself. At the end of the book, Ewing reaches the conclusion that 'for the human species, selfishness is extinction' (CA, 528), and the acuity of this belief has been mapped in the already-written futures of Sonmi and Zachry.

The connections that were plotted between geographically disparate characters in *Ghostwritten* are thus stretched across time in *Cloud Atlas*, where the recurrence of a comet-shaped birthmark and vague memories of previous lifetimes imply that many of the central characters are the same transmigrated soul. This metaphor of humanity's shared journey through time is spelled out in Zachry Bailey's narrative at the post-apocalyptic epicentre of *Cloud Atlas*:

> I watched clouds awobbly from the floor o' that kayak. Souls cross ages like clouds cross skies, an' tho' a cloud's shape nor hue nor size don't stay the same, it's still a cloud an' so is a soul. Who can say where the cloud's blowed from or who the soul'll be 'morrow? (*CA*, 324)

Just as clouds are ever-changing coalescences of wind-blown water molecules, *Cloud Atlas* suggests that the human species is at once infinitely protean and bound together in an inter-reliant community that spans the boundaries of ethnicity and nation. The conceit of literary metempsychosis already encountered in *Ghostwritten* therefore also provides the connective tissue of *Cloud Atlas*, but here its lifeblood is drawn from a different source, which supplies a thematic coherence to the text. Whereas in *Ghostwritten* the multiplication of perspectives and subjectivities rendered its ethical underpinnings decidedly ambiguous – its competing voices each offering a specific view of the world – nested narratives in *Cloud Atlas* are linked by the twin refrains of the Nietzschean will to power and the eternal recurrence of human subordination.

In Ewing's phrase 'the entropy written into our nature' (*CA*, 528) is the imperative that animates the novel, pitching individual acts of resistance against a vision of what he calls the 'many-headed hydra of human nature' (*CA*, 529). If, during the first half of the text, humanity appears to be shackled to its apocalyptic destiny – the animus that compels the strong to subjugate the weak ultimately begetting the Hobbesian nightmare of mutual destruction – the reversal of this forward momentum opens up an alternative perspective. Rather than the future being impossible to resist – an outcome genetically hard-coded and already etched into the trajectory of history – as the interrupted narratives are resumed, in reverse order, the novel argues the case for ethical choices made by individuals and societies reasserting the potential for enlightened political agency. As Ewing recognizes, a single life may amount to no more than 'one drop in a limitless ocean' of human history, and yet 'what is any ocean but a multitude of drops?' (*CA*, 529).

6. Cloud/Ocean: The Multitude of Drops

Repeating the opening question of the novel but in the present rather than the past tense, the conclusion to *Ghostwritten* finds Quasar asking again 'Who is blowing on the nape of my neck?' (*G*, 436). Like such shorthand concepts as the 'butterfly effect', used to describe the behaviour of complex, non-linear systems, small perturbations in one part of this matrix of novels produce unpredictable air currents to waft across the fictional field as each story releases its influence like an opened gas canister. For instance, the 'spectral' (*CA*, 425) masterpiece composed by Robert Frobisher in *Cloud Atlas* haunts a future Luisa Rey, who we first met in *Ghostwritten*, and reverberates through the 'Solarium' section of *Black Swan Green*. Similar intertextual connections ripple through Mitchell's writing to coalesce in suggestive patterns. At the level of character, the effect is of a curious intersection of lives that influence each other in a community of interdependence that takes the globe as its frame of reference. Yet, from the perspective of any one particular viewer immersed in their own time and space, the sparks produced by the contact-points of crisscrossing lives and narratives are often so subtle as to be practically invisible, such that the connections are unfathomable other than intuitively.

One way of approaching this may be as a literary expression of Hardt and Negri's concept of the global multitude. In their works *Empire* (2000) and *Multitude* (2004) Hardt and Negri suggest that the ultimate extension of the circuits of production and exchange has propagated a new logic of structure and rule, which they term 'Empire'. This regime incorporates the entire world within its open, expanding frontiers, regulating the flows of commodities and labour while seeking to exert its control over all human interactions, even human nature itself. The multitude is the other side to these global networks of power; it is the productive, creative subjectivities of globalization whose movements, modulations of form, and processes of mixture and hybridization express the desire for liberation from the hierarchies imposed by transnational capitalism. In a similar way, Mitchell's narrators are connected through common needs and desires that have little regard for the borders and boundaries that parcel up their world. Though separated from each other by enormous geographical and temporal distances, their struggle against various forms of subordination is presented as a universal impulse. Hardt and Negri (2000: 60) describe the multitude as 'constellations of singularities', and this also seems an approximation of the version of subjectivity dominant in these novels. While the characters remain embedded in the material conditions of their existence, their narratives couched in the ideological and moral atmospheres of their time, the final lines of Adam Ewing's journal, and also of *Cloud Atlas*, articulate the possibility of opening up new paths of becoming, away from seemingly localized misery and exploitation. Ewing affirms both the necessity of the ethical struggle towards a more equitable world and the capacity of individuals to actively shape their collective history. He finally pledges himself to the Abolitionist cause, deciding that 'Belief is both prize & battlefield, within the mind & in the mind's mirror, the world' (*CA*, 528).

7. Looking for Connections

'All those wideworlders in transit, all those misplaced thrown-away people ... How do they know who they are?' (*G*, 357) asks Mo Muntervary while on the run from the authorities in *Ghostwritten*. This is a question that is framed in various ways throughout the novel. On one level, the formal dislocations of Mitchell's texts mirror the sense of atomization articulated by many of the characters as they struggle to find roots in an increasingly fluid and unstable world; yet Mitchell also reaffirms the traditional role of narrative in shaping the discontinuities of lived experience. In *number9dream*, Eiji's search for the father he has never known is also a search for meaning in his own life; he believes that discovering the identity of his absent parent will complete his own. As Eiji drifts through the labyrinthine streets of Tokyo, a self-styled private detective on the hunt for clues, his quest is characterized by unexpected detours, including the re-establishment of contact with his estranged mother. For much of the novel, the hazy figure of Eiji's father is little more than a symbolic projection wherein naive fantasies of love and forgiveness commingle with feelings of resentment. Unsurprisingly, considering the all-encompassing nature of his paternal search, Eiji's voyage through the city spawns a succession of surrogate paternities, from his landlord, Buntaro, to the Yakuza 'father' who 'educates' him in the ways of the violent criminal underworld that thrives in Tokyo's shadows. Eiji's febrile imagination conjures up a range of romantic scenarios in which multiple conspirators keep him apart from the parent whom he believes to be a high-profile public figure. He prefers these fantasies to a more plausible, and emotionally debilitating, reality. When Eiji finally comes face to face with his father, his dreams of fulfilment dissolve into a crushing sense of bathos opening the way to a reconciliation with his mother and the memory of his twin sister (*n9d*, 372–4).

However, instead of closing the circle of Eiji's voyage in a gesture of mythic homecoming on the island, the 'ending' of *number9dream* merely marks the beginning of a further stage in the journey. After drifting off to sleep in his grandmother's house, Eiji is awoken from a peculiar dream – which alludes to, among other things, the creation myth of Japanese Shintoism – by a radio announcement that a massive earthquake has struck the Tokyo region causing widespread destruction and severing all lines of communication.[7] If for much of the book the distinction between dream and reality has been indefinite, here the actuality of the event is painfully affirmed, with Eiji's fantasies appearing finally to give way to a catastrophic eruption of the real into his dreamworld:

> I would give anything to be dreaming right now. Anything. Are the airwaves and cables jammed because half the phone users in the country are trying to call the capital, or because Tokyo is now a landscape of rubble under cement dust? Outside, a century of quiet rain is falling on all the leaves, stones and pine needles of the valley. (*n9d*, 418)

In this i(nte)rruption, whose language echoes that of Gabriel Conroy at the end of Joyce's 'The Dead' watching the snow that is general all over Ireland, *number9dream* rejects the traditional closure of the *Bildungsroman* in favour of the dissemination and dispersal of narrative, like a shower of rain.[8]

Eiji's girlfriend Ai suggests to him that 'maybe the meaning of life lies in the act of looking for it' (*n9d*, 288). This underlines the text's implication that identity is determined through becoming and the search for meaning: *number9dream* is a quest narrative composed of alternative somnambulant identities conjured by an islander without family; in *Ghostwritten* it is proposed that 'the human world is made of stories, not people' (*G*, 386); and *Cloud Atlas* articulates a similar conflation of narrative and subjectivity as storytelling and memory, life and fiction, merge into each other. Yet although Mitchell's characters shape themselves and the world through the stories that they tell, the recurrence of particular images, thoughts and experiences gives their narratives an intertextual, already-read quality whose effect is to undercut the notion of distinct, self-authored identity. In this context, the title of Luisa's Rey's section of *Cloud Atlas* takes on a new stratum of meaning: 'Half-Lives' is as much an allusion to the dispersal of subjectivity and text as a reference to radioactive decay. In Mitchell's writing, people and stories are constantly reciting and recomposing both themselves and each other. While reading the last eight letters Frobisher wrote to Sixsmith in *Cloud Atlas*, Luisa Rey wonders whether 'molecules ... of Robert Frobisher's hand, dormant in this paper for forty-four years' may now be 'swirling in my lungs ... in my blood' (*CA*, 453), an image which combines the transmission of narrative with the transmission of corporeal identity. Buttressed by Nietzchean eternal recurrence – whose 'elegant certainties' (*CA*, 490) are at the heart of Frobisher's music – *Cloud Atlas*, like *number9dream*, hypothesizes identity as at once singular and multiple. Each narrator is necessarily circumscribed by the specificity of their place in history, but profound moments of perception are achieved when the novel's characters catch sight of the larger epic encompassing their own story.

8. Fiction/Fabulation

> For a moment I had an odd sensation of being in a story that someone was writing ... (*G*, 56)

In Mitchell's writing, the multitudinous characters are thus interconnected but the overall effect is to insinuate that these stories are merely selected actualizations of myriad possible 'untold tales' within one fictional universe. Characters and events seem at once to be distinct and yet tied to each other in ways that reveal a small part of the pattern while implying that nothing less than the full multitude of interwoven stories would be sufficient to explain the world, which exists as much in the interior imagination as in external materiality.

The chapters in *number9dream* are loosely thematic. In an author's note, Mitchell lists the successive connecting principles as 'imagination, memory, the moving image, nightmare, fiction, meaning and dreams (he confesses to not yet knowing the theme of the penultimate chapter)' (Dutta, 2001: 21). The work's title, and its epigraph taken from Don DeLillo's *Americana* (1971) ('it is so much simpler to bury reality than it is to dispose of dreams'), anticipate the fact that the various connecting themes are all both modes of perception and alternatives to social reality. All the novels are like *number9dream* in that they could be read as an elaborate succession of solipsistic reveries or fabulations within a multifaceted vision of life as 'one river of sound' as Lennon's *number9dream* expresses it. In *Modernity at Large*, Arjun Appadurai (1996: 27–47) captures this fluid quality of global relations with the analogy of planetary space as an amalgam of shifting landscapes, or, better, seascapes, composed of financial, cultural, technological and demographic movements. These distinct but confluent dimensions provide the globally defined fields of possibility for the production of a constellation of 'imagined worlds'. Eiji's narrative demonstrates similar qualities: each segment of the novel evokes a distinct narratorial texture that keys into a different mode of reality. This layering of disjunctive textual scapes constructs a fractal geometry of current cultural formations in a floating world, for which, in the novel, modern Tokyo is the focus.

Just as distinction between fantasy and reality appears insufficient for an appreciation of Mitchell's texts, the duality of material and immaterial does not seem an adequate way of framing the complex intertwinings of organic and technological networks whose dynamic interplay structures Eiji's world in *number9dream* as he shifts fluidly between the different scapes of modern subjectivity, cycling through versions of himself. In 'The Language of Mountains is Rain',

Eiji dreams the world but also 'a mind in eight parts' (*n9d*, 417), mirroring the structure of the novel and intimating the polyphonic quality of consciousness-levels.[9] Similarly, the disparate characters who emerge from the volatile tumult of the city are no less unstable. They are oddly refracted through Eiji's memories and desires or appear to represent alternative versions of himself. This is a model of ontological instability where multiple imaginary dimensions interpenetrate each other, raising complex system questions rooted in language and pre-social identity, such as where Eiji's consciousness ends and the external world begins. Underpinning this is the suspicion that stories may exist in different minds or media even though they connect across frames; which is to say all is fiction, or rather, all is story.[10]

9. Storyteller

In a 2006 interview with Robert Birnbaum for *The Morning News*, Mitchell outlines his view of the novel as an aggregation of shorter pieces:

> I think all novels are actually compounded short stories. It's just the borders get so porous and so squished up that you no longer see them ... And I do structure my novels in that way. One of the commandments of *Black Swan Green* was to write a novel made of chapters that are theoretically extractable short stories ... Short stories have a background white noise that creates the illusion that the world is much bigger than the mere 10 or 15 pages, and I wanted to see if I could sync up the white noise of the background of short stories. And another model for the novel, which I indulge myself by trying to sneak into all of my books, is provided by the postcards Jason buys at the tourist shop, the 13 postcards ... and when you put them end-to-end, the background is one continuous whole. That's the village and the background plots happening in *Black Swan Green*, yet the foreground dinosaurs are the themes of each separate, individual story ...

A sequence of individual postcards that together create one picture-string describes not just *Black Swan Green* but Mitchell's common approach to his fiction. The stories frequently foreground writing as connection: the reincarnated characters in *Cloud Atlas* forge links with each other through the act of reading and writing; similarly the figure of the ghostwriter in Mitchell's first novel is another iteration of this idea of narrative transmission, which commingles the spectrality of identity and text, each bleeding into the other. 'Study of Tales' in *number9dream* deepens this meditation on textuality and identity. Eiji holes up from the Yakuza in a quiet suburban house owned by his landlord's mother's sister who, it transpires, is a 'fabulist' (*n9d*, 228). In a room 'sentient with books' (*n9d*, 210), Eiji immerses himself in the manuscript of a surrealistic fable featuring three part-human and part-animal characters. The fable is characterized by a playful linguistic excess whose Joycean inspiration is pointedly referred to by the 'stream of consciousness' (*n9d*, 256) in which the protagonist, Goatwriter, swims near the end of the story. The, at times, childlike experimentation with words and the punning allusiveness of the prose clearly foregrounds the materiality of language; both its referential and rhetorical functions.[11] Eiji asks himself at one point whether 'I am a book too' (*n9d*, 210); it is intimated that his immersion in the books that line the study is issuing in the dispersal of his corporeality – 'I gather up any sign of me and stuff it into the plastic bag under the sink. I must clean up traces of myself as I make them' (*n9d*, 213). This sense of dissolution into textuality and the putative serenity of the aesthetic is ambiguously mirrored in Goatwriter's quixotic quest for 'the truly untold tale' (*n9d*, 207) that can only be accomplished by sloughing off his material body in the sacred pool. In this chapter's words, 'Reality is the page. Life is the word' (*n9d*, 267) – Mitchell's fiction offers an understanding of being as an artistic endeavour, the inscription of the self framed as a unique performance from which uniquely singular meaning emerges.

Co(da)nclusion

'I left my Walther PK in my last fantasy' (*n9d*, 27) says Eiji in the first chapter of *number9dream*. This chapter takes the form of a series of daydreams conjured by Eiji's febrile imagination. In one particular fantasy, he is going to see a surrealist arthouse film (similar in its use of dream imagery to Hitchcock's collaboration with Salvador Dali in *Spellbound* [1945]) called, like the chapter and the building Eiji has been watching, 'Panopticon'. In the film, an asylum inmate named Voorman believes he is God.[12] This delusion of grandeur mirrors not only that of the fantasist Eiji but also of the novelist. Voorman makes Belgium disappear and then takes over the asylum by swapping identities with his doctor. Mitchell frequently explores the art of fiction through other media, usually music, but here he uses cinema. The fabulist who believes he is God reshapes the world to suit himself and makes even the map of the world conform to his desires. But if the image of the novelist as God seems to be another worrying will to power, remember that Eiji begins the second chapter of the novel trying to saw the head off the thunder God. Throughout Mitchell's novels there is a suspicion of the conflation of authorship and authority.

In *Ghostwritten*, although Quasar's monologue expresses rigid opposition to the interpenetrations and hybridizations emerging from fluid networks of globalization, the final part of the novel articulates the ineluctable imbrication of lives and narratives. In 'Underground', we descend into the mind of Quasar at the moment when he releases canisters of Sarin gas into a packed metro carriage, an event that has been alluded to a number of times in the novel but which has never been confronted directly. As the tenth chapter in Mitchell's 'novel in nine parts', this section operates as a kind of coda that loosely draws together the strands of the text. It presents itself as a node through which the rest of the stories pass, or perhaps as a journey into the underworld that threads together different levels of reality. The terrorist's struggle to escape from the carriage after setting the timer that will release the poison is rendered in dreamlike prose where people and objects take on a mythic resonance. In his panic, the integrity of Quasar's narrative begins to collapse and images alluding to each of the other chapters seep into consciousness (*G*, 434–5). As the real and the imaginary are increasingly confused, people and objects become peculiar echoes of the stories that we have just read (for example, a sailor has a glossy booklet entitled Petersburg, City of Masterworks, and a vinyl shopping bag 'bulges with a crayon-coloured web that a computer might have doodled. *The London Underground*'; G, 335). This interpenetration of voices, texts and sensations reveals the multiplicity of Quasar's identity and the fragility of the boundary between clean and unclean that structures his existence and divides him from the world.

In *Cloud Atlas*, a similar metaphor of connection is put forward in 'Half-Lives' by the nuclear scientist, Isaac Sachs. Sachs proposes a model of time as 'an infinite matrioshka doll of painted moments' (*CA*, 409), where at every instant we exist within the ever-accreting 'shells' of virtual pasts – one of which is also the real past – and encase within our present a multitude of possible futures, of which only one will ultimately come to pass. This also both mimics the novel's structure and provides another slant on the 'half-lives' of its narrators, whose truncated stories are only completed after the interventions of successive characters. This suggests that narratives (and lives) do not so much end as ceaselessly recycle themselves in new contexts, transposed into different but related forms: for example, Sonmi is granted her final wish to see the closing scenes of Cavendish's filmed memoir where the protagonist gains his freedom; Cavendish obtains the second half of *Half-Lives* for publication; Luisa Rey acquires the remaining correspondence between Frobisher and Sixsmith; and Frobisher encloses the concluding pages of Adam Ewing's journal with his final letter, which is also his suicide note. There is an ethics of fiction here in the assertion of human possibility, but we have also tried to argue that Mitchell's experimentation with structure parallels a wider aesthetic and cultural condition, and that the new stylistic directions of the novels express contemporary life through their multidimensional terrain of transmigratory dreamscapes.

Notes

1 Mitchell divulged this in an interview with James Naughtie (2007) at the Hay Literature Festival recorded for BBC Radio 4's 'Book Club' programme.

2 For an extended study of the palimpsest in relation to modern and contemporary literature, criticism and theory see Sarah Dillon's *The Palimpsest* (2007).

3 The phrase originates with Salman Rushdie's article 'The Empire writes back with a vengeance' (1982). The essay is also included in Rushdie's *Imaginary Homelands* (1990). It is now best known as the title to Bill Ashcroft, Gareth Griffiths and Helen Tiffin's *The Empire Writes Back: Theory and Practice in Post-Colonial Literatures* (1989).

4 The noncorpum makes an allusion to a 'writer in Buenos Aires' who 'suggested a name for what I am' – this is, presumably, Jorge Luis Borges, whose eclectic fictions may well provide the imaginative stimulus for Mitchell's own creation.

5 Deleuze and Guattari explain the concept of the rhizome in the Introduction to *A Thousand Plateaus* (1988). The rhizome is a web or network put forward in opposition to the traditional philosophical model for thought of the tree. Deleuze and Guattari also conceive of the work of art in different terms to those of the root-book with its leaves and branches, central trunk, flowering and deep rootedness. Instead, Deleuze and Guattari write of the 'principal characteristics' of the rhizome: 'unlike trees or their roots, the rhizome connects any point to any other point, and its traits are not necessarily linked to traits of the same nature; it brings into play very different regimes of signs, and even nonsign states ... It is composed not of units but of dimensions, or rather directions in motion. It has neither beginning nor end, but always a middle (milieu) from which it grows and which it overspills ... The rhizome operates by variation, expansion, conquest, capture, offshoots' (Deleuze and Guattari, 1998: 21).

6 This is particularly resonant in the dream connections that characters, such as Quasar in 'Okinawa' and Margarita in 'Petersburg', make with each other, sharing a planetary fate that inclines towards catastrophe or equanimity.

7 The myth has it that the earth and heavens were one cloud, some lighter parts rising to become heaven and others sinking to become muddy water. Later, Izanagi and his wife/sister Izanami created the Japanese islands by whipping a spear in the ocean.

8 Mitchell's text is punctuated with a number of allusions to its novelistic architecture, which are also meditations upon the nature of temporality and identity. In 'Letters From Zedelghem', Robert Frobisher toils away on the composition that, at the tender age of twenty-three, he knows to be his masterwork, an artistic gesture that encompasses his life and will stand as the enduring monument to it. In one of his epistolary outpourings to his college lover, Rufus Sixsmith, he describes his magnum opus

as a 'sextet for overlapping soloists' in which each part is interrupted by another played on a different instrument that speaks 'in its own language of key, scale and colour' (*CA*, 463). Frobisher's piece, whose arrangement sketches the novel's overarching framework in miniature, is pointedly named the *Cloud Atlas Sextet*. Like *Ghostwritten* and, to a lesser extent, *number9dream* and *Black Swan Green*, *Cloud Atlas* could be read as a compendium of short stories or loosely connected episodes, but the image of Mitchell's novel as a musical composition suggests that each of its narratives should be understood as symphonic movements of a larger whole.

9 See also Jerome Urquhart's 2001 interview with Mitchell for the author's explanation of the novel's constituent parts.

10 It is sometimes implied that all the stories are films/books/dreams/ games and so on, but ultimately stories. The end of 'Petersburg' says that 'none of this really happened' (*G*, 261), and earlier in 'Mongolia' Caspar thinks of a film he's seen 'about art thieves in Petersburg' (*G*, 166). This leads to an ontological spiral: if 'Petersburg' is a film then what is the status of Timothy Cavendish in *Cloud Atlas*? And then of Neal Brose in *Black Swan Green*, or Huw Lllewelyn, or the mystery of Luisa Rey? Referentiality spirals off across the fiction playing a game of mirrors between the novels.

11 Though there is not the space to engage with the point in more depth here, the parallels with Joyce in 'Study of Tales' provoke wider comparisons with *Ulysses* (1922) in particular. Indeed, there are thematic and stylistic correspondences between the two texts, not least in the overall architecture of Mitchell's novel that is similarly a presentation of a young man's quest for a father-figure and a portrait of a city.

12 The intertextuality of Mitchell's novels is shown in the poster for the movie, which depicts 'a row of screaming Russian dolls' (*n9d*, 26) that prefigures this recurring metafictional trope in *Cloud Atlas* (*CA*, 26).

Works Cited

Appadurai, Arjun (1996) *Modernity At Large: Cultural Dimensions of Globalisation*. Minneapolis: University of Minnesota Press.

Ashcroft, Bill, Griffiths, Gareth and Tiffin, Helen (1989) *The Empire Writes Back: Theory and Practice in Post-Colonial Literatures*. London: Routledge.

Birnbaum, Robert (2006) 'David Mitchell', *The Morning News*, 11 May, URL (consulted August 2010): http://www.themorningnews.org/archives/ birnbaum_v/david_mitchell.php

Bradford, Richard (2007) *The Novel Now: Contemporary British Fiction.* Oxford: Blackwell.

Chambers, Iain (1994) *Migrancy, Culture, Identity.* London: Routledge.

Deleuze, Gilles and Guattari, Félix (1988) *A Thousand Plateaus: Capitalism and Schizophrenia,* trans. Brian Massumi. London: Athlone.

Dillon, Sarah (2007) *The Palimpsest.* London: Continuum.

Dutta, Shomit (2001) 'Eiji, Anju, Ai and Goatwriter', *Times Literary Supplement,* 5109(2 March): 21.

Hardt, Michael and Negri, Antonio (2000) *Empire.* Cambridge: Harvard University Press.

Hardt, Michael and Negri, Antonio (2004) *Multitude: War and Democracy in the Age of Empire.* London: Hamish Hamilton.

Iyer, Pico (2006) 'Books: Thirteen Ways to Be 13', *Time,* 16 April, URL (consulted September 2009): http://www.time.com/time/magazine/printout/0,8816,1184057,00.html

Iyer, Pico (2007) 'The Time 100: David Mitchell', *Time,* URL (consulted September 2009): http://www.time.com/time/specials/2007/article/0,28804,1595326_1595332_1616691,00.html

Lodge, David (1996) *The Practice of Writing.* Harmondsworth: Penguin.

Naughtie, James (2007) 'Book Club: Cloud Atlas – David Mitchell', BBC Radio 4, 3 June, URL (consulted June 2010): http://www.bbc.co.uk/radio4/arts/bookclub_archive.shtml

Rushdie, Salman (1982) 'The Empire writes back with a vengeance', *The Times* (3 July): 8.

Rushdie, Salman (1990) *Imaginary Homelands,* Granta, Penguin: Harmondsworth.

Urquhart, Jerome (2001) 'You May Say He's a Dreamer', *Independent,* Features, (24 March): 11.

3

'OR SOMETHING LIKE THAT'
Coming of Age in *number9dream*

Kathryn Simpson

A young man's coming-of-age experience is a recurrent theme in David Mitchell's novels. In *Ghostwritten* (1999), Satoru falls in love at first sight in a chance encounter with Tomoyo; their romance runs the risk of failure but finally they overcome the barriers put in their way and Satoru, a 'slow worker' when it comes to romance, is able to attain independence and sexual maturity (*G*, 57). Jason Taylor in *Black Swan Green* (2006) similarly undergoes several rite of passage experiences, which include challenging and exposing the school bullies and experiencing a sexual awakening and his first kiss. Although Orito is not Jacob de Zoet's first love in *The Thousand Autumns of Jacob de Zoet* (2010), the intensity of his unrequited desire for her is a new experience and one that retains its power and alters the course of his life.[1] In *number9dream* (2001), the quest for identity is the central preoccupation and dynamic of the narrative. Eiji Miyake, like many other male protagonists of coming-of-age narratives, is on a quest to find his father, a quest that he is convinced will confirm his identity as a young man and secure him a place in society. As Kenneth Millard (2007: 15) comments, the father's absence in coming-of-age narratives means that 'the desire for a relationship with the father dictates the shape of the protagonist's journey'.[2] For Eiji, this takes him on a literal journey from his rural island home to the massive, chaotic postmodern city of Tokyo. This is simultaneously a metaphorical, emotional and psychological journey during which events act as a series of tests of his manhood, strength, heroism, skill, loyalty, intelligence and judgement. In keeping with other more traditional coming-of-age narratives, Eiji experiences the key rite-of-passage events: he falls in love and has experience of death and sex. Eiji also comes to recognize his quest is a search for meaning – for a way of interpreting the past so that he can find a new meaning for his own life. Unlike more conventional versions of such coming-of-age narratives, however, in Mitchell's novels the process of reaching maturity is incomplete; if 'the journey is one of the most common metaphors for individual maturation' (Moretti, 1987: 93), Mitchell's protagonists remain in transit.[3]

Eiji's coming-of-age experience is also complicated by the fact that his is a double quest in which the overt and acknowledged search to find his father is intertwined with the more implicit, less tangible, quest to understand his twin sister's death. This quest to reconcile his feelings of guilt and his devastating sense of loss about his twinned self, who 'had grown with me cell by cell, day by day' (n9d, 291), is the more profound (and least clearly resolved) aspect of his experience.[4] These interconnected, twinned quests have an ethical dimension and both *seem* to enable Eiji to come of age, to begin to recognize himself as an individual, to realize his potential for intimate relationships beyond his familial context, and to find again a sense of harmony with another person. What also becomes apparent is that these twinned quests function as a strategy via which Eiji seeks to achieve a sense of self not premised on loss, as it has been up to this point.'[5]

The humanist concerns of *number9dream*'s coming-of-age narrative are fundamentally at odds with the knowingly postmodern qualities of the novel. Indeed, in many ways, the *Bildungsroman* is, if not exactly a metanarrative in the Lyotardian sense, a totalizing, centralizing narrative structure premised on the notion of progress that postmodern theory and aesthetic practices work to disrupt and undermine, treating such narratives with 'incredulity' (Lyotard, 1984: xxiv). In his seminal study of the *Bildungsroman*, Franco Moretti characterizes it as a narrative form that works to codify the new paradigm of modernity arising in Western Europe towards the end of the eighteenth and throughout the nineteenth century. It is, he argues, 'the "symbolic form" of modernity' (Moretti, 1987: 5), which attempts to impose pattern and meaning on the protean dynamism of the newly emerging capitalist culture. Although Moretti (1987: 177) claims that by the end of the nineteenth century 'The *Bildungsroman* is over', he also argues that it is not a static form but one that responds to specific cultural, historical and economic contexts in different ways, as his tracing of the generational and geographical developments and differences indicates. Taking on his point that 'the concept of the *Bildungsroman* has become ever more approximate' (Moretti, 1987: 15), it might be possible to read *number9dream* as a postmodern *Bildungsroman*: it questions the viability of the conventional coming-of-age quest for self-knowledge and a secure sense of identity in a postmodern, late capitalist context even as it simultaneously tantalizes the reader with this possibility.

As Linda Hutcheon (1987: 10) might argue, *number9dream* 'use[s] and abuse[s], install[s] and then destabilize[s]' the narrative 'convention' of the *Bildungsroman*. Mitchell's novel destabilizes and questions traditional literary forms (through the wildly exaggerated aspects of Eiji's quest for his father, for example), but does not entirely reject nor cynically dismiss the *Bildungsroman*'s central concerns. Rather, the knowingly postmodern qualities of the novel are held in productive tension with the more humanist and ethically focused aspects of Eiji's quest, so that the novel might be said to engage in a process of redefining the coming-of-age narrative through a postmodern frame. The novel employs traditional literary devices for exploring and revealing different aspects of the protagonist's identity – not least the conceit of the literal journey (which functions as a trope to explore the process of development), the inclusion of dreams, allegorical tales and fairytale motifs – alongside spectacular postmodern devices and techniques, such as parody, pastiche, intertextuality and the blurring of boundaries between reality, virtual reality and fantasy, which work to draw attention to the self-conscious fictionality of the text.[6] As a postmodern *Bildungsroman*, the narrative works with and through the postmodern towards something meaningful – plural, ambiguous, contingent and uncertain, but nonetheless poignant and significant – for Eiji and for the reader. In other postmodern fiction, Eiji's fantastical, surreal and mass-media infused experiences might work to distance the reader and to empty his human story of meaning; here, such narrative elements work to articulate his profound sense of loss and his painful quest to understand and acknowledge this and, ultimately, to find people he can trust and love.

Whether Eiji achieves this or not is without certainy: his narrative radically disrupts any sense of success in his quest for definite meaning and full self-knowledge (experienced as 'maturity'), a fulfilment so central to the *Bildungsroman* tradition.[7] His identity remains 'in process', indeterminate, and open to possibility, as the blank pages of the final chapter attest. This deviation from the closure of the traditional *Bildungsroman* is echoed in the wandering, episodic structure of the novel as a whole. Although overall there is a sense of onward movement, this is far from straightforward and linear: the narrative resembles the twisting of a kaleidoscope so that the elements of the narrative are continually reshaped into new patterns but remain connected (often in unexpected ways). Indeed, the movement of twisting is an apt metaphor, describing as it does both the twisting of traditional forms the novel undertakes, and the way in which Eiji's narrative circles back on itself. Eiji redirects his quest for paternal origins in order to renew his relationship with his mother and to return home in a 'perfect reversal of the way [he] imagined things to be' (*n9d*, 382), only to (possibly) return again to Tokyo and to Ai.

Two key elements of this postmodern *Bildungsroman* are explored here: first, the telling of tales, tales which are often simultaneously more telling and revealing than Eiji the narrator is aware; second, the recurrence of twinning, doubling and substitution of characters, but also of narrative events, and in the form of linguistic play. These complicate Eiji's coming-of-age experience and problematize any sense of there being a single individual identity for Eiji, as they ultimately work to constitute a fluid, provisional and contingent postmodern 'identity'.

Telling Tales

Composed of various fantasies, dreams, memories and media-drenched narrative episodes, *number9dream* adopts a self-referential approach to its own construction and status as fiction. It cleverly pastiches a variety of styles and genres, takes pleasure in linguistic and conceptual play, and generates a sense of ontological uncertainty as the narrative shifts between not only different locations but seemingly different worlds – what Mitchell has referred to as 'multiple reality frames' (Min, 2002). At the heart of the novel is a self (aware) fantasist extraordinaire for whom telling the story of his own life inevitably draws on the multiplicitous influences of the postmodern world. In many ways Eiji is typical of a postmodern decentred subject, wherebyhis experience and construction of his 'self' is shaped by plural sources of influence so that he might be described as 'a flux of contextualized identities' in Hutcheon's (1988: 59) words. More specifically, he is also in many ways the embodiment of postmodern youth and this is evident in the ways in which his daydreams and fantasies are not only richly infused with, and shaped by, postmodern media forms, but also in his use of mass-media technology as one of the tools for his own self creation.[8] In Eiji's telling of his tale the reader is faced with the profound uncertainty about what Eiji's 'reality' is, as boundaries between what seems real and fantasy and/or nightmare constantly slip and slide. This effect is intensified as Eiji demonstrates his unreliability as a narrator, not least through his own awareness that 'daydreams translate into reality … Not very well, not very often' (*n9d*, 4), but also as he draws attention to his own fictionality in his reference to himself as a book to be read (*n9d*, 253). The novel explores what a young man's reality might be as it stages the generation of this reality via the different modes, processes and scenarios through which experience is mediated.

All the tales that comprise this coming-of-age narrative are telling and the tales told by others and embedded into Eiji's narrative also play an important role in redirecting Eiji's quest. They reveal Eiji's identity to be under construction and generate sympathy for him. From the outset of the novel, the importance and centrality of fantasy to Eiji's ongoing creation of his identity is apparent. His heroic fantasies of gaining access to the high-security PanOpticon building and so to his father are clearly informed by thriller and espionage films; his quickly changing choice of cigarette brands indicates the powerful sway of media-fuelled consumer society in helping to construct identities that are only ever provisional. Paradoxically, the fantasies of action-hero success with which the novel begins serve to prolong Eiji's procrastination and his actual attempt to see Akiko Katō results in utter failure and humiliation. However, this failure works to highlight the function and importance of daydreams and fantasies in any coming-of-age experience, as they facilitate the figuring and refiguring of the self and desires, and the testing out of different possibilities for action. Crucially, the fantasy and surreal worlds in which Eiji's different versions of himself are played out are not simply showy postmodern additions to a linear narrative of development; rather, they form the episodic and palimpsestic 'reality frames' of Eiji's quest towards maturity. As such, they inform his perception and interpretation of the literal and metaphorical journey-quest he is undertaking.

Like other postmodern fictions, however, *number9dream* teases at and tests structures of authority, playing with the idea of Eiji as the author of his own narrative. Although at one level the whole novel could simply be composed of Eiji's fantasies (and indeed could be the recounting of eight of his dreams), he is in many ways also an author without authority and feels overtaken by the plot.[9] He points out that the number of coincidences in his experience is suspiciously high – 'Something is too wrong. All these coincidences are too weird' (*n9d*, 140) – and when he finally decides to trust his life story to chance, this leads him for the second time into a violently nightmarish Yakuza trap in which Tsuru, the Yakuza godfather, again asserts his control (albeit briefly) over narrative events. In a postmodern sleight of hand, this experience with the Yakuza literalizes Doi's philosophy that, 'The human condition is a card game, man. Our hand is dealt in the womb … Some days, you got a strong hand. Other days, your winning streaks end in bad gongs. You bet, call, bluff' (*n9d*, 351–2). Trusting to the 'magic' of coincidence (*n9d*, 364) and chance, Eiji's success in his quest to meet his father, achieved via 'a card trick that Tokyo has performed' (*n9d*, 370), is profoundly anticlimactic, so much so that it derails the teleological drive organizing such coming-of-age narratives. Eiji's obsessive quest to find his father sustains a centralized concern with 'origin, oneness … and monumentality … that work[s] to link the concept of center to those of the eternal and universal' (Hutcheon, 1988: 58), but this is ironically undermined by his success in this aspect of his quest, leading him to become aware of the multiple and conflicting points of origin available to him.

Having said this, an important part of Eiji's thrilling and simultaneously troubling negotiation of the boundaries between the seemingly real and fantasy realms is the encounters he has, and the relationships he builds, with several father figures. All of these offer dramatically differing versions of, and perspectives on, the father–son relationship and on the tale he thinks he is telling of his quest for his father. These encounters, and his escapist fantasies, function as distractions from his anxieties and loss but, importantly, they also work to bring the complexities of Eiji's emotional, sexual and psychological development to the surface. Eiji's obsession with finding his father leads him to be lured twice into traps set by the Yakuza and his experiences take on a surreal and horrific quality; the boundaries between Eiji's sense of known reality and the nightmarish, sadistic, cyberpunk world of gangster stories and films are blurred. If Yuzu Daimon is in some ways a demonic substitute sibling, Mr Morino, the head of one of two rival crime syndicates, functions as a kind of demonic surrogate father figure. His vicious rivalry with his 'sibling' head of the other syndicate leads to unspeakable acts of violent revenge. In this reality frame, the fairytale elements common to traditional English *Bildungsroman* narratives – with the accompanying polarizations of good and evil and the meting out of rewards and punishments, as Moretti (1987: 185) describes – become savagely twisted. Eiji is a Faustus character who, desperate for the knowledge he desires, signs a contract of loyalty to this Yakuza 'father' in blood and so is bound to be a Yakuza son until midnight (*n9d*, 183).[10] However, in this bond he is also a very unlucky Cinderella, as Morino cynically remarks, 'Guns and fairy godmothers. They make your wildest wish come true' (*n9d*, 192). Mr Morino promises all the ordinary kinds of 'father–son' activities Eiji could have wished for: 'we could spend the rest of the day together. Go bowling. An outing to a dog show. A bite to eat, and afterwards a get-together with some old friends. Midnight comes around, we give you a lift home' (*n9d*, 182–3). However, these activities are violently distorted and Eiji is forced to witness and participate in horrific events that are profoundly disturbing. His saviour from death in the explosion that ends Eiji's ordeal, Suhbataar (or 'Leather Jacket' as Eiji refers to him), advises him that 'To survive' this experience he 'must persuade' himself that it was 'another man's nightmare into which [he] accidentally strayed' (*n9d*, 202).

Eiji's second encounter with the nightmarishly violent underworld of the Yakuza leads him to being trapped and forced to play cards, the stakes being body organs. This time he *has* stepped into someone else's nightmarish experience – that of Kozue Yamaya's son who was kidnapped and his organs sold to wealthy Japanese parents (*n9d*, 337). That Kozue's son was also called Eiji (and his name also written using the same unusual kanji; *n9d*, 339) makes Eiji a double for this earlier lost son, so that the nightmare simultaneously is and is not his own. His odd sense of dissociation and uncanny doubling when he fails to recognize the image of himself playing this game of chance projected onto a screen compounds this duality and liminal sense of identity: he feels the screen Eiji Miyake 'is operating Miyake by remote-control. I look at myself on the screen. Myself stares back, I never knew I looked like that' (*n9d*, 359). At what is in many ways a defining moment in Eiji's coming-of-age experience (one which leaves Eiji 'wide, wide awake'; *n9d*, 363), this postmodern *Bildungsroman* privileges uncertainty and provisionality. The discontinuity between Eiji and his screened 'performance' of 'being' Eiji 'textualize[s]' the generic liminality of this novel by incorporating the traditional *Bildungsroman* elements (self-recognition and awareness) that it simultaneously contests 'in the performances of [its] characters and examinations of subjectivity' (Lee, 1990: 83).

Eiji's terrifying ordeal comes to an end when Tsuru has a stroke and, in a darkly comic moment, dies face down on a hotplate. This dramatic deflation of the power of this Yakuza father also anticipates Eiji's disappointment when he meets his own father later in the chapter. In an allusion to L. Frank Baum's *The Wonderful Wizard of Oz* (1900), Tsuru not only plays 'god' by creating the illusion of a disembodied voice behind a screen (*n9d*, 358), but he is also exposed as a fake deity and only a mere human by a runaway dog. As for the characters on a quest to see the wizard, this nightmare functions as

Suhbataar has already suggested – as a message 'sent by who, or what, we *really* are, underneath'; 'nightmares are our wilder ancestors returning to reclaim land. Land tamed and grazed, by our softer, fatter, modern, waking selves' (*n9d*, 190). It acts as a caution not to forget our true selves. Eiji's ethical stance against the violent, all-pervasiveness of commodification works to metaphorically reclaim such a land (a 'territory of the self'), which has greater moral integrity. His actions are also in the spirit of a celebration of his friend Suga's skill. Following Kozue Yamaya's advice to 'Act with your eyes open, as your conscience dictates' (*n9d*, 338), Eiji releases the information she has sent him, exposing the extent of Yakuza corruption and trade in body parts using Suga's 'Mailman' computer virus.[11] This act of revenge on behalf of his namesake is only possible once Eiji has finally met his father. In doing so, he makes good his promise to Anju and attains the goal of his teleological quest, but he nonetheless finds himself literally walking in circles. The implication of this paradoxical outcome is that his quest has been circular and futile all along.[12] Although what he finds in his father he no longer wants (*n9d*, 375), this meeting does allow Eiji to feel 'release' to believe that he 'can go now' to make his life as he wants it to be and to take ethical action: 'I am a plague-spreader. Only this plague might cure something' (*n9d*, 378).

In stark contrast to the demonic Yakuza fathers and to his absent biological father, other more positive characters act as father substitutes, not least, Eiji's landlord, Buntarō and Eiji's grandfather, Takara Tsukiyama. Crucially, both of these figures offer Eiji alternative narratives, tales which impact on Eiji's coming-of-age experience and changing sense of his identity as they provoke new ways of thinking and perceiving himself, his life and his quest. The experiences of reading the fables in the 'Study of Tales' and Subaru's journal draw Eiji's narrative closer to a more traditional *Bildungsroman* narrative in terms of the revelation of Eiji's interior state. In keeping with the conventions of such narratives, these chapters are typically inward looking, drawing attention to the emotional and psychological development of Eiji as an individual: the fables lead Eiji closer to the unacknowledged aspect of his quest (to understand and accept Anju's death –

the 'untold tale', perhaps) and Subaru's journal prompts Eiji to discuss with Ai what the meaning of their lives might be.

Buntarō's increasingly excited contemplation of his role as father-to-be and his determination to be a good father act as a foil for everything Eiji discovers about his own father. It is Buntarō who searches for Eiji when he goes missing with the Yakuza, and he and his mother, Mrs Sasaki, also provide Eiji with a safe haven in which to hide and recover following his ordeal.[13] From Buntarō Eiji also 'inherits' the 'Study of Tales', the fables Buntarō's aunt began writing for him as a child. These allegorical tales play a key symbolic role in Eiji's experience of coming to terms with the loss of his twin sister/self and so coming of age as an individual capable of finding new ways to love and be loved. Following his first life-threatening experience with the Yakuza, Eiji goes into hiding and this experience forces him to learn to need others again, a dependency he has spent the nine years since Anju's death trying to avoid (*n9d*, 217). Buntarō is a key figure Eiji comes to need, and he sees him with an ordinary, filial affection: 'Here comes my saviour, leaping over the flooding drain with a newspaper held over his head. His bald patch glistens in the rain' (*n9d*, 242).

Although he continues with his quest to find his father (contacting and meeting the detective Morino used to get the information on Eiji's father), Eiji's active quest and obsession with his father becomes suspended to an extent. The conditions of Eiji's hiding place mirror this sense of suspension in that there are no clocks or calendars with which to measure the external passage of time (*n9d*, 213). This detail, along with the pragmatic necessity for Eiji to hide all material evidence of his presence in the house, suggests a shift to a more internal (emotional and psychological) 'reality frame', somewhere between waking and dreaming. In this sense, like Goatwriter, Eiji finds himself in the 'real world margins', suspended in an unknown place and time (*n9d*, 215). In a sense, Eiji goes into a figurative as well as a literal hiding here, moving away from being the active author-constructor of his own narrative as Goatwriter takes over, ghost writing and symbolically glossing Eiji's quest and literally opening up a new representational aspect of it. Goatwriter himself embarks on a number of quests to find the various things he has lost, all of which are crucial to his identity, to his ability to create, and to his ability to fulfil his overarching quest to find and articulate the 'truly untold tale' (*n9d*, 207). In many ways, Goatwriter's quests function metaphorically to represent Eiji's questioning of what he needs to secure his own identity and to author his own, as yet incomplete, untold tale.

As the title of the chapter – 'Study of Tales' – suggests, the fables included here are tales about fiction itself – a point which the *Guardian* reviewer, Steven Poole (2001), remarks is 'symptomatic of Mitchell's greatest fault: he explains too much', calling this chapter 'wastebasket-fodder'. However, Poole's attack misses the point, failing to take into account the fact that the novel plays with the reader's expectations of postmodern fiction (in this case via the deliberate use of self-referentiality) as it simultaneously plays with the expectations of what should be included in a coming-of-age narrative for boys – 'sadistic action movie, detective story, cyberpunk thriller' as Poole lists them, but also war story, video games and awakening sexuality. As with the other overtly postmodern techniques Mitchell employs, the self-referential style here moves beyond simply being a display of skill and has an ethical quality and a humanist significance.[14] In the treatment of both the more traditional and the fantasy narratives that constitute it, *number9dream* alerts the reader to the importance of making a study of tales. At the same time, Mitchell wryly anticipates his critics having Goatwriter warn about the dangers of postmodern over-theorizing and analysis, which can, to condense Goatwriter's concern, lead critics to 'de ... struct' him and his tales (*n9d*, 238).[15]

This chapter, more than the others, revels in the kind of linguistic play typical of children's rhymes and fairytales; however, as is traditional for such literary forms, the Goatwriter's fable also acts as a cautionary tale. It clearly resonates with both Eiji's overt quest to find his father (his obsession with the origins of his own life story), and the unspoken aspect of Eiji's quest, the desire to understand and accept the death of his sister. Goatwriter's obsessive quest for the originary 'truly untold tale' acts as a warning that to pursue a quest for origins to the limits is actually to embrace death; death is the only truly untold tale, a tale only fully understood by an experience that cannot be narrated. Eiji has come close to death on his quest for his father but it is Goatwriter's tale of the ghost girl that works to recall the more profound aspect of his quest and Eiji's persistent sense of his twin's ghostly presence: with Anju's dare-devil agility, the girl skips off a high wire above 'the unending cataract of Saturn' (n9d, 232) only to vanish in the moonlight before she hits the water.[16]

Indeed another ghostly narrative (Eiji's great uncle Subaru's war journal that Eiji inherits from his grandfather) is significant to Eiji's coming-of-age quest in a number of ways: it brings to his consciousness not only the possibility that his quest to find his father might be 'just a vague ... passing ... nothing', but, importantly, the fact that he 'never did discover' the reason Anju died (n9d, 291). Written during Subaru's preparation as a pilot in the Kai Ten programme during the Second World War, this journal registers the dramatic historical, economic and cultural shifts in Japan since the war, making Eiji realize that the Japan his great uncle died to defend no longer exists. However, this journal is precious to Eiji's grandfather and is a gift loaded with significance: it is premised on the vital importance Eiji's grandfather places on bloodline and family honour, as well as cutting to the heart of what motivates Eiji's own quest – to find where he came from as the key to who he is. As Eiji's grandfather passionately explains: 'Bloodlines are the stuff of life. Of identity! Knowing who you are from is requisite of self knowledge' (n9d, 274). Although 'the pencil marks (of the journal) are fading away to ghost lines' (n9d , 281), the journal inscribes, and substitutes for, his great uncle's body – his brother and family will have the journal in place of a body to bury and mourn over. As Subaru writes, 'This journal is my solace, my meaning, and my body. The sea is a fine tomb. Do not mourn immoderately' (n9d, 275–6).

Importantly, these 'ghost lines' act as a means through which Eiji can contemplate more fully the impact of Anju's death; he can begin to reassess what he values and what he considers to be the meaning of his life ahead. Interspersed with the entries of Subaru's journal are the most heart-wrenching memories of Anju. Reading Subaru's account of the last weeks, days and minutes of his life triggers Eiji's recollection of the days immediately following Anju's death when he ran away

to the interior of the island, lost his sense of time and longed to be
turned into a cedar tree by the forest lord:

> I climb ... A graveyard of trees, a womb of trees, a war of trees ... I
> am not afraid. You have to value yourself to be afraid ... I want the
> forest lord to turn me into a cedar ... When I wake, stiff, not a tree but
> a snot-dribbling boy again, throat tight with a cold, I sob and sob and
> sob and sob and sob and sob. (*n9d*, 290–1)

These memories are recounted using the present tense suggesting
how very present his grief is still – an effect perhaps created by the
fact that Subaru and Anju have similar deaths.[17] However, what marks
a significant turning point for Eiji is his realization that his identity
is not made by himself or by his parents, but that he is a product of
the historical and cultural context in which he grew up (*n9d*, 310).
Later, when Eiji visits Anju's grave, he reads their great uncle's journal
to her, a fitting way to signal Eiji's acceptance of her death and his own
distance from this: although all three have the same birthday (9 September), the similarities of Anju's and Subaru's deaths suggest that,
for Eiji, Anju is now part of another era and that he can finally lay to
rest his grief and loss and say goodbye.

Although Subaru's journal prompts Eiji to discuss with Ai what
the meaning of their lives might be, they revise and develop their
ideas about what constitutes this meaning. They settle on the view
that meaning is always contingent and relative to experience ('Experiences, influences, diseases, divorces.'), and that it depends on the
perception of the self and the purpose of one's life: 'Maybe the truest
difference between people is exactly this: how they see why they are
here' (*n9d*, 299, 300). This instability means that Eiji's decisions fluc-
tuate and experiential markers of transition are never definitive. This
is evident especially in his attempts to come to terms with the loss of
his twin (of another 'self'), and in the many ways in which his desperate longing to rewrite the past and to rescue Anju are played out
(notably in his relationships with Ai and Yuzu). Their names suggest
distinctive subject positions (I and you), but their significance for Eiji
is inextricably bound up with his loss of Anju: Ai and Yuzu continue
the process of twinning and doubling, which abound in this narrative

and which problematize Eiji's coming-of-age experience, generating ambiguity, uncertainty and the sense of identity being decentred, dispersed and in process.

Anju/Yuzu/Ai (Anju)

Eiji's experience of remembering his childhood with Anju is evocative and moving and this probing of inner experience, and its emotional significance, forms an important component of traditional *Bildungsroman* narratives. In the aptly titled chapter, 'Lost Property', Eiji's work at the Lost Property Office at Ueno Station brings his own hidden losses to the surface through the narrative's juxtaposition of a number of apparently disparate events. The discrete narrative sections shift between accounts of Eiji's daytime work, the deeply personal and painful experience of his dream-memories of the time of Anju's death, and the range of difficult and conflicting emotions that surface during a sleepless night. These emotions are indicated by the events of this night, which include the phone call from a 'weird guy' wanting to order a pizza (who, as Eiji discovers later, is very likely to have been his father), his reading of a letter from his mother in which she recalls her wish to kill him as a child, and his own phone call to the clinic in which his mother was staying in an attempt to contact her. These all serve to demonstrate Eiji's present-time confusion. Throughout the chapter there are also frequent suggestive connections between Eiji's present-day experience and his dream-memories, creating the sense of a residue of association and affect. Sometimes it is the discussion of memory itself that initiates a shift to memory of Eiji's childhood ('My memory is the most regular visitor' [*n9d*, 51], 'I like how you can study reflected faces, so deeply you can almost leaf through their memories' [*n9d*, 57]); sometimes it is a repetition of themes, for instance, death with the dying cockroach in Eiji's apartment and the suicide of Mr Aoyama: 'Aoyama jumps from the ledge./Aoyama is no longer alive but not yet dead./His body cartwheels, and falls for a long, long time' (*n9d*, 89). Images of falling and cartwheeling pervade the present-time sections of the chapter and these are clearly associated with Anju: with her daredevil antics and her cat-like agility ('Anju climbed trees like cat. A summer puma'; *n9d*, 44); with her death, but also with Eiji's sense of her continued presence. This relationship is also partially played out in Eiji's attachment to the cat he has unofficially adopted: at one point it looks likely the cat may have died, but she returns to Eiji, snuggles in to the curl of his body and looks at him with her 'Cleopatra eyes' (echoing descriptions of Anju's behaviour and eyes in two of Eiji's dream-memories; *n9d*, 92, 51).

Unlike the typographical mark of a solid diamond that distinguishes Eiji's dream-memories from the immediate present (and which creates the effect of being startled awake, often accompanied as this shift is by reference to time), the mark distinguishing the shift from present to distant past is a fractured diamond shape. This helps to create a sense of slipping into these dream-memories – they are triggered by events in Eiji's present-day experience – but also suggests that the life-changing events these dream-memories recall are present with Eiji all the time. Two of the losses reported to the Lost Property Office that Eiji remembers here – the lost little girl and the woman who had lost her 'pictures', meaning her memories – compound the links between Eiji's present, his past and his powerful feelings of loss as they work to literalize his loss of Anju. This makes clear that Anju is a part or 'property' of him that he has physically lost forever, but who remains an important emotional and psychological prop to his sense of self.[18]

The 'Lost Property' chapter operates in three temporal frames – the distant past recalled though Eiji's dream-memories of his childhood, the recent past and present of his experiences at work, and the immediate present of his sleepless night. Although the chapter is framed by two sections which follow on from each other chronologically and which recount Eiji's decapitation of the thunder god (an act of revenge for Anju's death and so a marker of Eiji's acknowledgement of this), these sections, like the dream-memories, are narrated in the present tense. This creates a temporality that undermines any sense of the 'pastness' of the past, signalling Eiji's perpetual sense of loss, grief and inability to accept Anju's death. Eiji 'wakes' abruptly from dream-memories to the immediate present reality of the time recorded on the Fujifilm clocks opposite his 'capsule', but these markers of 'real' time also serve to draw attention to the temporal slippage Eiji's experience of loss creates, as one example illustrates: 'Fujifilm says two o'clock has come and gone. A single night is stuffed with minutes, but they leak out, one by one' (*n9d*, 53). The Fujifilm clocks (one which records the time at the present moment and one set 45 minutes ahead to the time when the photos will be processed) function both as a temporal anchor to the material present but also signify the double time in which Eiji exists: for him time runs in the present and the past, and his future is always uncertain and in process (*n9d*, 43–4).

That the clocks measure the time taken for the processing of photographs is also significant: photographs function as an anchor to a specific time and place (the moment in which the image was captured on film), but also signal what is irretrievably lost (that specific moment has changed as soon as the photograph is taken). As Roland Barthes (2000: 79) argues, photographs always record not only the past, but what has passed: photographs create a temporal paradox, a 'perverse confusion' in being 'the living image of a dead thing' and so create the illusion of a permanence of presence captured in the 'this-has-been' of the past.[19] This double moment of perception and response functions as yet another form of doubling in the novel: the photograph of Anju that Eiji takes 'out to the balcony' so as to 'drink [his] coffee in her company' (*n9d*, 90) is another indication that Anju is 'alive' to him, her ghostly presence preserved in her photograph, even as this unchanging image is testimony to her lack of life. Photographs also represent doubleness in the way they serve as a reminder that even the most personal, individual, intimate and real aspects of experience (as recorded by this mimetic medium as 'reality in a past state: at once the past and the real' [Barthes, 2000: 82]) are mediated, especially in a postmodern culture. 'Real' experiences are saturated by what Baudrillard calls 'simulacra', so that what is experienced as a sense of an essential self (as evidenced by the powerful memories and emotions photographs help to consolidate) is at least in part technologically produced.[20] However, although this novel accepts that memories, like 'pictures', can be manufactured and 'processed', and that identity remains always in process, this postmodern *Bildungsroman* still allows for the meaningfulness of memory as an important aspect of identity. Eiji's memories indicate that his sense of loss is perpetually present and his longing to rescue Anju pervades his fantasies as well as forming a key role in his relationships with Ai and Yuzu, and in the rite-of-passage experiences he has.

Eiji's meeting with Yuzu on the former's twentieth birthday is (over)loaded with significance in relation to Eiji's quest to find his father, his inability to accept Anju's death, and his coming-of-age experience, given that Yuzu's birthday gift leads to Eiji losing his virginity.[21] They meet as Eiji plays a Zax Omega video game for the first time, an experience he interprets in relation to his own construction of himself and the quests in which he is engaged. This blurring of fiction and reality is evident in the way in which the chapter begins:

> I catch a glimpse of my father being bundled into an unmarked van parked across the baseball field. I would recognize him anywhere. He hammers on the back window, but the van is already through the gates and disappearing into the smoking rubble of Tokyo. I leap onto our patrol stratobike, take off my baseball cap and rest it on the console. Zizzi flashes me a peppermint smile and off we zoom. (*n9d*, 97)

The game involves the player / Zax in the rescue of his father accompanied by the virtual sex symbol, Zizzi Hikaru, and it ends at the point at which the father is exposed as an 'imposter' and the Zizzi character begs not to be left behind (*n9d*, 98). Eiji overlays his own emotional fantasy onto this virtual reality game, the generic father becomes a substitute for his own, and Zizzi is both the love/sex interest and a substitute for his sister.[22] Eiji plays out his anxieties, loss and guilt through this game: his father may be an imposter and unable to fulfil Eiji's needs; and the intensity and complexity of his feelings for Anju mean he is compelled not to leave her behind in his past, but to carry her with him as his only intimate relationship.

Given the emotional intensity Eiji attributes to the Zizzi character at this point, it is significant that it is Yuzu's imitation of Zizzi's voice that interrupts Eiji's immersion in the video game ("'Honey,'" mimics a voice over my shoulder, "don't quit now!'"; *n9d*, 98). This first meeting is followed quickly by a second when Eiji goes back to the games centre to retrieve his baseball cap that he had left on the games console. Both of these meetings associate Yuzu with Anju (he mimics

Zizzi who substitutes for Anju in Eiji's fantasy, and he wears Eiji's cap which is Eiji's gift from Anju and his most precious talisman) and set up the complex significance Yuzu will have for Eiji's emerging identity. At the start of this evening, both Eiji and Yuzu acknowledge their fluid or uncertain state and their feeling of not being 'themselves'. Eiji's experiences first at the Merry Christmas Bar and then at Yuzu's father's exclusive club, the Queen of Spades, lead Eiji to be intoxicated not only with alcohol but also with the way his sense of identity unravels further. As Eiji, looking at the reflected images in the club lift, remarks, 'stay in here long enough and you'd forget which one was you' (*n9d*, 111). Yuzu's significance is complexly multiple: he is at once a brother-figure, a role model and a substitute for Anju.[23] As such, he is also a kind of alter ego/double for Eiji himself as his name 'you/zu' suggests.

Eiji's loss of his virginity is a key rite-of-passage experience. It overtly marks a significant stage in his quest for identity and carries significance for the more implicit goal of his quest which is to accept his sister's death. Drunk and stoned, he and Velvet share a first kiss which seems to last 'for nine days and nine nights' and later he and Coffee have sex (*n9d*, 117). Eiji's disappointment with this culturally celebrated marker of maturity gives rise to a comically outraged response: '*That* groin sneeze was sex? That was no Golden Gate bridge to a promised land. It was a wobbly plank across a soggy bog. Nobody even gives you a badge to sew on' (*n9d*, 120). However, the way this experience is described takes on a more complicated significance for Eiji: the nine days and nine nights of his first kiss recall the time that seems to pass while the thunder god decides whether or not to accept the young Eiji's deal. His experience and description of sex in terms of swimming, diving, surfacing and gasping for air, then finally falling and not waking before hitting the ground, all recall Anju – her death-defying leaps from tree branches, their discussion of the myth of falling in dreams and, of course, her death by drowning. This rite of passage experience, then, takes on heightened and complicated significance for Eiji. In part it marks a new awareness of separation from Anju: death by drowning literally separates Eiji from his twin and his new experience as a young man *should* confirm this symbolically. However, the fact that this new experience is described in terms of Anju's experiences puts the separation this rite-of-passage event should signify into question and suggests that his attainment of individuality and maturity are not so readily achieved as other coming-of-age narratives suggest.[24]

Although Eiji does not have an external marker of this rite-of-passage experience – a badge of manhood, as it were – he is able to act in a heroic way to defend Ai when, back at the Jupiter café, she is accosted by an irate customer. His 'first head-butt' is ironically described as 'An historic occasion' by Ai (*n9d*, 131), but his reward is to know her name so that their romance can begin. However, despite the sense of progression that Eiji's loss of his virginity and his first act as a 'heroic' figure indicate, to a certain extent he finds himself back at the beginning – he is in the Jupiter café, playing out his fantasies about meeting his father, this time through the video game belonging to the old customer he met on his first visit there. Eiji is moving onward towards maturity at the same time as he is simultaneously back at the beginning of his quest.

This circularity and ambiguity about his 'progress' on his twinned quest is central to Eiji's increasingly intimate and important relationship with Ai. She plays a key role in Eiji's quests: she is instrumental in Eiji finding his grandfather and getting access to information about his father; she procures him the job at Nero's Kitchen through her flatmate, Sachiko Sera, which finally leads to Eiji's meeting with his father; importantly, she also helps to redirect his quest towards his mother, with her view that Eiji's life 'could be a whole lot richer with [his mother] in it' (*n9d*, 349). Once Eiji has told Ai about Anju, she claims to understand his feelings and his dreams with 'perfect pitch' (*n9d*, 400). However, Eiji's romance with Ai is far from straightforward and, rather than acting to confirm his maturity, it further reveals Eiji's complex, palimpsestic and incomplete coming-of-age experience. Eiji's firstly imagined and later anticipated rescues of Ai frame the novel as a whole and these narrative repetitions and plot circularity paradoxically suggest that Eiji both attains a degree of maturity and separation from the past and Anju, while at the same time work to undermine a sense of linear progression. This creates the effect of a profound uncertainty about any sense of this process of Eiji's coming of age being complete.

In one of Eiji's first fantasies he rescues Ai from death by drowning and a crocodile attack in his imagined freak flooding of Tokyo. In his fantasy Ai, grateful and distraught, looks into the water from the 'stone whale' and watches helplessly as Eiji drowns and sinks 'in slow, sad circles' (*n9d*, 20). This fantasy serves to reverse the fact of Anju's death and erase Eiji's guilt: Eiji is able to save Ai/Anju but only at the expense of his own watery (though heroic) death. Both Ai and Eiji himself are substitutes for Anju in this fantasy – a complex intertwining that remains central (and problematic) in Eiji's coming of age. Peter Childs's suggested word play with 'Ai Anju' – I and you – underscores this interconnection and teases at the troubling, ambiguous and perhaps impossible process of attaining an individual sense of identity as 'I'. This substitution and intertwining also temporarily relieves Eiji's sense of guilt and responsibility for Anju's death (since he rescues Ai/Anju in this fantasy), as well as revealing his ongoing sense of the loss of this intimate bond with another, twinned, self (since he dies in this fantasy so they still cannot be reunited). The complex duplication and substitution (Ai/I Anju) also signals the impossibility of an intimate bond with others as being distinct from that with his twin.

In contrast, Eiji's anticipated return to Tokyo to find Ai when the city is hit by an earthquake is testimony to Eiji's success in attaining maturity and independence, as is his journey to meet his mother and his return home to his grandmother's house. Eiji, like the hero of a traditional coming-of-age narrative, has, through his various experiences, attained a more adult perspective on the world.[25] He no longer sees his parents simply as relative to his needs and desires, but as ordinary, flawed individuals; his perception of his home and his past has changed and the 'frame' of his vision is altered so that he can now see 'the whole' (*n9d* 415); he can finally acknowledge the death of his twin and be able to distinguish his romantic and sexual desires for Ai as distinct from his intimacy with Anju.[26]

Eiji seems to have found peace and a new sense of his individual identity. At the same time this sense of linear progression is put into question by the fact that Eiji's journey home is one taken almost en-

tirely in a dream state. He dreams vividly in what are surreal confla-
tions of his experiences in Tokyo, his past and his unconscious desires.
Moreover, his guilty anxiety and his chance meetings with Mrs Persimmon further blur the boundaries between dream and real experience. Dreams are often assumed to be coded 'texts' and, post-Freud,
are read as symbolic of unconscious desires and so as self-revelatory.
These assumptions about dreams *seem* to coincide with Eiji's return
to the 'interior', to the geographical and emotional territory he sought
to escape in his quest to find his father: here he returns to the heart of
his past, his memories, and his familial connections which are key to a
sense of identity. However, as alternative forms for constructing a narrative of the self, dreams are revealed to be far from straightforward:
Eiji's return journey is beleaguered by too many pieces of advice and
conflicting ideas about the significance of dreams from the truck
drivers who drive him home and from Mrs Persimmon. The effect
is counter-productive so that the dreams and the various modes of
analysis modelled here serve only to maintain the complexity and
uncertainty of Eiji's experience. Eiji's dreams are *too* obvious and
overloaded, and that is possibly the point. Like a typical *Bildungsroman* hero, Eiji returns home with a new perspective generated by new
experience, but not with the full self-knowledge and understanding
such return journeys typically assume and that dreams supposedly
help to realize.

Finally, rather than looking to the future, the dream he slips into as
he waits for his grandmother is still a dream of origins, of the mythic
origin of Japan which comes to focus on Anju's death. This again puts
the success of his quest into question as it indicates that what remains
central to his unconscious is an ongoing anticipation of an explanation for his sister's death: this explanation is impossible to obtain and
yet it blocks any movement into an independent future. His dream
is significantly interrupted by the radio announcement of a massive
earthquake in Tokyo and, wishing he were actually dreaming this catastrophic news, Eiji is finally awake to the reality of his life and to his
individual identity and desires. The reader is left to interpret the final
words of the novel, 'And I begin running' (*n9d*, 418), but, given Eiji's
new sense of maturity and his separation from the past, we might as-

sume that he is running back to Ai. Despite this massive impetus to leave the past behind, however, the novel ends with a state of suspension: Eiji is suspended between Yakushima and Tokyo, between a past that is closed to him and a profoundly uncertain future represented typographically by the blank pages of the final chapter.

Alison Lee (1990: 83) argues that postmodern fiction both 'inscribes a superficial layer of recognizable conventions' (in this case, of the *Bildungsroman*) while at the same time refusing to 'subscribe unquestioningly to the wiles of (a particular) genre'. *number9dream* functions between generic identities in this way and the final insistence on a liminal identity for the hero of this postmodern *Bildungsoman* is consistent with this. Eiji is neither one of the hero figures he imagines he is in his fantasies, but nor is he not one of these heroes either; his identity fluctuates somewhere in between so that at the end of his coming-of-age narrative he is finally poised to become the action hero he imagined himself to be at the beginning of the novel. Whether he can make this transition, however, is not revealed and a secure sense of identity remains unrealized.

Towards the end of the novel, Eiji recalls that, after his sister's death, he had the sense that the 'Real' and ideal 'Eiji Miyake' existed elsewhere and that he and this real self simply dreamed one another:

> When I began my serial uncle visits, post-Anju, I imagined that there lived somewhere, in an advertland house and family, the Real Eiji Miyake. He dreamed of me every night. And that was who I really was – a dream of the Real Eiji Miyake. When I went to sleep and dreamed, he woke up, and remembered my waking life as his dream. And vice versa. (*n9d*, 407–8)

Eiji's quest for his father and to understand Anju's is represented in a narrative form in which the real, imagined and virtual worlds collapse into one another, and the boundaries between dream, nightmare, fantasy, memory and the illusory and hallucinatory are hard to detect or sustain. The question that finally hangs over the novel is whether Eiji will or can ever stop dreaming. It remains unclear whether, in a postmodern, hyperreal world, it is possible to represent a character that can fulfil the goal of a traditional coming-of-age hero and become *the* definitively 'Real Eiji Miyake'. As the initials of his name suggest, in a postmodern *Bildungsroman*, the 'REM' is perhaps always an impossible dream and identity always provisional, contingent and in process – always simply 'something like that' (*n9d*, 3).

Notes

1 Two parallel phrases encapsulate the enduring impact of his love and desire for her: the first narrates their literal separation as she fails to gain entry to Dejima and his protection – 'The well-oiled bolt slides home' (*TA*, 169); the second, the final sentence of the novel, movingly and metaphorically reunites them as Jacob dies – 'A well-waxed paper door slides open' (*TA*, 469).

2 Millard (2007) discusses two American coming-of-age novels in relation to these ideas: Russell Banks's *Rule of Bone* (1995) and Brady Udall's *The Miracle Life of Edgar Mint* (2001).

3 Satoru travels to Hong Kong and we have hints of his ongoing development through the glimpses other characters have of him; Jason moves from *Black Swan Green* and although he feels that his life 'doesn't *feel* very alright', the final words of the novel make clear that 'That's because it's not the end' (*BSG*, 371); Eiji remains suspended geographically and temporally. This is the case in other postmodern coming-of-age narratives such as Hanif Kureishi's *Buddha of Suburbia* (1990), in which Karim's coming-of-age experience is similarly narrated in an episodic way and is focused on the need to define his identity in relation to his father. Kureishi's text includes Karim's disturbing and pleasurable rite-of-passage experiences, the excitement and opportunities he finds in the city, and uses pop culture – especially music – as a medium to relate these coming-of-age experiences. Jeanette Winterson's *Oranges Are Not The Only Fruit* (1985/1990) shares a similar slippage between fantasy and realism in its representation of the complexity of the coming-of-age experience, a temporary return home and an ending, like that of *Buddha*, which leaves the protagonist's quest for identity incomplete.

4 Eiji blames himself for Anju's death not only because her fatal swim to the whalestone rock was in part inspired by his own storytelling and daydreaming about finding their father, but largely because of the 'deal' eleven-year-old Eiji makes with the thunder god (*n9d*, 52, 70). In this deal, the god would help grant him his wish (to be a football star and so

bring his parents back together) in exchange for 'Anything' Eiji can give – his success in the school football match coincides with his sister's death.

5 Eiji's father was absent from his life, his mother was estranged and subsequently rejected by Eiji following Anju's death. He is also aware that his grandmother blames him for the loss of Anju. Following Anju's death, he adopts a nomadic life, moving between visits with his various family members and loses any secure sense of home. This unsettled life and experience of being displaced seems apt, however, as a response to the profound sense of disturbance caused by the loss of the central relationship of his life, that with Anju.

6 Like much postmodern fiction, *number9dream* sets up endless teasing possibilities for speculation about interconnections between reality and fiction, and the title is a significant example. It alludes to John Lennon's song of the same title, which was released on the album *Walls and Bridges* (1974), a title that also seems significant for a narrative concerned with overcoming barriers and making new connections as Eiji quests for his sense of identity. The album cover itself reproduces a drawing Lennon made when he was eleven showing boys playing football, which again seems to teasingly echo the football game in which Eiji plays when he is eleven and which, for him, is the defining experience of his life.

7 This is the case for nineteenth-century *Bildungsroman* heroes such as Charles Dickens's Pip in *Great Expectations* (1861) and the eponymous David Copperfield, and also for Charlotte Brontë's Jane Eyre. James Joyce's Stephen also announces his independence, maturity and greater self-knowledge at the end of *A Portrait of the Artist as a Young Man* (1916), though this is more ambivalent than for the earlier heroes. Later twentieth-century *Bildungsroman* heroes, such as Jeanette in *Oranges Are Not the Only Fruit* and Karim in *The Buddha of Suburbia*, reach maturity but, similarly to *number9dream*, the endings of their coming-of-age journeys are much more uncertain and open ended.

8 See Côté and Allahar (1994: 22–3) for a discussion of this more generally.

9 Salman Rushdie's Saleem Sinai in *Midnight's Children* (1981/1995), though for different reasons, is also a first-person narrator whose grip on his own narrative is at times tenuous if not lost entirely. As Saleem complains, 'And there are so many stories to tell, too many, such an excess of intertwined lives events miracles places rumours, so dense a commingling of the improbable and the mundane' (Rushdie, 1981/1995: 9). Rushdie's

novel as a whole privileges the complexity and multiplicity of versions of the same 'truth'.

10 Eiji desires to know his father and Morino's detective's file on his father containing 'Name, address, occupation, résumé, personal history, pix – colour, black-and-white – itemized telephone bills, bank accounts, preferred shaving gel' would seemingly deliver his father in his entirety (*n9d*, 183).

11 'Mailman' is a gift Suga makes to Eiji with 'a proud-father beam' and his virus is significantly described as being his child-creation (*n9d*, 347).

12 This recalls the man Eiji observes walking the three circuits of the same streets at the beginning of the novel, a detail that adds to the doubling at work in Eiji's narrative, and which also confirms the narrative's circularity by returning the reader to the beginning of the novel and the start of Eiji's quest (*n9d*, 23–4).

13 It is also through Buntarō that Eiji got his job at the Lost Property office at Ueno Station, perhaps suggesting that early on Buntarō recognized Eiji's need to reconcile his loss.

14 There is a similar self-referential moment at about the mid-point of *The Thousand Autumns of Jacob de Zoet* where the storyteller's art is demystified ('Tricks of the trade, you see?'; *TA*, 260), while the importance of narratives to feed the emotions, the imagination and the soul is simultaneously asserted. Although there is a degree of cynicism in the process of the composition of (and motivation for) the stories written here (which follows a Propp-like method of assembling narrative elements), the fact that 'Storytellers are not priests who commune with an ethereal realm, but artisans, like dumpling-makers, if somewhat slower' (*TA*, 260) highlights the nurturing power of narratives.

15 As Goatwriter exclaims, 'The critics will de-re-un-in(con)struct me!' (*n9d*, 238).

16 Anju is explicitly associated with ghosts in other parts of the novel, such as in Eiji's dream-memories of their childhood where she likens herself to ghosts (*n9d*, 47, 58).

17 Both die by drowning and both are driven by their faith in the power of myth: Anju dies because of local myth of the whalestone coming to life to fulfil her dreams, and Subaru dies defending myth of Japan as a nation.

18 An interesting comparison here could be made with 'Unborn Twin' – a textual but never physical presence – in *Black Swan Green* who continu-

ally speaks to Jason in his mind, and advises him, particularly at moments of indecision or crisis. [Ed.]

19 Madame Crommelynck's views on photographs in *Black Swan Green* similarly resonate with these ideas. Looking at a photograph of her younger self, she reflects on her friend's words that, 'By slicing out *this* moment and freezing it ... all photographs testify to time's relentless melt' (*BSG*, 199). In doing so, they trouble any single or linear sense of time: as Madame Crommelynck continues, 'Photographs make me forget if time is forwards or backwards. No, photographs make me wonder if there *is* a forwards or backwards' (*BSG*, 199–200). [My thanks to the editor for drawing my attention to this comparison.]

20 As Baudrillard (2004: 1) states, 'Simulation is no longer that of a territory, a referential being, or a substance. It is the generation by models of a real without origin or reality: a hyperreal'.

21 Twenty is the official age of majority in Japan and there is a coming of age day in which those who have reached twenty are given symbolic gifts to mark the transition into adulthood.

22 Zizzi is similarly a sex symbol in Eiji's earlier masturbatory fantasies (*n9d*, 47–8). Although this detail might lend itself to the suggestion of incestuous desires, what it more obviously suggests is Eiji's profound sense of guilt and loss, feelings intensified by his sense as a child of being somehow responsible for Anju and his fear of her death. In one of his dream-memories in 'Lost Property', for instance, the scene of the two children high up in a tree, his fear of Anju falling and his awareness that their grandmother 'would murder [him]' if she fell are all telling indications of his persistent sense of his responsibility for her, and therefore for her death (*n9d*, 46).

23 He is, initially, the kind of successful and sophisticated young man Eiji aspires to be, as Eiji remarks: 'Yuzu Daimon is a final-year law student, a native of Tokyo, and the finest pool player I have ever met. He is brilliant, truly' (*n9d*, 103).

24 In *Oranges Are Not the Only Fruit*, for example, Jeanette's first sexual experience is of monumental proportions (as the biblical allusion implies): 'we hugged and it felt like drowning. Then I was frightened but couldn't stop. There was something crawling in my belly ... And it was evening and it was morning; another day' (Winterson, 1991: 86). In *Buddha of Suburbia*, Karim's first sexual experience with Charlie is similarly dramatic: 'There was dancing in my streets. My flags flew, my trumpets blew!' (Kureishi, 1990: 17).

25 Compare, for example, Dickens's *Bildungsroman* heroes in *Great Expectations* and *David Copperfield*, and also Charlotte Brontë's *Jane Eyre*.

26 Both Jeanette in *Oranges Are Not the Only Fruit* and Karim in *The Buddha of Suburbia* are also able to see their parents as flawed but endearing and this is a sign of their maturity. Like Eiji, Jason in *Black Swan Green* similarly realizes that his parents are individuals with needs of their own and this alters his perception of his relationship to them: 'I noticed a new need that's normally so close up you never know it's there. You and your mum need to like each other. Not love, but like' (*BSG*, 246). [My thanks to the editor for drawing my attention to this comparison with *Black Swan Green*.

Works Cited

Barthes, Roland (2000) *Camera Lucida*. London: Vintage.

Baudrillard, Jean (2004) *Simulacra and Simulation*, trans. Sheila Faria Glaser. Ann Arbor: University of Michigan Press.

Childs, Peter (2009) 'David Mitchell's Novels in Nine Parts', paper presented at the David Mitchell Conference, St Andrews, September 2009.

Côté, James E. and Allahar, Anton L. (1994) *Generation On Hold: Coming Of Age In The Late Twentieth Century*. New York and London: New York University Press.

Hutcheon, Linda (1987) 'Beginning to Theorize Postmodernism', *Textual Practice* 1(1): 10–31.

Hutcheon, Linda (1988) *A Poetics of Postmodernism: History, Theory, Fiction*. New York and London: Routledge.

Kureishi, Hanif (1990) *The Buddha of Suburbia*. London: Faber and Faber.

Lee, Alison (1990) *Realism and Power: Postmodern British Fiction*. London and New York: Routledge.

Lyotard, Jean-François (1984) *The Postmodern Condition: A Report on Knowledge*, trans. Geoff Bennington and Brian Massumi. Manchester: Manchester University Press.

Millard, Kenneth (2007) *Coming-of-age in Contemporary American Fiction*. Edinburgh: Edinburgh University Press.

Min, Toh Hsien (2002) 'The Illusionist's Dream', *Quarterly Literary Review Singapore* 1(2), URL (consulted August 2010): http://www.qlrs.com/interview.asp?id=173

Moretti, Franco (1987) *The Way of the World: The Bildungsroman in European Culture*. London: Verso.

Poole, Steven (2001) 'I think I'm Turning Japanese', *Guardian*, 10 March, URL (consulted August 2010): http://www.guardian.co.uk/books/2001/mar/10/fiction.davidmitchell

Rushdie, Salman (1981/1995) *Midnight's Children*. London: Vintage.

Winterson, Jeanette (1985/1991) *Oranges Are Not the Only Fruit*. London: Vintage.

4

REMEDIATIONS OF 'JAPAN' IN *NUMBER9DREAM*

Baryon Tensor Posadas

Circulations of 'Japan'

Just as any other nation, 'Japan' exceeds the boundaries that its name formally designates. Subsumed under its name is not merely a singular or monolithic entity that is reducible to a geographic location or the putative cultural essence of a set of traits and practices that can simply be identified and demarcated; rather, it is at once a space constituted in and as fantasy. In other words, 'Japan' is a signifier that is overcoded and overdetermined by a shifting constellation of relations through which it is imagined, along with their consequent discursive contestations and complications. This has a long history of manifestations, taking on various guises that range from – as Susan Napier has catalogued in *From Impressionism to Anime* (2007) – the *Japonisme* of late nineteenth-century art, to its modernist articulations, to the imaginings of postwar science fictions.

In the contemporary conjuncture, one domain wherein this has taken on a particular visibility is in recent Hollywood films. The past decade has been witness to several Hollywood films that use Japan as their setting – *The Last Samurai* (2003), *Lost in Translation* (2003), or *Memoirs of a Geisha* (2005), for instance – and, with this, have consequently attracted considerable controversy and criticism over their representations of the nation they take up in their respective narratives. Rob Marshall's *Memoirs of a Geisha*, for instance, was subject to critical responses in Japan and China, stemming in part not only from the controversies surrounding its casting of Chinese actresses for the principal roles (McCurry, 2005), but also for presenting a 'condescending and naive' (Bell, 2005: 1) picture of the culture it purports to represent. Similarly, in the wake of the release of Sophia Coppola's film, *Lost in Translation*, critic Kiku Day (2004: 3) wrote a scathing review in the *Guardian* accusing the film of anti-Japanese racism, pointing to 'one-dimensional and dehumanized' representations of the Japanese in the film. Taken together, these controversies indicate the extent to which contemporary representations of Japan are still haunted by the specter of Orientalism.

While I sympathize with these criticisms to a certain extent, I must call into question the underlying assumptions of the assertions made in them. More often than not, the objections raised against these films are founded on questionable notions of accuracy and discourses of authenticity. What such an approach implicitly presupposes is that there is such a thing as a discrete and identifiably authentic 'Japan' out there, outside of the discursive practices through which its image is produced. This frame of analysis cannot but reproduce the reifying logic of Orientalist fetishizing of cultural identities that such readings purport to critique. It is a crucial (if at times overlooked) component of Edward Said's seminal critique of the historical discourse and practice of Orientalism. As Said writes in *Orientalism* (1979: 273): 'My whole point about this system is not that it is a misrepresentation of some Oriental essence – in which I do not for a moment believe – but that it operates as representations do, for a purpose, according to a tendency, in a specific historical, intellectual, and even economic setting'. The task then is not simply to dismiss these fantasies of the Orient as inaccurate portrayals (regardless of whether or not this is in fact the case) but, more importantly, to recognize how, through these fantasies, desires are constituted and structured. This makes it imperative to articulate the problem of what function such desires serve at the historically specific junctures in which these representations are produced and circulated.

For Said and his analysis of representations of the historical 'Orient' – that is, the Middle East – the sociopolitical milieu at large is the history of colonialism. Needless to say, this cannot simply be extended to representations of Japan in the present moment. To do so would fail to account for not only the different position Japan occupies in the global imaginary geography, but also, and more importantly, the changes in the political and economic structures of the contemporary context. The implication here is not that the problem of Orientalism is inapplicable to the case of Japan. Rather, as Richard Minear (1980: 507–17) has suggested, attention to the specificity of the context of Japan – as object of an Orientalizing gaze despite not having been directly colonized – productively enables the possibility of thinking through Orientalism as it operates in discursive regimes other than formal colonialism. Such is the case in the contemporary conjuncture, after all, which historian Arif Dirlik characterizes as a passage from colonial modernity to a global modernity, the latter of which marks on the one hand the end of formal colonialisms and on the other is at once the transnational generalization and deepening of the logic of colonial modernity itself, 'the internalization by societies globally of the premises of a capitalist modernity, deeply entangled in colonialism, to which there is now no viable alternative' (Dirlik, 2005: 7).

Despite these shifts in the structures of power in the present, what remains unchanged is the fundamental point: countries and cultures, in other words, are not merely static preexisting entities that exist a priori to their representations. Rather, especially in the present juncture, they are image-commodities that are trans-nationally produced and circulated, and as such, are necessarily imbricated in the structures of global modernity. The two examples noted earlier are illustrative. In the case of *Lost in Translation*, Kôichi Iwabuchi suggests that, in order to be fully understood, the film's representation of Japan and the subsequent responses to it both need to be situated within the intensifying transnational circulation of images via media and culture industries through which national and cultural identities are branded and trafficked (Iwabuchi, 2008: 544). Similarly, in her discussion of Arthur Golden's novel *Memoirs of a Geisha* (1997), from which the subsequent film was adapted, Anne Allison crucially observes that although the novel certainly re-stages a history of geisha fetishizing in Euro-America, the popularity of Golden's novel is not attributable to its seeming authenticity; that is, its classic unmasking of a mysterious Orient. Instead, in alignment with the centrality of disguise and foregrounding of performativity embodied in the figure of the geisha, what attracts readers to the novel is its very play on fictionality and the *momentary* identification with the fantasy of otherness this facilitates. For Allison (2001: 392–3), this hints at a readerly desire for commodified and easily exchangeable cultural identities. The point here is that a rigorous critique of such Orientalist fantasies and cultural fetishisms demands that the mechanisms of such commodity fetishisms be accounted for. In particular, the function they serve in buttressing the structure of relations that are constitutive of the contemporary conjuncture warrants examination.

It is against this backdrop that David Mitchell's second novel *number9dream* first appears and in such terms that it can be productively read. Set in Japan with a Japanese protagonist, an all too easy critical conclusion would be that the novel reproduces imagery that may be characterized as 'techno-Orientalist'.[1] Such a reading is invited in particular by the proliferation of what are by now stereotypical images of a hypermodern Tokyo in the text.[2] These are derived from the deployment of 'the Orient' and specifically of 'Japan' as privileged signifiers for the increasing incursion and mediation of technology into the human body and human perceptual systems in contemporary science fictions like Ridley Scott's *Blade Runner* (1982) and William Gibson's *Neuromancer* (1984). However, *number9dream* resists such a reading: although it partakes in *Blade Runner*-inspired cyberpunk motifs to represent its Tokyo setting, its self-reflexive hypermediation of these motifs calls attention to the pervasiveness of the circulation of cultures as image-commodities. In effect, this brings to the foreground the very mechanism of repression and displacement onto the Other of which techno-orientalist imagery is symptomatic. Moreover, the novel implicitly positions itself as a kind of intertextual doppelgänger of the fiction of Murakami Haruki, who is himself a transnational writer not easily fixed to a national positioning. A plethora of winking allusions to several of Murakami's novels – including *A Wild Sheep Chase* (Hitsuji o meguru bôken, 1982; trans. 1989), *Norwegian Wood* (Noruwei no mori, 1987; trans. 2000) and *The Wind-up Bird Chronicle* (Nejimakidori kuronikuru, 1994–5; trans. 1997) – call into question notions of fixed origins and authorship.[3] Taken together, what these narrative strategies suggest is that this is a novel that does not simply make a naive attempt at representing an imagined truth or essence of

'Japan'. Rather, it recognizes the impossibility of locating a 'Japan' not already mediated and subsumed under the logics of global modernity. In doing so, it opens up a productive space to articulate a politics of cultural translation that is attentive to the unevenness of the immaterial labor of fantasy production.

Remediation upon Remediation

number9dream literally begins with a fantasy:

> It is a simple matter. I know your name, and you knew mine, once upon a time: Eiji Miyake. Yes, *that* Eiji Miyake. We are both busy people Ms. Katô, so why not cut the small talk? I am in Tokyo to find my father. You know his name and you know his address. (*n9d*, 3)

These opening lines, and the scene that unfolds subsequent to them, are imaginary. Presumably in preparation for the scenario's eventual enactment, they are rehearsed in advance by the protagonist and narrator of the novel (Eiji Miyake) as he waits in the Jupiter Café adjacent to a building called PanOpticon where his father's lawyer (Akiko Katô) is evidently employed.

The novel's opening scene sets up several key elements of the narrative. First, it establishes through proper nouns – naming the place (Tokyo) and the two characters – that the narrative takes place in Japan; it also serves to set up the primary narrative thread of the novel wherein the protagonist Eiji Miyake is in search of his estranged father. Second, and more importantly, the opening lines foreshadow a key feature of the narrative of *number9dream*: the tendency of the protagonist Eiji to slip into elaborate fantasies. More often than not, these fantasies come with little preparation or marks of transition in the novel, in effect blurring the borders between Eiji's experiences and fantasies and making it effectively impossible to mark the distinctions between them.

Aside from the sheer absurdity of the scenarios depicted in Eiji's fantasies – in one case a flood washes over Tokyo and Eiji ends up getting killed and has his funeral attended by various ambassadors and dignitaries and no less than Yoko Ono – there are often few clues that the scene described is one of the protagonist's fantasies until it is resignified by the following scene. This narrative structure produces a nagging sense of unreliability in the narration on the reader's behalf, since the reader is never certain whether what she or he is reading is fact or fiction, within the imaginative world of the novel.

More importantly, what makes Eiji's fantasies even more interesting is that they make use of tropes derived from mass-media cultural artifacts. For instance, the first extended excursion into Eiji's daydreams takes on the pattern of an action scene in a cyberpunk science fiction film, with Eiji storming the PanOpticon in search of Akiko Katô. Smoothly following on from the scene in the Jupiter Café, it is made to appear that Eiji attempts to infiltrate the PanOpticon. Bluffing his way past security to reach the office of Akiko Katô, he is then finally able to utter the lines from the novel's opening that he has been rehearsing. Following this statement by the narrator, the novel then proceeds to an exchange and confrontation with the aforementioned Ms. Katô, eventually ending with Eiji shooting Akiko Katô, only to have it subsequently revealed that he has killed nothing more than a mechanical simulacrum. The following passage occurs near the end of this fantasy:

> Akiko Katô closes the door with her ankle, and levels a Zuvre Lone Eagle.440 at the spot between my eyebrows. Dumbly, I look at the Akiko Katô still slumped in her chair. The doorway Katô laughs, a grin twisted and broad. Emeralds and rubies are set in her teeth. 'A bioborg, dummy! A replicant! You never watched *Bladerunner*?' (*n9d*, 11–12)

This citation of Ridley Scott's film *Blade Runner* in this early scene can be understood as a self-referential gesture pointing towards the novel's significant borrowing of tropes and rhetorical strategies from the cyberpunk genre.[4] Among these, *number9dream* adopts the particularly noteworthy technique of surplus signification, seen in the parade of brand-names, arbitrary proper nouns, and an excess of detail, which a number of critics have noted to be characteristic rhetorical strategies in science fiction and especially in cyberpunk.[5] Mitchell's novel deploys a dazzling barrage of disorienting images in order to represent its Tokyo setting as an image-saturated space wherein it is no longer possible to trace signs to their referents and any sense of a coherent meaning becomes impossible. An illustrative example appears during one of Eiji's repeated periods of waiting in the Jupiter Café as he plots his next move. He glimpses a giant video screen on the neighboring NHK building and rattles off a montage of discontinuous scenes that flash on it:

> Missile launchers recoil, cities catch on fire. A new Nokia cellphone. Foreign affairs minister announces putative WW2 Nanking excesses are left-wing plots to destroy patriotism. Zizzi Hikaru washes her hair in Pearl River shampoo. Fly draped skeletons stalk an African city. Nintendo proudly presents *Universal Soldiers*. The kid who hijacked a coach and slit three throats says he did it to stand out. (*n9d*, 125)

Mitchell's *number9dream* is certainly not the first text to depict Tokyo in such terms so as to present it as a site of the disappearance of meaning. Evocations of images of Tokyo specifically, and Japan generally, have permeated cyberpunk from its very beginnings. This is evidenced by the prominent place these geographical locations occupy in the genre's seminal texts, be it the geisha images projected onto the giant video screens on the sides of buildings in Ridley Scott's *Blade Runner* or in the setting of the opening chapter of Gibson's *Neuromancer* in the greater Tokyo area (specifically, Chiba City). Other texts, be it literary and cinematic, have taken up similar imagery. Chris Marker's quasi-documentary film *Sans Soleil* (1983), for example, evokes a similar excess of signification through the use of techniques such as rapid montage sequences marked by jarring juxtapositions and incongruous intercuts. These are techniques that, as Scott Bukatman (1993: 27) has suggested, borrow heavily from the rhetoric of science fiction, and particularly the then emergent language of cyberpunk, to communicate the experience of dislocation. Moreover, through its notable focus on the large number of video screens on the sides of buildings in Tokyo's many downtown cores, the film produces an image of the city as a disorienting spectacle; as Catherine Russell (2002: 215) has argued, in films such as Marker's and others, the persistent attention to the 'omnipresent projection of advertisements and music videos in the various city centres suggest how the city is a screening space, a discursive site – an imaginary city'.

The prevalence of the move to take Japan as an object of vision in media and fiction, inflected by the rhetoric of cyberpunk, is what has led to the identification of the genre as an exemplary manifestation of techno-Orientalism. In Lisa Nakamura's (2002: 63) characterization, these techno-orientalist images and stereotypes are typically formed out of the juxtaposition of high-technology with anachronistic imagery of a traditional Japan (for example, samurai and geisha) that paradoxically become signifiers of the future rather than the past. Similarly, Ueno Toshiya (2002: 228) suggests that, 'in "Techno-Orientalism", Japan not only is located geographically, but also is projected chronologically ... Japan has been located in the future of technology'. As Wendy Chun (2006: 177) has articulated in her development of the concept, techno-Orientalism 'seeks to orient the reader to a technology-overloaded present/future ... through the promise of readable difference, and through a conflation of information networks with an exotic urban landscape'. Through the mediation of techno-Orientalist imagery what is enabled is the treatment of the contemporary experience of dislocation in late capitalist modernity in a culturally fetishized form; specifically, it is rendered graspable as something quintessentially Japanese.

For Ueno (2002: 228), techno-Orientalism functions as a kind of image producing machine, through which 'Western or other people misunderstand and fail to recognize an always illusory Japanese culture, but it also is the mechanism through which Japanese misunderstand themselves'. In other words, techno-Orientalism is not reducible to misrepresentations, to the production of images of Japan. Rather, it is the very production of 'Japan' as aestheticized spectacle, as image – and for that matter, as image-commodity – itself. For example, William Gibson had never set foot in Japan at the time he wrote the seminal cyberpunk text *Neuromancer*. According to Tatsumi Takayuki, however, following its publication (and relatively rapid translation into Japanese), the novel had the effect of significantly reconfiguring Japanese self-representation, particularly in its own science fiction. This effect blurs distinctions between (mis) perceiver and (mis)perceived, confusing any attempt to locate an authentic and original 'Japan' outside of a transcultural intermediation. As Tatsumi (2006: 111) writes, 'Gibson's Chiba City may have sprung from his misperception of Japan, but it was this misperception that encouraged Japanese readers to correctly perceive the nature of postmodernist Japan. In short, the moment we perceive cyberpunk stories which misperceive Japan, we are already perceived correctly by cyberpunk'.

Techno-Orientalism works in this sense on the basis of remediation, defined by Jay David Bolter and Richard Grusin (1999: 56) as the redeployment and embedding of one medium, or several other media (and their systems of representation), into another. Cyberpunk, as a genre constituted precisely in acts of remediation, turns out not surprisingly to be at the centre of the discourse. Livia Monnet (1997: 227) succinctly summarizes this character of the genre when she points out that cyberpunk texts 'partake of, and contribute to, the extraordinary information overload in global technocapitalism at the turn of the twenty-first century: cyberpunk is an encyclopaedia of parodies, pastiches, remediations and revisions of media texts and mediated cultural practices from several histories and cultural legacies'.[6] To put it another way, both thematically – with its focused attention on the social impact of hypothetical human-machine mediatic interfaces – as well as formally – with its appropriations of film noir styles, its incessant citation of fetishized image-commodities in the form of brand name dropping, and constant cross-referencing and cross-pollination with other texts in the genre – cyberpunk is always already intermediated. To these then might be added the reproduction and remediation of the discursive and spectacle productions of 'Japan' thus rendering it not merely as a site *to be* represented, but as itself a site *of* representation; in other words, 'Japan' becomes an extension of the economy of textuality and visuality, a part of the same assemblage of technologies as cinema, television, and other media forms.

Against this backdrop, what is most striking about Mitchell's *number9dream* is how, in its remediation of cyberpunk, it at once brings to the foreground the remediating logic built into the constitution of cyberpunk itself. Its use of the genre's tropes of image-saturation and excessive signification cannot be reduced to the borrowing of a grammar with which the space of Tokyo can be represented; it is not merely an attempt to unproblematically produce Japan as spectacle. By punctuating these acts of remediation, on the one hand, by calling attention to their precedents through citation, and, on the other, mapping them on to the fantasies of its protagonist Eiji, the novel arguably demonstrates a cognisance of the status of these received representations of Japan as circulating image-commodities. Or, to put it in the terminology of Bolter and Grusin, *number9dream* performs these acts of remediation of cyberpunk's rhetorical strategies with little attempt at constructing an illusion of immediacy. Rather, the text calls attention to the act of mediation itself by highlighting a logic of hypermediation.[7] In effect, rather than uncritically partaking in the discourse of techno-Orientalism, the novel is actually about the operations of techno-Orientalism.

The stakes of *number9dream*'s remediation of cyberpunk tropes can be clarified when viewed in conjunction with the narrative structures of Mitchell's preceding novel *Ghostwritten* (1999), as well as his subsequent novel *Cloud Atlas* (2004). The former is organized around multiple vignettes each set in a different location; the latter is structured as a set of multiple nested stories within stories. Through these narrative performances, both of the novels gesture toward the inadequacy of singular narratives for capturing the complexity of the structural relations – now transnational in scale – through which lived experience is constituted. In other words, they exhibit a cognisance of the unrepresentability of their totality, in line with Fredric Jameson's (1991: 51) characterization of the conditions of social life in the present. At a glance, in contrast to *Ghostwritten* and *Cloud Atlas*, *number9dream* appears more conventional in its narrative structure. It features neither multiple locations nor multiple stories that coalesce into a larger totality but instead deals largely with a single protagonist and is organized around a single narrative trajectory. But it is here where its remediations of cyberpunk tropes become significant. Following Jameson, if Tokyo is always already experienced as image, as representation, then as a consequence of the transnational traffic of image culture, it is also paradoxically rendered unrepresentable – it exists only in the totality of the constellation of relations through which these images are produced and circulated. The parade of shifting signifiers (whether fictional or in reference to actual image-commodities) through which the city is represented produce a dizzying effect upon the text's reader that renders it opaque. More importantly, congealed in each of these signifiers, in each of these circulating image-commodities, are social relations whose origins are always already somewhere else. In foregrounding – in hypermediating – the operations of these image-commodties, the novel makes visible the structuring force of the constellation of relations through which the space of Tokyo is rendered unrepresentable.

Intertextual Doppelgängers

The issues highlighted by Mitchell's remediation of cyberpunk are further punctuated by another set of remediations that *number9dream* foregrounds: its numerous citations and allusions to the fiction of Japanese author Murakami Haruki.[8] For example, descriptions of Ai Imajo – the waitress with the perfect swan-like neck and love interest of protagonist Eiji Miyake – are reminiscent of Murakami's description of the character Kiki, the girl with perfect ears in his *A Wild Sheep Chase* and *Dance Dance Dance* (Dansu dansu dansu, 1988; trans. 1994). Also, Goatwriter – who appears as a character in a children's book that Eiji reads while he is in hiding from the Yakuza – recalls not only the disembodied ghostwriter of Mitchell's previous novel *Ghostwritten*, but to a certain extent also the Sheep Man (*Hitsuji-otoko*) from the same two Murakami novels noted earlier. In addition, the isolated psychiatric institution where Eiji's mother stays reminds the reader of the institution featured in *Norwegian Wood*.

As in my previous discussion of *number9dream*'s remediation of cyberpunk texts, over and above the obvious referencing of Murakami's fiction, what is more significant is Mitchell's appropriation of, and embedding into his own narrative, several rhetorical strategies that commonly appear in Murakami's fiction. While *number9dream* flashes allusions to several of Murakami's writings, in terms of its narrative strategies, the text it borrows from the most is Murakami's *The*

Wind-up Bird Chronicle. Space considerations make a summary of the complex and multilayered narrative of this novel difficult, but, at its most basic, the primary narrative thread involves the narrator and his quest to recover his estranged wife from a kind of 'mental prison' of his brother-in-law Noboru Wataya, an upstart politician and TV pundit. Stories by an old World War II veteran told to the narrator about covert operations in Nomonhan form the second major narrative thread. A third narrative thread appears near the end of the novel with the narrator acting as a kind of supernatural healer. The similarity between the two texts, *The Wind-up Bird Chronicle* and *number9dream*, are difficult to overlook: the primary narratives in both of the novels involve a quest for a missing person; both novels also feature metafictional devices in the form of a story within a story (the Goatwriter sections in *number9dream* and Akasaka Cinnamon's stories in *The Wind-up Bird Chronicle*); finally, both novels have the protagonists reading extended personal accounts of the experiences of soldiers during World War II.

When all these elements are considered, it does not seem to be much of a stretch to suggest that *number9dream* takes on the position of an intertextual doppelgänger of Murakami's novel. My point in highlighting this is not to imply that Mitchell's novel is nothing more than a derivative or inferior copy of Murakami. Such an argument would reinscribe a privileging of notions of originality, a point which the very concept of the doppelgänger and its confusion of categories of identity and difference calls into question. On the contrary, a closer look at the specific aspects of Murakami's fiction that appear in *number9dream*, coupled with an analysis of how these are reconfigured in Mitchell's deployment, shows that, like Mitchell's foregrounding of cyberpunk rhetorical strategies, the novel focuses on this intertextuality, addressing the very problem of originality. To elaborate upon this point, it is worth noting a key point of difference between the two novels. While both involve searches for missing persons, the object of the quests differs in the two novels: in *The Wind-up Bird Chronicle*, the protagonist Okada Tôru searches for his missing wife; in *number9dream*, in contrast, a missing father is the object of the search (one which is, tellingly, ultimately aborted). While this may initially seem like a trivial point of difference, the quest for the father (and its associated concepts of genetic lineage and origins) in *number9dream* resonates with the problem of origins brought into the spotlight by the text functioning as an intertextual doppelgänger of Murakami's fiction.

Metafictional questions of origin and authorship take centre stage in the section of the novel when Eiji is in hiding at a writer's residence following his run-in with the Yakuza. Here, scenes of Eiji waiting for, and occasionally meeting with, other characters are interspersed with scenes from a manuscript of a children's story that Eiji reads. This section of narrative in *number9dream* opens with Goatwriter hearing fragments of 'the truly untold tale' and then scribbling them down with the same pen used by Sei Shonagon. 'The truly untold tale' is presented as a holy grail of stories, reminding us of the cliché that there are no longer any truly original stories, that all tales written now have already been told before. The following day, however, Goatwriter's manuscript containing the fragments of the truly untold tale he had heard and written down is stolen. He finds out later that the pen of Sei Shonagon, which he calls the tongue of his imagination, is also stolen. The three characters then go on a quest to find the thief.

Throughout this section, Mitchell lets loose a series of in-jokes about the writing process and profession: Goatwriter describes the place where the events unfold with the words '[i]nky landscape. paperpulp sky ... we are in the margins' (*n9d*, 206); later, he drinks water from a literal 'stream of consciousness' (*n9d*, 256). Eventually, they find themselves trapped in the spider Queen Erichnid's literal website. Queen Erichnid tells them that she intends to digitize Goatwriter and assimilate his writing talents. Goatwriter asks Queen Erichnid 'Where is the creative fulfillment in passing off another's stories as your own?' (*n9d*, 246). While Goatwriter asks this, he himself cannot claim to be producing an original story. Even the 'truly untold tale' he writes is not his own. He merely hears fragments of it in the whispers of the wind and the songs of birds and attempts to reconstruct it in writing. His pen (the tongue of his imagination) is not his own either but the pen of Sei Shonagon. The last scene of the Goatwriter section emphasizes this point very well. After his encounter with Queen

Erichnid, Goatwriter disappears in search of the 'truly untold tale'. When he begins writing again in his hideaway, he is surprised to find that the pen of Sei Shonagon is speaking to him. In response to his question of when it began to speak, the pen says 'Since *you* learned to unblock your ears' (*n9d*, 267). 'Unblocked ears' is a quotation from Murakami's *A Wild Sheep Chase*, where the phrase appears as the title of the chapter wherein Murakami's narrator first meets an unnamed character identified only as the girl with perfect ears. She appears plain under normal conditions but, when she pulls back her hair and unblocks her ears, she takes on an almost magical radiance. By quoting and recontextualizing this phrase from Murakami in *number9dream*, Mitchell in effect simultaneously performs the idea of writing as a web of quotations as he thematically depicts it in the Goatwriter section.

Another scene later in the novel serves to echo this point. In yet another of Eiji's fantasies, he dreams he is having a conversation with John Lennon in Ueno park. He asks John Lennon what the song 'Tomorrow Never Knows' is about. This results in the subsequent exchange between them:

> John pulls a philosopher pose. 'I never knew.'
> We giggle helplessly. 'But you wrote it!''
> No, Eiji, I never...' He dabs his tears away. 'It wrote me!' (*n9d*, 398)

With this statement, *number9dream* proclaims its allegiance to a conception of authorship as a function produced by the text, not as an origin of the text, or as an arbiter of its meaning. The implications of this are made clear in the rest of their conversation. John Lennon tells Eiji that '#9dream' is a descendant of 'Norwegian Wood'. One can of course read this literally as Lennon talking about songs he has written, but it also simultaneously points to the title of the novel itself (*number9dream*) and the title of Murakami's most famous novel *Norwegian Wood* whose title draws from the John Lennon song. As such, Lennon's observation also functions as a self-referential comment on the novel's intertextual reworking of Murakami's text.

Just as Mitchell extensively cites and borrows from Murakami's fiction, Murakami himself is known for his constant citation of other

texts, along with a plethora of pop-cultural references and remediations. Aside from *Norwegian Wood*, Murakami's *South of the Border,
West of the Sun* (Kokkyô no minami, taiyô no nishi, 1992; trans. 1999)
references the Nat King Cole song in the first part of its title. Similarly,
the short story 'The 1963/1982 Girl from Ipanema' (1963/1982-nen
no Ipanema-musume, 1982; trans. 2002) cites the famous bossa nova
song. Perhaps the most often discussed (and at times criticized) feature of Murakami's fiction is its constant citation of other texts, be it
in books that characters read or films they see or music to which they
listen. This particular trait of Murakami's writing has incited Masao
Miyoshi (1991: 235) to go so far as to call Murakami's fiction nothing
more than a 'sophisticated stylization of trivia'. Other critics, in Japan
and the USA, noting this, as well as his constant citation of western
cultural artifacts and brand-name goods, comment upon the 'un-Jap-
anese' feel of Murakami's writing.[9]

   If one takes Murakami's own pop-cultural and intertextual remediations into account, Mitchell's reworking and doubling of Murakami in *number9dream* brings to attention the multidirectional
nature of transnational flows of cultural artifacts and representations.
Murakami's representation of contemporary Japan is itself heavily
infused with what is conventionally thought of as western cultural (and media) artifacts; conversely, Mitchell's remediation of
them in effect blurs the lines between what is 'Japanese' and what
is not. In Mitchell and Murakami, the very name 'Japan' is inevitably tangled with various intermediations. In this sense, the repeated
remediation of imagery, tropes, and rhetorical strategies performed
by *number9dream* is reminiscent of Jean Baudrillard's (1993: 198)
ideas on simulacra: 'all hold-ups, hijacks and the like are now as it were
simulation hold-ups, in the sense that they are inscribed in advance in
the decoding and orchestration rituals of the media, anticipated in
their mode of presentation and possible consequences'. Baudrillard's
point can be extended to address the problem of transcultural experience and the representations thereof: how one experiences difference
is already anticipated and intermediated by preceding images and orchestrations.

Mitchell's doubling of Murakami's fictions – and the consequent troubling of notions of originality that the performance of such a doubling entails – can be understood as affecting the production of a narrative that is less about any actual Japan and more a self-referential narrative about the fantasy of 'Japan', that is, about the impossibility of an authentic and original experience of 'Japan' outside of its global traffic as an image-commodity. Through its positioning of itself as a doppelgänger to Murakami Haruki's fiction, and through its remediation of cyberpunk rhetorics (both of which are formed through further remediation of other texts that preceded them, and so on and so forth), *number9dream* gestures at the impossibility of locating an authentic, unmediated, and original Tokyo or Japan. Even a 'real' lived experience of Japan is rife with the interventions and remediations of its previously encountered orchestrations and representations.

Cultural Politics of the Japanoid

In its remediation of cyberpunk rhetorical strategies and in its calling to task of the desire for originality and authenticity through the transcultural doubling of Murakami, *number9dream* is a text that embodies cultural critic Tatsumi Takayuki's concept of the 'Japanoid' – a 'post-80s hyper-creole subjectivity transgressing the boundary between the Japanese and non-Japanese, and in so doing, naturalizing the very act of transgression' (Tatsumi, 2002: 16). The idea of the Japanoid brings Donna Haraway's theory of the human-machine hybridity of the cyborg into relation with the transracial and transcultural hybridity of the postcolonial figure of the Creole. For Tatsumi, the emergence of the notion of the Japanoid is a particular consequence of the contemporary condition, wherein 'the interracial identity ... at the turn of the nineteenth century developed into a cyborgian identity ... at the turn of the twentieth century' (Tatsumi, 2006: 29). While *number9dream* certainly appears to confirm Tatsumi's key arguments, at the same time the critical question to raise here is what larger stakes might be implicated in such a performance?

Much of Tatsumi's articulation of the concept of the Japanoid is indebted to the work of postcolonial theorist Homi Bhabha, in particular, his discussion of mimicry and ambivalence. In *The Location of Culture* (1994), Bhabha offers a broad critique of the production of binary oppositions such as colonizer/colonized, civilized/savage, arguing that they are the fundamental mechanism through which colonial power operates. Bhabha's discussion aims to show that the imposition of these various bifurcations upon the colonized are never quite complete – that is, they are necessarily and structurally ambivalent. The key example addressed is the practice of colonial mimicry. For Bhabha (1994: 122), colonial mimicry generates an image of a 'reformed, recognizable Other, *as a subject of difference that is almost the same, but not quite*' (emphasis in original). In doing so, it imposes an identity upon the colonized subject so as to discipline and regulate otherness in the service of reproducing empire in the role of intermediary. In this sense, it is 'one of the most elusive and effective strategies of colonial power and knowledge' (Bhabha, 1994: 122). Necessary to this operation is the constant production of slippage between identity and difference, since otherwise the subservient position of the colonized intermediary subject cannot be maintained. As a consequence, mimicry bears within it the potential to become an immanent threat to the logic of the colonial order – the constitution of a hybrid identity causes a rupture in the demarcation between original and mimic, between the very positionalities of colonizer and colonized it operates to enforce. Although Japan was never formally subject to colonization, Tatsumi suggests that a similar logic underpins the intercultural traffic between Japan and its ('Western') Other. Analogous to Bhabha's discussion of colonial mimicry, in Tatsumi's view, the Japanoid functions not as 'a failed attempt to achieve originality, but as a counter-strategy that radically problematizes the very origin of originality' (Tatsumi, 2006: 10).

Aspects of Tatsumi's discussion of mimicry and his notion of the Japanoid are compelling; not least, in recognizing that Japan always already exceeds itself. Tatsumi resists the reduction of Japan to a putative cultural essence. He is too uncritical, however, of the science fictions and postmodernist texts he examines in his analyses and by extension the material conditions of the world in which they emerge. In his celebration of a certain kind of multicultural hybridity, what

Tatsumi fails to recognize is how the production of these hybridities is very much a component of the operations of power in late capitalist modernity. In this respect, his conception of the Japanoid suffers from the same problems and limits that trouble Bhabha's work on colonial mimicry. In *Imperial Leather* (1995), Anne McClintock recognizes that hybridity and colonial ambivalence, at least in particular contexts, may indeed have subversive potential. At the same time, she contends that, 'the lyrical glamour cast by some postcolonial theorists over ambivalence and hybridity is not always historically warranted' (McClintock, 1995: 67). Specifically, McClintock criticizes Bhabha's model of colonial hybridity and ambivalence as too formally abstract. She argues that this abstraction elides the material differences in social, political, and economic power wielded by colonizer and colonized, and the differences between mimicry that is disruptive and mimicry that is all too often violently enforced. While a subversive potential may very well be structurally embodied in colonial mimicry, to what extent this potential in fact materialized into an active resistance in colonized sites is open to question. Mimicry and hybridity were just as easily deployed as an operation of power as opposed to its resistance, thus calling into question whether ambivalence is in itself inherently subversive. As McClintock writes:

> But if mimicry always betrays a slippage between identity and difference, doesn't one need to elaborate how colonial mimicry differs from anti-colonial mimicry; if colonial and anti-colonial mimicry are formally identical in their founding ambivalence, why did colonial mimicry succeed for so long? (McClintock, 1995: 64)

For McClintock, a symptom of the problems with Bhabha's conception of colonial hybridity is its ahistorical articulation. It collapses the complexity of colonial histories into a singular Eurocentric narrative trajectory that fails to account for the historical specificity of different locations. As a consequence, instead of subverting the tropes of linear development and modernization, Bhabha unwittingly reinscribes them: 'If the theory promises a decentering of history in hybridity, syncretism, multidimensional time and so forth, the singularity of the term [postcolonial] effects a recentering of global history around the single rubric of European time. Colonialism returns at the moment of its disappearance' (McClintock, 1995: 11).

McClintock's criticisms of Bhabha can also be leveled at Tatsumi's discussion of the Japanoid. In extending the notion of postcolonial hybridity to the context of Japan, Tatsumi constructs a historical trajectory of mimicry that passes through three stages: 'the essentialist myth of originality and imitation, the late capitalist synchronicity between different cultures, and the multicultural and transgeneric poetics of chaotic negotiation' (Tatsumi, 2006: 9). However, in constructing this historical trajectory, Tatsumi elides the history of Japan's own colonial empire. Paying attention to this calls to task not only Tatsumi's uncritical celebration of the hybridity of the Japanoid, but also his assertion of its novelty in the present moment. One need only to look at the cultural policies enacted by imperial Japan upon its colonial subjects in the 1920s as a case in point. These took the shape of an ideology and practice of imperial multiculturalism and culturally enforced hybridity, in part as a consequence of Japan's peculiar status as a non-white, non-western colonial empire.[10] As Mark Driscoll (2005: 164) has cogently explained, the history of the Japanese colonial empire is marked by 'pluralist innovations in colonial governance ... that might be said to have preceded, or at least usefully compared to, modes of governance in other multiethnic societies'. Tatsumi's analysis of the Japanoid overlooks what Driscoll (2005: 172) has characterized as 'postcoloniality in reverse – the fabricated inversion assigned to East Asia of the normalized Euro-American trajectory of globalized multiculturalism'. The normal Eurocentric postcolonial narrative from ethnoracial homogeneity to multicultural postcoloniality is thus reinscribed since this movement is in fact historically reversed in East Asia. As a consequence, in the Japanese context the production of hybrid subjectivities can be seen to function as a mechanism of rule.

In characterizing and celebrating what he sees as the creativity of cross-cultural literary transactions in the contemporary moment, Tatsumi's argument implies that the present is at a posthistorical moment that Homi Bhabha (1994: 18) has described as an 'unhomely world'. In order to affirm the novelty and creative potential of what he sees as the hybridity of the transgeneric and transnational literary transactions of the present, Tatsumi must at the same time pose the idea of a fixed and essentialized originality as a foil. He does so without accounting for how, in the contemporary conjuncture, new logics and distributions of power may very well be in operation and essentialist notions of origins may no longer be the proper object of critique. On this point, it is worth referencing Michael Hardt and Antonio Negri's (2000: 45) criticism of postcolonial theories for failing to recognize that the contemporary moment sees a fundamentally new 'mode of the production of identity and difference', one wherein the defence of difference and hybridity is not necessarily opposed to, but rather buttresses, the logic of the capitalist imperial machine. In *Empire* (2000), Hardt and Negri argue that:

> postcolonialist theorists in general give a very confused view of this passage because they remain fixated on attacking an old form of power and propose a strategy of liberation that could be effective only on that old terrain ... What is missing here is a recognition of the novelty of the structures and logics of power that order the contemporary world. (Hardt and Negri, 2000: 145–6)

In a similar vein, Arif Dirlik (2002: 429) argues that, 'preoccupation with colonialism and its legacies makes for an exaggerated view of the hold of the past over contemporary realities, and an obliviousness to the reconfiguration of past legacies by contemporary restructurations of power'. What is therefore required is an analysis situated in the specificities of the structure of relations present in the historical moment in question. Such an analysis would need to be attentive to how the discourse of multicultural hybridity is nonetheless itself increasingly becoming a highly commodified spectacle, and an alibi for the uneven development that is at the core of the very logic of capitalist modernity. Given that these are *image*-commodities, to speak of unevenness means also to recognize the unevenness in symbolic exchanges and scopic regimes. As Rey Chow (1991: xiii) once noted, 'since the West owns not only the components but also the codes of fantasy, the non-West is deprived not only of the control of industrial and commercial, but of imaginary productions as well'.

number9dream partakes of and reproduces the techno-Orientalizing logic of the Japanoid, as any contemporary text that engages with the category 'Japan' unavoidably does. However, in its self-referentiality to this logic, *number9dream* puts it under erasure. In the first instance, through its mapping of the techno-Orientalist tropes of cyberpunk, the text recognizes the embeddedness of such an imagination of 'Japan' in the global order of production through which the imaginary is constituted and subsumed by the logics of capital, what Neferti Tadiar's (2005: 5–8) calls the transnational system of 'fantasy-production'. In doing so, it offers a literary critique of the cultural politics Tatsumi advances in his analysis. In the second instance, the novel's status as an intertextual doppelgänger of Murakami Haruki's writing is uncanny. For Freud, the figure of the doppelgänger is intimately tied to the experience of the uncanny. In one of its many manifestations, the uncanny is created by the return of that 'which is familiar and old-established in the mind and which has become alienated from it only through the process of repression' (Freud, 2000: 243). Ueno Toshiya (2002: 235) links techno-Orientalism specifically to the uncanny, characterizing the former as a kind of defense mechanism against the latter in the form of a projection or displacement, a 'shock projected onto the other'. By troubling the relations between self and other, between familiar and unfamiliar, in its capacity as an intertextual and transcultural doppelgänger, *number9dream* enacts a resistance to this displacement; it performs an uncanny interruption of the fantasy of techno-Orientalism.

Repeated interruptions of the narrator Eiji's fantasies structure the narrative in *number9dream*. Every time the story seemingly begins to take shape, every time Eiji's quest seemingly begins to move in one direction or another, something provokes it abruptly to end. Another set of salient interruptions also appears on a different register. At various points in the narrative, events that highlight all manner of violence built into the structural logic of Japan and its place in the world erupt to expose what has been repressed in the slick images of techno-Orientalist fantasy. The character of Miriam – a Korean club hostess involved with the Yakuza – hints at the complexities of the colonial history between Japan and Korea and its continuing repercussions. This is given particular emphasis when at one point she tells the narrator, 'Tell him my country stopped being a Japanese colony at the end of the last war!' (*n9d*, 136). The journal of the *kaiten* suicide submarine pilot Tsukiyama Subaru that Eiji reads calls to mind the disavowal of the history of war constitutive of the postwar social order of Japan (*n9d*, 275–316). Finally, the letter from Kozue Yamaya telling the story of the murder of her son and her captivity as a sex slave in payment for her husband's debts brings into focus the base of brutal violence and exploitation upon which the highest orders of finance capital is built (*n9d*, 333–8). Through these interruptions, the novel calls attention to the unevenness and asymmetrical relations through which the social factory in the contemporary global order is constituted in both its material aspects and its immaterial and imaginative production. Although *number9dream* might be unable to articulate a way out of this alienated imaginary, the novel nevertheless gestures toward such a desire, toward a project of claiming a 'freedom of imagination', as Partha Chatterjee (1993: 13) explains, when the ninth chapter (the titular number 9 dream) at the end of the novel remains blank, yet to be written.

Notes

1 In 'Techno-Orientalism: Japan Panic', David Morley and Kevin Robbins (1995: 141) extend Edward Said's conception of Orientalism to consider the production of new stereotypes and imagery of Japan in response to the global dominance of Japanese high-tech companies. While it is in the work of Morley and Robbins that the term originates, other cultural critics have subsequently developed the concept further. One such critic is Ueno Toshiya who characterizes techno-Orientalism as the late twentieth-century global information capitalist mutation of the colonial Orientalism of the late nineteenth century. It melds racialized (and at once also gendered) alterities with the uncanny of a machinic automaton (Ueno, 2002: 228–9).

2 The most obvious examples are the emphasis on the gargantuan video screens attached to the sides of buildings in descriptions of the city (*n9d*, 3) and the incessant attention placed on the endless crowds and pulsating neon in the scenes that take place in Shibuya, one of Tokyo's major entertainment districts (*n9d*, 99). Also worth noting is the narrator's habit of

marking technology with recognizably Japanese brand names: the video screens are specifically labeled 'Panasonic'; a clock across the street from the narrator's room is named 'Fujifilm' (*n9d*, 53)

3 Alongside the novel's stylistic echoing of Murakami's fiction, some examples of these intertextual citations include a reference to 'unblocked ears' in the Goatwriter sequence (*n9d*, 267), which recontextualizes a detail from *A Wild Sheep Chase* (Murakami, 1989: 45) and a citation of the Beatles song 'Norwegian Wood' doubles as a citation of the Murakami novel that shares its title (*n9d*, 398). I discuss these intertextual references in greater detail later.

4 Cyberpunk is a sub-genre of science fiction that emerged in the 1980s. It is characterized by its attention to the penetration of technologies into human bodies and perceptual systems and employs a narrative style heavily influenced by hard-boiled detective fiction and film noir. Larry McCaffery (1991: 1–16) provides a useful overview of cyberpunk and its relations with science fiction as a whole, as well as postmodernist writings from the 1980s, in his introduction to *Storming the Reality Studio*.

5 In 'About 5750 Words', Samuel Delany (1977: 11–13) cogently describes the critical role that textual detail (and especially incongruous verbal juxtaposition) plays in establishing science fictional worlds through language. While Delany discusses science fiction in general and not the specific characteristics of cyberpunk, Brian McHale (1992: 149–50) correctly notes that, 'there are few, if any, absolute novelties in cyberpunk SF; all the motifs ... have precedents in earlier SF, and some are very widely attested, to the point of constituting routine SF formulas and clichés'. Where cyberpunk is distinct is in its intensification of these motifs and rhetorical strategies. One example McHale (1992: 154) highlights is its world-building: 'instead of microworlds spaced out along a narrative itinerary, here they have been collapsed together in the heterotopian space of a future megalopolis'.

6 For example, writing of William Gibson's prose in *Neuromancer*, Scott Bukatman (1993: 171) asserts that, 'the space of the text is deeply cultural in origin, explicitly contoured by other writers, genres and voices. The heavily referential space of the text thus removes that origin to a site *outside* the subject and *inside* the technologies of information'.

7 Bolter and Grusin (1999: 21–44) identify two tendencies in acts of remediation: what they call immediacy (wherein the act of remediation is effaced to create the illusion of transparency for the production of real-

ity effects) and hypermediacy (wherein the act of remediation is fore-grounded in the text).

8 While I discuss these two sets of quotations/remediations separately here, it is worth noting that Livia Monnet identifies cyberpunk tropes (among several other intertextual references) in Murakami's writing as well. She suggests that whether or not they overtly make use of the genre conventions of cyberpunk fictions, in their constructions of parallel spaces and virtual worlds Murakami's narrative strategies nevertheless exhibit a keen parallel awareness of the implications of information technologies for contemporary social relations (Monnet, 1997: 340).

9 Matthew Strecher (2002: 5) succinctly summarizes many of these criticisms of Murakami. Jay Rubin also notes that the apparent sense of Murakami's 'internationalism' among his English language readers was perhaps further emphasized by Alfred Birnbaum's English translation of *A Wild Sheep Chase*, which deliberately omitted many references specific to 1970s Japan in an effort to bridge the time lag (the translation appeared in 1991, in contrast to the 1982 publication date of the Japanese text). See Rubin (2002: 273–89).

10 On this point, the work of Ôguma Eiji is essential. Key to his discussion is how the notion of Japan as a homogenous ethnoracial nation became the hegemonic discourse only in the postwar period; prior to that, under the context of a multiethnic empire, Japan often represented itself as hybrid at its origins.

Works Cited

Allison, Anne (2001) 'Memoirs of the Orient', *Journal of Japanese Studies* 27(2): 381–98.

Baudrillard, Jean (1993) 'The Evil Demon of Images and the Precession of Simulacra', in Thomas Docherty (ed.) *Postmodernism: A Reader*, pp. 194–9. New York: Columbia University Press.

Bell, Josh (2005) 'Turning Japanese: Memoirs of a Geisha is a Whitewashed Fairy Tale', *Las Vegas Weekly*, 22 December, URL (consulted August 2010): http://www.lasvegasweekly.com/news/archive/2005/dec/22/turning-japanese

Bhabha, Homi (1994) *The Location of Culture*. London: Routledge.

Bolter, Jay David and Richard Grusin (1999) *Remediation: Understanding New Media*. Cambridge, MA: The MIT Press.

Bukatman, Scott (1993) *Terminal Identity: The Virtual Subject in Postmodern Science Fiction*. Durham, NC: Duke University Press.

Chaterjee, Partha (1993) *The Nation and its Fragments*. Princeton, NJ: Princeton University Press.

Chow, Rey (1991) *Woman and Chinese Modernity: The Politics of Reading Between West and East*. Minneapolis: University of Minnesota Press.

Chun, Wendy Hui Kyong (2006) *Control and Freedom: Power and Paranoia in the Age of Fiber Optics*. Cambridge, MA: The MIT Press.

Day, Kiku (2004) 'Totally Lost in Translation', *Guardian*, 24 January, URL (consulted August 2010): http://www.guardian.co.uk/world/2004/jan/24/japan.film

Delany, Samuel R. (1977) 'About 5750 Words', *The Jewel-hinged Jaw: Notes on the Language of Science Fiction*, pp. 1–16. Elizabethtown, NY: Dragon Press.

Dirlik, Arif (2002) 'Rethinking Colonialism: Globalization, Postcolonialism, and the Nation', *Interventions* 4(3): 428–48.

Dirlik, Arif (2005) 'The End of Colonialism? The Colonial Modern in the Making of Global Modernity', *Boundary 2* 32(1): 1–31.

Driscoll, Mark (2005) 'Conclusion: Postcoloniality in Reverse', in Yuasa Katsuei *Kannani and Document of Flames*, pp. 161–93, trans. Mark Driscoll. Durham, NC: Duke University Press.

Freud, Sigmund (2000), 'The Uncanny', in *The Standard Edition of the Complete Psychological Works of Sigmund Freud, Volume XVII*, trans. James Strachey, pp. 219–56. New York: W. W. Norton.

Gibson, William (1984) *Neuromancer*. New York: Ace Books

Haraway, Donna (1985) 'A Manifesto for Cyborgs: Science, Technology, and Socialist Feminism', *Socialist Review* 15(2): 244–75.

Hardt, Michael and Antonio Negri (2000) *Empire*. Cambridge, MA: Harvard University Press.

Iwabuchi, Kôichi (2008) 'Lost in TransNation: Tokyo and the Urban Imaginary in the Age of Globalization', *Inter-Asia Cultural Studies* 9(4): 543–56.

Jameson, Fredric (1991) *Postmodernism, or, the Cultural Logic of Late Capitalism*. Durham, NC: Duke University Press.

McCaffery, Larry (1991) *Storming the Reality Studio: A Casebook of Cyberpunk and Postmodern Fiction*. Durham, NC and London: Duke University Press.

McClintock, Anne (1995) *Imperial Leather: Race, Gender, and Sexuality in the Colonial Contest*. London: Routledge.

McCurry, Justin (2005) 'Geisha film incenses Japanese', *Guardian*, 29 November, URL (consulted August 2010): http://www.guardian.co.uk/japan/story/0,7369,1653009,00.html#article_continue

McHale, Brian (1992) 'Elements of a Poetics of Cyberpunk', *Critique* 33(3): 149–75.

Minear, Richard (1980) 'Orientalism and the Study of Japan', *Journal of Asian Studies* 30(3): 507–17.

Miyoshi, Masao (1991) *Off Center: Power and Culture Relations Between Japan and the United States*. Cambridge, MA: Harvard University Press.

Monnet, Livia (1997) 'Televisual Retrofutures and the Body of Insomnia: Visuality and Virtual Realities in the Short Fiction of Murakami Haruki', *Proceedings of the Midwest Association for Japanese Literary Studies* 3: 340–80.

Monnet, Livia (2002) 'Towards the Feminine Sublime, or the Story of a Twinkling Monad, Shape-shifting across Dimensions: Intermediality, Fantasy and Special effects in Cyberpunk Film and Animation', *Japan Forum* 14(2): 225–68.

Morley, David and Robins, Kevin (1995) *Spaces of Identity: Global Media, Electronic Landscapes, and Cultural Boundaries*. London: Routledge.

Murakami Haruki (1989) *A Wild Sheep Chase*, trans. Alfred Birnbaum. Tokyo: Kodansha International.

Murakami Haruki (1997) *The Wind-up Bird Chronicle*, trans. Jay Rubin. New York: Vintage.

Murakami Haruki (2000) *Norwegian Wood*, trans. Jay Rubin. New York: Vintage.

Nakamura, Lisa (2002) *Cybertypes: Race, Ethnicity, and Identity on the Internet*. London: Routledge.

Napier, Susan (2007) *From Impressionism to Anime: Japan as Fantasy and Fan Cult in the Mind of the West*. Basingstoke: Palgrave Macmillan.

Ôguma, Eiji (1996) 'Yûshoku no shokumin teikoku: 1920-nen zengo no nikkei imin haisô to Chôsen tôjiron' [The Coloured Colonial Empire: The Termination of Japanese immigration and the Occupation of Korea in the 1920s], in *Nashonariti no datsukôchiku* [Deconstructing Nationality], pp. 81–102. Tokyo: Shin'yôsha.

Rubin, Jay (2002) *Haruki Murakami and the Music of Words*. London: The Harvill Press.

Russell, Catherine (2002) 'Tokyo, the Movie', *Japan Forum* 14(2): 211–24.

Said, Edward (1979) *Orientalism*. New York: Vintage Books.

Strecher, Matthew Carl (2002) *Dances with Sheep: The Quest for Identity in the Fiction of Murakami Haruki*. Ann Arbor MI: The Center for Japanese Studies, University of Michigan.

Tadiar, Neferti Xina M. (2005) *Fantasy Production: Sexual Economies and Other Philippine Consequences for the New World Order*. Hong Kong: Hong Kong University Press.

Tatsumi, Takayuki (2002) 'The Japanoid Manifesto: Towards a New Poetics of Invisible Culture', *New Japanese Fiction, Special issue of Review of Contemporary Fiction* 22(2): 12–18.

Tatsumi, Takayuki (2006) *Full Metal Apache: Transactions Between Cyberpunk Japan and Avant Pop America*. Durham, NC: Duke University Press.

Ueno, Toshiya (2002) 'Japanimation and Techno-Orientalism', in Bruce Grenville (ed.) *The Uncanny: Experiments in Cyborg Culture*, pp. 223–36. Vancouver: Arsenal Pulp Press.

5

THE STORIES WE TELL
Discursive Identity Through Narrative Form in *Cloud Atlas*

Courtney Hopf

Introduction: How to Be in Two Places at Once

Several years ago at the Paris museum of modern art, the Pompidou Centre, I walked into a curious installation consisting of a square room lined on two sides with mirrors. It was a piece by artist Dan Graham (1974), entitled *Present Continuous Past(s)*. It consisted of a bare, mirrored, four-walled room, containing nothing except a video monitor on one wall with a video camera visibly mounted above it. When I entered the space it was empty of other people. I walked immediately over to the monitor and expected to see my image in it, but the screen remained blank. Assuming the camera was mounted too high to pick up my small stature, I jumped up and down and waved my hands above my head into the lens. Nothing happened on the screen. Disappointed with the installation, I turned around and meandered across the room, looking in the mirrors to see if I was missing the point. Seconds later, as I turned around again, I saw myself hopping in the air on the monitor, waving foolishly into the camera. In the instant it took me to realize that the video was on a time delay, I startlingly felt an uncanny sense of disembodiment, shock, and even shame.

What prompted this reaction? In some ways it was the interruption of my belief that I was entirely alone. For eight seconds I was blissfully ignorant of the act of surveillance, but my recorded movements felt ridiculous when I was forced to confront them having already concluded that I was unwatched and unnoticed.[1] In the instant that I recognized the purpose and structure of the installation, I underwent a strange moment of duplicated subjectivity, in which I experienced both the moment of eight seconds earlier as well as the moment of its representation, a jarring clash of the present continuous with the past. The time-delayed video continued to run, allowing me to relive my experience of realization, and my experience of the experience of realization through an endless succession, but also through the veil of my actual, present moment in time. I was, in fact, both subject and object.

Intertextual references and allusions in literature can be considered in the same light as *Present Continuous Past(s)*. When a complicated text draws a link between themes, images, characters or ideas, the reader's recognition of that link is itself a kind of doubling – an inhabiting of both the present moment of reading and the remembered moment of what has already been read. Of course, any act of reading in general is a process of subjective doubling, though it unfolds over an extended time rather than arresting the reader in a jarring moment of recognition. Focalization allows readers to see through the eyes and minds of characters; omniscient narration grants them access to information a single character cannot possess. When we read, we experience a conflation of subject and object because we produce meaning in concert with the text, and we do so by maintaining positions both 'inside' and 'outside' the narrative.[2]

The work of David Mitchell particularly lends itself to this sort of readerly interaction, as it consists of a boundless and ever-expanding world that spans across all his novels. Characters, themes, objects and stories consistently reappear and reconstitute themselves from narrative to narrative and novel to novel. These repetitions incite moments of recognition that serve to transform the literary subject and to encourage reader agency in the process of narrative meaning-making. In this essay, I will use three different modes of narratological analysis to examine Mitchell's oeuvre, all of which underline the interactions between text and reader. I will demonstrate how Mitchell's work strives to blur the line between subject and object as well as the distinction between life and narrative. In the first section, I focus on the prevalence of readers and interpreters in and across all of Mitchell's novels, paying particular attention to how characters in *Cloud Atlas* (2004) experience uncanny and unsettling moments of recognition that are mirrored by the external reader's experience of the text. The second section engages with an ongoing debate about narrative identity, and the extent to which life and narrative can co-mingle. The third section examines the multiple narrative levels of *Cloud Atlas* and interrogates the role of the objects passed from level to level. These transgressions of diegetic levels – or metalepses, to use the narratological term – serve to establish the ontological hierarchy of the novel. I appropriate the concept of remediation – the representation of one medium within another – to demonstrate how *Cloud Atlas* enacts not just the repurposing of a variety of media, but a remediation of the reading subject. Each of these methods demonstrates explicitly how Mitchell's novels enact a transformation of the reader as a literary subject, and how the process undergone by the subject is mirrored through character and plot within the novels themselves.

Diegetic and External Readers

David Mitchell's novels are populated with readers and writers who draw special attention to their narration: rather than just relaying 'what happens', his narrators *perform* their discourse, always emphasizing the process of storytelling as a transformative act. From his first novel, *Ghostwritten* (1999), it was clear that Mitchell is concerned with how our lives are 'pre-ghostwritten by forces around us' (*G*, 296). Though not every narrator of the novel is literally a writer – Marco the ghostwriter of 'London' is the only one – they are all accomplished storytellers, each drawing from an established discourse and vernacular in an effort to order and make sense of the world around them, to write their lives into meaning. Quasar from 'Okinawa' has bought into a cult mythology that places him in the role of the heroic, loyal warrior, saving the world from those who are 'unclean'. Margarita Latunsky from 'Petersburg' is a virtuoso self-deceiver, spinning lies about who she is and what she does with such aplomb that even she believes in the falsities.[3] The *noncorpum* of 'Mongolia' derives all he knows about his origins from a single folk tale, and we might say that Mo Muntervary of 'Clear Island' renders the theories of impenetrable quantum physics intelligible by describing them in words instead of numbers: 'Quantum physics speaks in chance, with the syntax of uncertainty' (*G*, 373). While this ghostwriting, this shaping and making sense of experience through language, takes the form of ruminations on chaos theory, quantum mechanics, spirituality, history, technology, and fate, it is the metaphor of storytelling that ties this disparate list of forces together.

The proliferation of storytellers continues in Mitchell's subsequent offerings. In *number9dream* (2001), the protagonist Eiji Miyake glosses the surface of the unsatisfying real world with genre conventions from science fiction to gangster films – he often does this as a coping mechanism for the challenges he faces and the memories that haunt him. Similarly, *Black Swan Green* (2006), in many ways Mitchell's 'straight story' and certainly his most autobiographical one, is the tale of the birth of a writer, in which words and narratives become a refuge from adolescent difficulties. Most recently, *The Thousand Autumns of Jacob de Zoet* (2010), set in Edo period Japan, highlights linguistic translation as its own kind of storytelling, and the slippages and nuances both inscribed and lost as narratives move from language to language. *Cloud Atlas* (2004), Mitchell's most popular and commercially successful novel, is also perhaps his most ambitious experiment in narrative form and the possibilities of storytelling. In each section of the novel, there is a character who reads the story of another character, and who in turn has their story read by someone else. Repeatedly, these characters experience uncanny moments of recognition that they cannot explain, and again and again the source of that recognition is narrative discourse. The act of reading is revealed to have infiltrated their consciousness in a way they could not possibly have anticipated, and it affects their perception of the diegetic level they occupy, the world that is 'real' to them.

These uncanny moments of subjective doubling are not unlike the process encouraged by *Present Continuous Past(s)*. The characters experience the pull of another version of the self; they sense a knowledge, the source of which they cannot identify. In *Cloud Atlas*'s 'Half Lives: The First Luisa Rey Mystery', reporter Luisa Rey is making a quick getaway from her hotel room on sinister Swannekke Island when she is struck with the feeling that she has done this before: 'A swarm of *déjà vu* haunts Luisa as she stuffs her belongings into her overnight bag. *Robert Frobisher doing a dine and dash from another hotel'* (*CA*, 142). Luisa has been entranced by Frobisher's letters, and unsettled by 'the dizzying vividness of the images of places and people … [they] … have unlocked. Images so vivid she can only call them memories' (*CA*, 121). Her sense of connection with Frobisher comes from her realization that she possesses the same comet-shaped birthmark as him, but the possibility that this indicates a metempsychosis plot is not particularly explored or validated within the novel.[4] Instead, Luisa's reaction to the letters is the response of a lover of words who has encountered a kindred spirit. She is also not the only character to feel an uncanny connection with a discursive construction. In the following tale, 'The Ghastly Ordeal of Timothy Cavendish', the narrator awakens after suffering a stroke with his mind full of muddled words: 'A stroke? Two-stroker? Stroke me? Margo Roker had a stroke. Margo Roker?' (*CA*, 370). Though Cavendish does not realize it at the time, Margo Roker is a tragic character from the Luisa Rey mystery, which he had been reading before his stroke. She becomes intertwined with the foreign personages surrounding him at the retirement home, and as he stumbles toward awareness she is arguably just as 'real' to his muddled consciousness as they are.

It must be noted that the position of these characters as discursive constructions is continually highlighted by the embedded structure of the novel, which resembles a Russian doll. A passing reference to this concept is first made early in 'Letters from Zedelghem' when Robert Frobisher mentions the composer Vyvyan Ayrs's *Matruschyka Doll Variations* (*CA*, 52). Later, in 'Half Lives: The First Luisa Rey Mystery', the metaphor is fleshed out by Isaac Sachs when he employs it to think about how time alters perception, and thus identity and truth:

> One model of time: an infinite matrioshka doll of painted moments, each 'shell' (the present), encased inside a nest of 'shells' (previous presents) I call the actual past but which we perceive as the virtual past. The doll of 'now' likewise encases a nest of presents yet to be, which I call the actual future but which we perceive as the virtual future. (*CA*, 409)

Sachs's thoughts eerily echo the shape and effect of *Present Continuous Past(s)*, and most importantly they emphasize that when memory and narrative intertwine to constitute identity, we experience it cognitively as a spatial process as much as a textual one – memory is a virtual world. The Russian-doll style embedding of each narrative reinforces how discourse over time is palimpsestic – new layers may be 'painted' on, but this does not erase the layers below. Similarly, each character's existence is secured beyond their individual chapters by their textual transmission to a 'higher' diegetic level: Frobisher 'exists' in his letters, Cavendish in his memoir, Sonmi in her orison. As beings shaped in and of discourse, the characters are shown to influence each other across these diegetic boundaries, whether they have encountered each other's narratives or not.

This is most evident in 'An Orison of Sonmi~451', when Sonmi – a clone in a post-apocalyptic future – remembers a moment she cannot place: 'The ford gathered speed, weight and weightlessness. I remember the drop: it shook free an earlier memory of blackness, inertia, gravity, of being trapped in another ford; I could not find its source in my own memories' (*CA*, 330). Sonmi simultaneously remembers a sensation yet cannot locate the root of her memory, reflecting an experience that is perhaps more bodily than cognitive. She is remembering – impossibly because she has not read the novel – Luisa Rey's drop from a cliff after being run off the road by the assassin Bill Smoke.[5] Similarly, in 'Letters from Zedelghem', Vyvyan Ayrs dreams of a Papa Song's eatery from Sonmi's world, and he, too, has no idea where it comes from, though the music in the café becomes the basis for one of his sonatas: 'I dreamt of a ... nightmarish café, brilliantly lit, but underground, with no way out. I'd been dead a long, long time. The waitresses all had the same face. The food was soap, the only drink was cups of lather' (*CA*, 80).

In addition to reinforcing the notion that these characters are constituted in and of literature, their uncanny intertextual recognitions serve to more firmly bond the experience of the external reader to that of the diegetic readers. With access to all of the narrative levels, the reader is guided through a series of encounters – not unlike those experienced by each main character – with every intertextual reference acting as a moment of forced subjective doubling. As the novel progresses, this doubling becomes iterative, and the matryoshka doll metaphor is once again apt, because it emphasizes how these references are absorbed into the subject, allowing her to create an ever-growing web of connections. The palimpsest that results problematizes the reading process and encourages additional blurring of subjectivity – as the reader progresses through the novel, she is placed in a new subject position as the character who is encountering each narrative, a process that is perpetually shifting and continually layering on top of itself. As each text is discovered and read by a subsequent narrator, another diegetic level is created and the reader reads *as* Luisa, *as* Cavendish, *as* Sonmi, and so on. In effect, by foregrounding narrative levels at such an extreme, the novel encourages the reader to see herself as just another such level, and to imagine the self as a discursive construction as well. Positioned with access not just to all the narrative levels, but to their overlapping characters and themes, the reader is in a privileged position as the only figure who can connect all of the novel's intertextual references, and is thus granted a greater interpretive agency than the diegetic readers can access.

Life as Narrative

That the instances of narrative level transgression in *Cloud Atlas* appear in the form of dreams and fleeting senses of déjà vu should give us pause. Though every character reads and absorbs a story that captures them, those acts of consumption neither influence the style through which they narrate, nor the form their personal story takes. (In contrast, this mode of inflected narration occurs with dizzying results in *number9dream*.) Instead, the influence of each text is felt tangentially, through a nagging sense of recognition, a dream, a moment brushed off as déjà vu. The subjective and unconscious influence of the stories problematizes the notion that 'life' or 'experience' can somehow be entirely separated from 'narrative'. However, the debate about the relationship between life and narrative has become a fixture in contemporary narrative theory. Roland Barthes (1977: 79) famously stated that, 'narrative is international, transhistorical, transcultural: it is simply there, like life itself', but the distinction between where narrative ends and life begins has remained a thorny one. It is generally agreed that a suitable definition of narrative must include the act of representation, and certainly this draws a clear dividing line between the narration (representation) and that which is narrated (the real to be represented).

In the digital era, however, the notion of 'reality' is just as blurry-edged as the notion of narrative, and more and more the convergence of media, storytelling and real world experience is challenging the idea that life and narrative are such distinct entities. For example, many fictional characters from today's films and television shows have online identities through social networking sites, websites like Twitter, and blogs. Fans can interact with these fictional constructions on exactly the same level as they do with their 'real' friends. Viral marketing through 'Alternate Reality Games' encourages fans to participate in the world-building of their favourite fictional universes by planting puzzles in the physical domain (such as complex codes in newspapers, fictional television commercials and websites, and even live 'meet-ups' in real world locations) that tie in with the fictional narrative. And, of course, that ultimate misnomer, 'reality' television, has completely rewritten the rules of what can be presented as factual in the mass media.[6] Mitchell's novels engage with contemporary culture by challenging our ideas about how readers can interact with a text – they *depict* that challenge in their plots, as detailed earlier, but through their style and structure they also simultaneously encourage the reader to *experience* these slippery conceptions of narrative, identity, and subjectivity.

Certainly, aside from the fact that they quite literally *are* discursive constructs, the characters in Mitchell's fiction bear the signs of identities organized by the proliferation of contemporary narratives. In *number9dream*, the novel that most overtly engages with hypermodernity, Eiji Miyake regularly invokes the rhetoric of his multimedia world, from science fiction tropes to action movie quips. His identity as a person built out of media culture reflects an identity built by narrative. Oliver Sacks (1985/1998: 110) famously asserted that 'it might be said that each of us constructs and lives a "narrative," and that this narrative *is* us, our identities'. Jerome Bruner (1987/2004: 694) later concurred with this in his essay 'Life as Narrative', in which he stated that narratives 'achieve the power to structure perceptual experience, to organize memory, to segment and purpose-build the very "events" of a life'. As noted, nearly all of Mitchell's characters are storytellers of some kind, and we can see, through thinking about life as narrative, that this impulse is not simply escapism, but the very assertion of identity – the need to write (or tell) oneself into being. Some of Mitchell's characters are unaware of how the story they construct for themselves is predicated upon their social context, but Eiji Miyake is an exception. He is constantly constructing fantasies in which he is the protagonist, but he is also well aware that his identity is structured by the narratives that surround him. Even his daydreams, themselves parodies of film and television, reflect his personal awareness of their own derivative nature, as when, in one such daydream, his nemesis spits out: 'You got hold of the wrong script, child' (*n9d*, 10). His identity is so erected in narrative that it is also already a metanarrative.

In recent years, some theorists have argued against the 'psychological narrativity thesis' proposed by Bruner and Sacks, noting that while many people experience their life and identity through a sequential narrative frame, there are certainly others who do not. In 'Against Narrativity' (2004), for example, Galen Strawson asserts that people are either fundamentally 'diachronic' (tending to view the self as continuous over time) or 'episodic' (tending to lack a sense of a consistent self that was there in the past and will be present in the future).[7] Regardless of whether one sees identity as organized through narrative or not, it would be impossible to argue that narrative plays *no* role in our memories and daily lives. Strawson (2004: 433) insists, 'I have no significant sense that I – the I now considering this question – was there in the further past', but certainly even in his protestations he is employing a form of storytelling to narrativize his experience. As James Phelan (2005: 208) notes, ' ... perhaps it's a meta-narrative: Strawson is the man who tells himself he has no narrative identity'.

It seems evident that *Cloud Atlas* engages with the life as narrative thesis; in fact, we might view many of the novel's protagonists through the episodic/diachronic model. Where most of the narrators appear to be diachronic – in that what they narrate is heavily influenced by where they come from and where they hope to go – Robert Frobisher can be viewed through a more episodic frame. He, like Strawson, lives squarely in the present, with little sense that the 'I' he was in the distant past brings much to bear on the 'I' he is during his narration. He makes decisions based on his immediate needs and desires, living quite gleefully from moment to moment. This 'present-ness' is evident even in his writing style – he often drops the subject from his sentences, lending greater urgency and immediacy to his writing: 'Asked if I could borrow a policeman's bicycle for an indefinite period. Told me that was most irregular. Assured him I was most irregular' (CA, 48).

It is fitting, then, that Frobisher's story is presented through the episodic format of letters, which inject time and spaces – gaps, indeterminacies – into the narrative.[8] Adam Ewing's journal, too, involves gaps in time, but Ewing himself always fills them in. Frobisher's narrative is unique to Cloud Atlas in that the external reader never gains access to the letters Frobisher receives from Sixsmith in response, and must thus 'read into' Frobisher's writing to understand their relationship. To see both ends of the episodic/diachronic continuum, we might contrast Frobisher with a character like Sonmi, who essentially narrates her entire life with the immediacy of a real-time hologram recording. Sonmi's identity is eminently diachronic, and it is made more so by her existence as a 'genomed' clone who had virtually no identity for the first few years of her life. When asked to describe her 'ascension' to individual consciousness, she explains the very first 'symptom' was a voice that began speaking inside her head – a narrative identity, in effect. At the end of her narrative, Sonmi makes clear that not only was her entire revolutionary act of rebellion a conspiracy carefully orchestrated by the corrupt ruling government, but that she was aware of this fact throughout her participation with the ruse. Her telling of the tale to the Archivist reveals itself to be more narrative than life, instead of the other way around. For Sonmi, life and narrative conflate for reasons that are all too appalling. Hers is a simulacrum of life, just as her existence began as a simulacrum of humanity. She states flatly to the astonished Archivist, 'free will plays no part in my story' (*CA*, 365).

Although life becoming narrative has terrible implications for Sonmi, it is a freeing process for many of the other characters in *Cloud Atlas*. Cavendish's memoir allows him to justify his behavior, place blame on others, and eventually exploit his 'ordeal' for financial gain. Though she is constructed as 'written' by Hilary V. Hush, as a journalist Luisa also holds great reverence for the written word and its power to expose murder and corruption. Regardless of their way of constructing identity, every protagonist in the novel shares the desire to complete the narrative they began reading in the first half. For Sonmi, the desire to watch the end of Cavendish's *Ghastly Ordeal* represents one of the only true expressions of free will she will ever experience, and as Robert Frobisher aphoristically states, 'a half-read book is a half-finished love affair' (*CA*, 65). Whether she or he is diachronic, episodic, constituted within, or dependent upon, narrative, narrative is an essential component within every character's life, and the desire for narrative closure is a constant for these diegetic readers as well as for the external reader.

Metalepsis and the Remediated Subject

Narrative identity is both a figurative and a literal formulation in *Cloud Atlas*, in that each object passed from diegetic level to diegetic level – Ewing's journal, Frobisher's letters, Sonmi's orison – is essentially a textually-encoded version of the identity it contains. It is presumable at the start of the novel that the various protagonists occupy the same level of reality and the same universe. Given the chronological movement from Ewing's nineteenth-century sea voyage to Frobisher's early twentieth-century letters, it is completely logical that Frobisher would discover Ewing's journal. However, when Frobisher's ex-lover, Rufus Sixsmith, appears as a character in the Luisa Rey mystery, and this mystery is revealed to quite literally exist *as a novel* within Cavendish's story, it becomes clear that each of these narratives only exists within the narrative that follows them. Each subsequent story in the first half of the novel exists on a 'higher' diegetic level than the one that precedes it. 'Sloosha's Crossin' an' Ev'rythin' After', though it appears buried at the centre of the novel, is actually revealed to be the container of all the stories 'below' it.

When the textual construction of the novel is considered in this way, it also means that each of the objects passed from character to character constitute a metalepsis, a transgression across diegetic levels. One of the founding theorists of narratology, Gerard Genette (1980: 234–5), defines metalepsis as 'any intrusion by the extradiegetic narrator or narratee into the diegetic universe (or by diegetic characters into a metadiegetic universe, etc.) or the inverse'. We can broaden the semantics of Genette's definition by emphasizing that the transgressions and intrusions across narrative levels in *Cloud Atlas* appear in the form of objects, characters, and even the aforementioned dreams and moments of recognition. The merest twinges of knowledge experienced by various characters constitute metalepsis, as they are moments in which one narrative level intrudes on another.

The objects passed from protagonist to protagonist are of course the most visible examples of metalepsis, and they do not undergo the process unchanged. Each object is transformed in some way from level to level, and we might even consider this transformation a degradation, in that the objects lose the sheen of immediacy. As Frobisher notes when he reads Ewing's journal: 'Something shifty about the journal's authenticity – seems too structured for a genuine diary' (*CA*, 64). Naturally, the journal *is* inauthentic; it was edited into a manuscript by Ewing's son and has been transformed from a handwritten document to a typescript. Frobisher's letters undergo a transformation as well – while they remain essentially the same object, they are worn by the passage of time to become yellowed, faded and ragged from rereading. Luisa's narrative only comes to be understood as a physical object – a novel manuscript – once the reader sees it in the hands of Timothy Cavendish, and Cavendish's memoir shifts from a typescript to a narrative film. Even Sonmi's orison, though it remains an egg-shaped metal device, undergoes a transformation of meaning. In her world it was a recording device and data storage, but in Zachry's world it is the magical home of a goddess, and the root of a new religion.[9]

The transformative power of metalepsis extends beyond objects when we consider its impact on the literary subject. Debra Malina (2002: 2) notes that metalepsis is a particularly useful theoretical frame for reading postmodern literature, because 'it provides a model of the dynamics of subject construction in an age that has witnessed … the deconstruction of the essential self in favor of a subject constituted in and by narrative'. Malina's stance takes for granted that the narration of the self structures our understanding of identity, something to which, as discussed earlier, Galen Strawson would certainly object.[10] However, in an age where identity is seen not just as fragmented, but as heavily mediated, problematizing that discourse through metalepsis is an apt model. As a kind of narrative decoding device, metalepsis also provides an interpretive key when applied to the complex structure of *Cloud Atlas*. Malina (2002: 4) notes: 'because it traverses an ontological hierarchy, metalepsis has the power to endow subjects with greater or lesser degrees of "reality" – in effect, to promote them into subjectivity and demote them from it'. From this theoretical standpoint, *Cloud Atlas* privileges the power of oral storytelling, the only method of storytelling that requires no physical medium, by endowing the 'Sloosha's Crossin'' narrative with the highest degree of reality.

Notably, 'Sloosha's Crossin'' is also the only chapter to directly imply a 'receiver' within the narrative itself, as Zachry repeatedly refers directly to his listeners, and through the final postscript we learn that his son has retold the tale to his own 'young 'uns', continuing the oral tradition. In these final lines of the chapter (and, one might note, the telos proper of the entire 'plot'), we learn that Zachry himself is long gone, but his words remain. So does Sonmi's orison: 'Sit down a beat or two. Hold out your hands. Look' (*CA*, 325). As in the other chapters, the external reader is in the position of the 'receiver', but this time that reception is performed as an act of looking and listening rather than reading, thus reinforcing the 'reality' of this diegesis. In other words, this chapter is the first instance in which the 'I' of the text is not filtered through a physical medium, but simply the newer voices who have picked up the tale and retold it. The ironic result of the nested structure of *Cloud Atlas* is that the narrative buried at the centre of the text is granted the highest ontological authority; everything is contained within that which appeared to *be* contained. As noted earlier, the existence of the characters is secured by their transmission from one diegetic level to a 'higher' one, and thus, within the diegesis of 'Sloosha's Crossin'', every previous character exists as a discursive construction.

This framing mechanism has been used notably in fantastic texts like *Frankenstein* (1818) and *Dracula* (1897). In these novels, the letters and journals which function as external frames for the main story also act as a static context around an otherwise sensational narrative. They distance the reader in a way that lends itself to the suspension of disbelief, while stabilizing the bizarre events with a frame that serves to reinforce realism. From a narratological perspective, the function of the many levels of *Cloud Atlas* is quite the opposite of the framing in a novel like *Frankenstein*. Mitchell's multiple frames force the reader to inhabit various personas in order to fully understand each subsequent story, and they serve to destabilize, rather than reinforce, an ontologically coherent conception of the novelistic universe. Rather than being presented with the framing narrative at the outset, the reader is forced to continually reinterpret the novel's levels as she encounters each new narrative – she is not granted a full understanding of their hierarchical organization until reaching the centre of the book. In this way, we might consider the impact of the novel on the reading subject as *itself* a form of metalepsis, as the reader must undergo a transformation of consciousness with the start of each new frame. The process of reading through *Cloud Atlas* (and, I would argue, *Ghostwritten* and *number9dream*) is a process of continual *re*-framing and *re*-contextualizing that encourages the reader to adapt to new subject positions with increasing ease.

As noted, 'Sloosha's Crossin'' takes a privileged place in the text of *Cloud Atlas* because it is presented as oral narrative, and as a mode of transmitting information, oral storytelling is relatively un-mediated. Its medium is language, which is highlighted by the distinctive vernacular spoken by the characters of the chapter. This heavy dialect implies that the story has passed directly from Zachry's lips to his son's ears, and will continue to pass thus from generation to generation.

It will be mediated only by the teller's consciousness, not a physical medium like the stories that came before it, until more advanced media come into play and the cycle begins again. If we were to map the entirety of *Cloud Atlas* we would find that it is a literalization of Marshall McLuhan's (2003: 19–21) famous claim that one medium never replaces another, but merely ingests or consumes it, incorporating it into a new mode of being and communication. The movement in this novel is not, as it first appears, a teleological movement forward in time toward apocalypse, but rather the gradual consumption over time of different media of expression – letters eat diary, novel eats letters, film eats novel, and so on. It is oral storytelling that takes the privileged position at the top of this chain. If we were to describe the entire structure of *Cloud Atlas*, we would have to say that it is a story in which an oral narrative describes a national history that contains a hologram of a personal and political history that contains a film about a man who read a novel about a woman who read some letters one man received from another who found and read a journal written by another man. Each step in this process is an act of mediation, but it is also an act of remediation, because each medium is encapsulated in another.

The concept of remediation was developed by Jay David Bolter and Richard Grusin. At its simplest, it is the representation of one medium within another. Bolter and Grusin argue that the process of remediation causes a fragmentation of the subject because media is now so ubiquitous it has become essential to how we define the self:

> Whenever our identity is mediated in this way [through film, television, print, etc.], it is also remediated, because we always understand a particular medium in relation to other past and present media ... Because we understand media through the ways in which they challenge and reform other media, we understand our mediated selves as reformed versions of earlier mediated selves. (Bolter and Grusin, 2000: 231–2)

This passage rings particularly true if one considers the reincarnation plot implied by *Cloud Atlas*. The spiritual implications need not even come to bear, as each of the characters – each discursive construction

– is quite literally a 'reformed version' of an earlier mediated self. It is not only the characters who are remediated – the material construction of the novel constitutes a remediation of the reader as subject, because in order to read the embedded narratives *as* each narrator, the reader needs to enter the discursive world in which each text exists. To do so, she must regularly reframe and recontextualize each new narrating consciousness as well as each new medium that contains it. The process of contextualizing a sea voyage journal is very different from the process of contextualizing a hard-boiled detective novel or a post-apocalyptic narrative, but *Cloud Atlas* demands these constant shifts in perspective from the reader.

The concept of the avatar can be fruitfully deployed here to describe this action of discursively 'entering' a text. In contemporary media, avatars are graphical representations of users in a virtual domain, and they serve to help the users project an identity for themselves and each other. They also grant the user spatial access to the virtual world, 'eyes on the ground', as it were. In this way, *Cloud Atlas* enacts a remediation of reader subjectivity by providing a series of *narratological* avatars within the text, in the form of each narrating protagonist. More than mere focalizers, these characters constitute avatars specifically because of the novel's ontological embedding, drawing users *into* virtual worlds, and thus remediating reader subjectivity through narrative form.

A Thousand Traces

In the 'Mongolia' chapter of *Ghostwritten*, narrated by the bodiless entity who inhabits a series of human hosts, the *noncorpum* describes the differences between minds formed in the developed world versus those from the undeveloped world as follows:

> It was good to transmigrate out of a westernized head. However much I learn from the non-stop highways of minds like Caspar's, they make me giddy. It would be the euro's exchange rate one minute, a film he'd once seen about art thieves in Petersburg the next, a memory of fishing with his uncle between islets the next, some pop song or a friend's internet home page the next. No stopping. Gunga's mind patrols a

more intimate neighborhood. She constantly thinks about getting
enough food and money. She worries about her daughter, and ailing
relatives. (*G*, 166)

This comparison highlights the influence of the digital era on identity,
and how hyperlinks are not confined to mouse clicks, but have altered
the very procedures we use to think about the world.

Like cognitive hyperlinks, the moments of recognition experienced by characters in *Cloud Atlas* are replicated a thousand times
for the reader throughout all of David Mitchell's novels. From the
smallest allusion – as when Katy Forbes in *Ghostwritten* has a print in
her apartment of the same Delacroix stolen by the art thieves in 'Petersburg' – to the reappearance of a character three novels later – as
when the Neal Brose (who dies in *Ghostwritten*'s 'Hong Kong' chapter) reappears as a bullying teenager in *Black Swan Green* – the experience of reading Mitchell's novels is a process of meaning-making
through links, and those links encourage a destabilization of subject
positions.[11] Like the instant of recognition prompted by *Present Continuous Past(s)*, passing moments like these in Mitchell's novels train
the reader to inhabit multiple positions at once, making connections
across discursive worlds in what is ultimately a satisfying process in
the era of mass connectivity. This process is ongoing as each new novel is bound to introduce characters readers have seen before and to
expand upon or fully rewrite their histories and identities.

The numerous narrative worlds of Mitchell's novels inflect, influence, contradict and continually eddy around each other, jostling for
ontological supremacy one moment and receding from such dominance the next. Like tectonic plates, they thrust against each other
until one is edged below, only to force its way to the surface in another
time and place. There is no absolute teleology in Mitchell's universe
– despite the apparent cause and effect of random events in *Ghostwritten* or the chronological sequence of nested stories in *Cloud Atlas*
– because experience lies entirely at the level of discourse, and the
discursive multiverse that constitutes his oeuvre is persistently expanding and in flux. The narratives are concerned with perception,

with how we tell our stories and how those stories influence lives, histories, myths, and identities.

Writing about *Present Continuous Past(s)*, Hilde Van Gelder and Jan Baetens (2004) note, 'the discrepancy between subject and object of the experience ... the crucial question that artists ask themselves on conducting such experiments, is how it feels for the human body to become part of a device in which it is completely absorbed both physically and intellectually'. The characters in Mitchell's worlds experience how what we read becomes inseparable from what we live; how stories can haunt us like dreams or memories or past selves; how the reader will fill gaps in a narrative, as Wolfgang Iser (1978) noted, but also how a narrative can fill gaps in the reader; how stories can become confused with truth, and thus, to all intents and purposes, become truth. This experience is replicated in the act of reading Mitchell's novels, as readers experience the iterative subjectivity encouraged by remediation, metalepsis, and networks of reference. Mitchell's novels problematize the dichotomy that polarizes life and narrative, and force us to reconsider the power and possibilities of life *as* narrative and narrative *as* life.

Acknowledgements

I would like to thank Jennifer Brock, Ryan Fong, Colin Milburn and William Stephenson for their insightful comments and support.

Notes

1 Eight seconds is indeed the precise time of the delay, as described in an illustrated explanation of the piece on the German website *Media Art Net*. The installation was first exhibited in 1974; it was displayed more recently in the Pompidou Centre as part of a new media retrospective.

2 See the reader response criticism of Wolfgang Iser for an understanding of interpretation as the sum of the reader's interaction with a text, especially *The Implied Reader* (1974) and *The Act of Reading* (1978). Iser's theories introduced literary phenomenology into the then contentious debate regarding whether the book or the reader was the site of interpretive authority. For Iser, the answer was both: meaning was produced by interaction between text and reader. With his theory, Iser managed to

walk a difficult middle ground between two camps – one arguing rigidly for readerly subjectivity and the other for reading the text as a unified, closed object.

3 Not since Gerty MacDowell of the 'Nausikaa' chapter of James Joyce's *Ulysses* (1922) have we encountered a character so immersed in her own self-delusion, and so talented at narrating it. Indeed, the influence of *Ulysses* upon *Ghostwritten* is quite pronounced, given the trope of metempsychosis (the transmigration of souls), the wandering focalization, and the role of place in each chapter.

4 Though there is certainly room for this kind of reading of the novel (especially given its prominence in Mitchell's first novel, *Ghostwritten*), the idea is explicitly undercut by Timothy Cavendish, the editor-character who fittingly gets to voice this skepticism: 'One or two things will have to go: the insinuation that Luisa Rey is this Robert Frobisher chap reincarnated, for example. Far too hippie-druggy-new age' (*CA*, 373) and 'As an experienced editor I disapprove of backflashes, foreshadowings and tricksy devices, they belong in the 1980s with MAs in Postmodernism and Chaos Theory' (*CA*, 152), a degree which, perhaps not ironically, Mitchell himself possesses.

5 Sonmi, too, possesses the comet-shaped birthmark, as does Cavendish, but the reincarnation plot is again undercut by the fact that Luisa is a character in a novel within Cavendish's universe. Even if Sonmi and Cavendish could theoretically occupy the same universe, Luisa cannot. Thus, if these characters do possess some form of spiritual or supernatural connection, it is a connection that transgresses boundaries between 'reality' and literary discourse. This transgression only serves to underscore the power of the written word in Mitchell's work, since the characters exist in separate discursive universes, yet in this conception of the novel they would somehow be traversing those narrative levels. It is also worth noting that during her 'ascension' Sonmi spends nearly a year reading everything she can, so she may very well have encountered the Luisa Rey novel in her studies, though there is nothing in her narration to signify this.

6 For additional work on the role of contemporary media in narrative, see Henry Jenkins, especially *Convergence Culture: Where Old and New Media Collide* (2006), Marie-Laure Ryan (ed.), *Narrative Across Media: The Languages of Storytelling* (2004), and Janet Murray, *Hamlet on the Holodeck: The Future of Narrative in Cyberspace* (1997).

7 Strawson's article has reignited the debate about life and narrative, especially in narratological circles. Paul John Eakin has responded and expressed ambivalence about Strawson's thesis, maintaining that narrative plays an important role in how we understand our identities. Surely much of the debate arises from the slippery nature of the terms: much of the discussion has involved equating narrativity of identity with narrativity of experience, and these are certainly two different things. Eakin perhaps puts the entire question to rest when he points out that 'when it comes to self-knowledge, narrative is value neutral, available as an identity *resource* to Episodics and Diachronics alike' (Eakin, 2006: 185, emphasis added).

8 As noted earlier, Iser in *The Act of Reading* proposes that meaning is derived from an interaction between text and reader. He also discusses how any narrative will necessarily possess gaps or indeterminacies that leave room for reader interpretation. In effect, the text provides a schematic – the rules of the narrative – but the reader then fills in the indeterminate spaces of that schematic using the very rules it provides.

9 The term 'orison' itself embodies this double signification, as it means both 'oration' or 'speech' as well as 'prayer'. The most famous use of the latter comes from *Hamlet*: 'Nymph, in thy orisons, be all my sins remembered' (III.i).

10 This conception of identity as discursive or virtual and therefore disembodied has also been challenged by some postmodern and posthuman theorists. For example, see N. Katherine Hayles, *How We Became Posthuman* (1999) especially 'Toward Embodied Virtuality': 'I view the present moment as a critical juncture when interventions might be made to keep disembodiment from being rewritten, once again, into prevailing concepts of subjectivity' (Hayles, 1999: 5).

11 In *Black Swan Green* we learn of the roots of Brose's downfall, during this exchange with Jason's cousin Hugo: '"Money's *never* a problem, not if you've got half a brain." "No?" "Money? 'Course not. Identify a demand, handle its supply, make your customers grateful, kill off the opposition." Neal Brose memorized every word of that' (*BSG*, 74–5).

Works Cited

Barthes, Roland (1977) 'Introduction to the Structural Analysis of Narratives', in *Image–Music–Text*, trans. Stephen Heath, pp. 79–124. Glasgow: Fontana/Collins.

Bolter, Jay David and Grusin, Richard (2000) *Remediation: Understanding New Media*. Cambridge, MA and London: MIT Press.

Bruner, Jerome (1987/2004) 'Life as Narrative', *Social Research* 71(3): 691–710.

Eakin, Paul John (2006) 'Narrative Identity and Narrative Imperialism: A Response to Galen Strawson and James Phelan', *Narrative* 14(2): 180–7.

Genette, Gerard (1980) *Narrative Discourse: An Essay in Method*, trans. Jane E. Lewin. Ithaca, NY: Cornell University Press.

Graham, Dan (1974) *Present Continuous Past(s)*. Pompidou Centre, Paris, France. [Art Installation]

Hayles, N. Katherine (1999) *How We Became Posthuman: Virtual Bodies in Cybernetics, Literature, and Informatics*. Chicago and London: University of Chicago Press.

Iser, Wolfgang (1978) *The Act of Reading*. Baltimore, MD and London: Johns Hopkins University Press.

Jenkins, Henry (2006) *Convergence Culture: Where Old and New Media Collide*. New York: New York University Press.

Malina, Debra (2002) *Breaking the Frame: Metalepsis and the Construction of the Subject*. Columbus: Ohio State University Press.

McLuhan, Marshall (2003) *Understanding Media: The Extensions of Man*, ed. W. Terrence Gordon. Corte Madera, CA: Gingko Press.

Media Art Net. 'Present Continuous Past(s)', URL (consulted 21 June 2010): http://www.medienkunstnetz.de/works/present-continuous-pasts/

Murray, Janet (1997) *Hamlet on the Holodeck: The Future of Narrative in Cyberspace*. New York: Simon and Schuster.

Phelan, James (2005) 'Who's Here? Thoughts on Narrative Identity and Narrative Imperialism', *Narrative* 13(3): 205–10.

Ryan, Marie-Laure (ed.) (2004) *Narrative Across Media: The Languages of Storytelling*. Lincoln and London: University of Nebraska Press.

Ryan, Marie-Laure (2006) *Avatars of Story*. Minneapolis and London: University of Minnesota Press.

Sacks, Oliver (1985/1998) *The Man Who Mistook His Wife for a Hat: And Other Clinical Tales*. New York: Simon and Schuster.

Shakespeare, William (2003) *Hamlet, Prince of Denmark*. Cambridge: Cambridge University Press.

Strawson, Galen (2004) 'Against Narrativity', *Ratio* 17: 428–52.

Van Gelder, Hilde and Baetens, Jan (2004) 'On the Body as the Subject of Experience: Art as a Necessary Element of the Genesis of Knowledge',

Image and Narrative 5(9), URL (consulted 21 June 2010): http://www.imageandnarrative.be/inarchive/performance/vangelder.htm

6

CLOUD ATLAS
From Postmodernity to the Posthuman

Hélène Machinal

Cloud Atlas presents the reader with a number of characteristics that are typical of postmodern writing, not least, generic hybridity, a fragmented structure, interrupted narratives, and an emphasis on illusion and simulacrum. After probing into the ingredients of this postmodern recipe, this essay will contend that David Mitchell's novel is rooted in postmodernity but that it also transcends it by introducing a philosophical dimension that goes beyond the individual level to a more collective one. Despite its apparent fragmentation and discontinuity, the structure of the novel gradually leads the reader towards a reflection on humankind. In its emphasis on recurrence, transmission, heritage and memory, the novel bridges gaps, connecting stories and History, individuals and societies. In doing so, it highlights the shift from an ontogenic perspective, one which only takes into account an individual's finiteness, to a phylogenic perspective, one that widens the prospect to the human species. Thus, Mitchell invites the reader to reflect on the possible future of humanity. To do so, he inserts two narratives at the core of his novel – 'An Orison of Sonmi~451' and 'Sloosha's Crossin' an' Ev'rythin' After' – which, respectively, picture an Orwellian dystopia and a post-cataclysmic primitive society. Hence, *Cloud Atlas* takes us through a temporal journey beginning during the century in which philosophical reflection on the individual emerges and ending in future worlds, one in which human beings and clones cohabit. This progression enables a reflection on the possible political, social and ontological consequences of the third industrial revolution, that of biotechnology. Mitchell invites his readers to mentally project themselves into a posthuman world that

details what the human could become in a future society characterized by the annihilation of human identity, a subjection of the human
through technology, and a reduction of human beings to mere commodities. Through his elaboration of the social, political and environmental facets of this posthuman world Mitchell asserts the necessity
of pondering the future of humanity and explores what it means to
be human.

Postmodernity

The playful recourse to genres deemed characteristic of postmodern
fiction is clear in *Cloud Atlas*. The novel opens with 'The Pacific Journal of Adam Ewing', a diary written in the early nineteenth century
and obviously modelled on adventure stories typical of the rise of
the novel. An intertextual allusion to Daniel Defoe's *Robinson Crusoe*
(1719) and its famous footprint discovery scene can be identified by
the reader as early as the first sentence of *Cloud Atlas*: 'Beyond the
Indian hamlet, upon a forlorn strand, I happened on a trail of recent
footprints' (*CA*, 3). In 'Letters from Zedelghem', the epistolary mode
provides a link between the Enlightenment and the modernist period
in which this second narrative is anchored. The influence of Friedrich
Nietzsche's writing, a *fin de siècle* ambience, and the protagonist Frobisher's exploration of musical forms in his *Cloud Atlas Sextet*, are all
evocative of trends in modernist writing.[1] Whereas Frobisher himself
is modernist, according to Randall Stevenson's (1991: 25) definition,
in his attempt 'to contain the dark energies of historical nightmare
within subtle structures and complex chronologies; that is, by radical-
izing form', Mitchell's text is postmodern in that it 'not only radicalizes
forms, but also satirizes them, exposing their incapacities to connect
with reality and the possibilities for distortions which result' (Stevenson, 1991: 25). Such satire is evident from the very opening in that
the discovered footprint does not lead to an incarnation of otherness
as it does in the source text, but to Dr Henry Goose, 'surgeon of the
London nobility' (*CA*, 3). The beginning of the novel is thus marked
by an attack on the violence and all-pervasiveness of colonialism: 'His
nationality was no surprise. If there be any eyrie so desolate, or isle

so remote that one may there resort unchallenged by an Englishman, 'tis not down on any map I ever saw' (*CA*, 3). The ironic distance towards the genre thus introduced by the author is immediately made explicit and introduces a reflexivity in the text – a common stand-point shared by readers and author alike. Therefore '[the] heightened sense of artifice, [the] suspicion of absolute truth and [the] resulting inclination to stress the fictionality of fiction' (Ousby, 1988: 752) pre-sented by Ian Ousby as characteristic of postmodernity are certainly to be found in *Cloud Atlas*.

With 'Half Lives, the First Luisa Rey Mystery', we enter the rotten world of the American thriller featuring a reporter as a sleuth investi-gating big business scandal. Luisa Rey's story also introduces another medium, that of the visual arts – it recalls well-known films based on this genre and shot in the mid-1970s, such as *All the President's Men* (1976). The evocation of the cinema recurs in the following narrative, 'The Ghastly Ordeal of Timothy Cavendish': Cavendish reads 'The First Luisa Rey Mystery' and sees the novel as 'written in neat little chapteroids, doubtless with one eye on the Hollywood screenplay' (*CA*, 164). In addition, Cavendish constantly compares himself to a film star: Humphrey Bogart, Steve McQueen and Fred Astaire are all mentioned and, to put it in a nutshell, Cavendish declares 'I was a man in a horror B-movie asylum' (*CA*, 181). Finally, at the end of the second part of this story, a voice gives technical indications to a director called 'Lars', clearly paving the way for Sonmi's remark in the following tale about 'The Ghastly Ordeal' being a film: 'A picaresque entitled *The Ghastly Ordeal of Timothy Cavendish*, made before the foundation of Nea So Copros in a long deadlanded province of the abortive European democracy' (*CA*, 243)

The gradual encroachment of the virtual is also an asset of postmo-dernity as it clearly points to the illusory quality of what we consider as real. In this novel the reader is led to retrospectively change his per-ception of both the nature and the status of each text he reads as set narrative roles are never stable and constantly need to be reappraised. Fictive reality is constantly questioned and never stabilized as, with each new narrative, the reader–writer contract of suspended disbe-lief is questioned. We enter Adam Ewing's fictive reality and believe in it until we discover in the following narrative that Frobisher reads Adam Ewing's journal. Not only is Adam thus relegated to the status of fictive character but Frobisher also casts suspicion on the journal's authenticity: 'Something shifty about the journal's authenticity – seems too structured for a genuine diary, and its language doesn't ring quite true – but who would bother forging such a journal, and why?' (*CA*, 64). We then enter Frobisher and Sixsmith's fictive reality, the reliability of which seems to hold, as in the third narrative Sixsmith reappears as an older character, which corresponds to the time gap between Frobisher's letters and Luisa's adventures. Luisa herself discovers and reads Frobisher's letters so that she is placed in a reader's position although the latter does not question the validity of their fictive reality yet. With the fourth narrative, Luisa, Sixsmith and Frobisher are sent back to the illusory sphere of fiction, as 'Half-Lives' is revealed to be a novel submitted for publication to Timothy Cavendish: 'Bills, junk, moral muggings from charity fundraisers and a package addresses "FAO The Visionary Editor of 'Knuckle Sandwich'" containing a MS titled *Half-lives* – lousy name for a work of fiction – and subtitled *The First Luisa Rey Mystery*' (*CA*, 157–8). Reading Cavendish's narrative, we adhere to the potential stability of the fictive reality it presents until we discover that Cavendish is an actor in a film seen by Sonmi in a posthuman future (*CA*, 243).

In the first four narratives, the validity of fictive reality is questioned through the character-narrator and thanks to the metafictional play on genres. With the central two narratives, the prospect widens and we could point out an evolution from an individual perspective to a more collective one. Indeed, the connections between Sonmi's and Cavendish's narratives are not only to be found in the aforementioned passage.[2] When Sonmi relates her escape with Hae-Joo away from Taemosan University, she discovers in the mountains 'the carved features of a giant sitting in the lotus position' (*CA*, 345) whom she identifies as Cavendish. She then learns that Cavendish had become a deity in the pre-consumers society and is still considered as a divinity in the Abbess's colony (*CA*, 345–7). The emphasis on the process of fictionalization now applies to collectivity, as seen also in the central narrative in which Sonmi is a divinity and Sonmi's orison is deified by

Zachry. The emphasis on fiction and fictionalization gradually invades the novel as, on the one hand, each narrator becomes a fictitious character in the narrative that follows his or her own, and, on the other, the fictive reality we have taken for granted in each narrative is questioned in the next.[3] As Brian McHale (1987: 101) writes, 'a "world of fixed and discrete objects" is given and then taken away, with the dual effect of destabilizing the ontology of this projected world and simultaneously laying bare the process of world-construction'.

In 'Simulacra and Science Fiction', Jean Baudrillard (1991: 309) enumerates three orders of simulacra, of which Mitchell's writing could be said to correspond with the third: 'simulation simulacra: based on information, the model, cybernetic play. Their aim is maximum operationality, hyperreality, total control'. In this third order, the critical distance that separates the real from the imaginary begins 'to disappear and to be absorbed by the model alone' (Baudrillard, 1991: 309):

> Models no longer constitute an imaginary domain with reference to the real; they are, themselves, an apprehension of the real, and thus leave no room for any fictional extrapolation – they are immanent, and therefore leave no room for any kind of transcendentalism. The stage is now set for simulation, in the cybernetic sense of the word – that is to say, for all kinds of manipulation of these models (hypothetical scenarios, the creation of simulated situations, etc.), but *now nothing distinguishes this management-manipulation from the real itself: there is no more fiction.* (Baudrillard, 1991: 310, emphasis in original)

Cloud Atlas models reality, but in doing so, it produces its own reality, and destroys the very foundations upon which our old distinction between real and imaginary is based. Whereas 'the imaginary was a pretext of the real in a world dominated by the reality principle. Today, it is the real which has become the pretext of the model in a world governed by the principle of simulation' (Baudrillard, 1991: 310).

To understand the concept of hyperreality, one can look at the concepts of simulation and simulacra as theorized by Baudrillard in *Simulacra and Simulation* (1994): simulation implies the disappearance of frontiers between reality and representation; the simulacrum can be defined with reference to Deleuze's description of 'an image without a semblance' (Deleuze, 1990: 257). The gradual contamination and proliferation of simulacra leads to a state of hyperreality in which the image 'has no relation to any reality whatsoever: it is its own pure simulacrum' (Baudrillard, 1994: 6). In *Cloud Atlas*, the contamination of the virtual paves the way to Sonmi's narrative, which corresponds to a post-capitalist world in which the mass reproduction of simulacra leads to a 'world with an unreality and a free floating absence of "the referent"' (Jameson, 1990: 17). *Cloud Atlas* is symptomatic of this shift identified by Baudrillard, a move into the state of hyperreality in which 'it is not a question of parallel universes, or double universes, or even of possible universes: not possible nor impossible, nor real nor unreal. It is hyperreal. It is a universe of simulation, which is something altogether different' (Baudrillard, 1991: 311–12). In the hyperreality of simulation there is no difference between real and unreal, in the sense that even if that difference exists, it is a difference without affect. Baudrillard (1991: 312) summarizes that 'there is neither fiction nor reality – a kind of hyperreality has abolished both' and concludes the observation with the assertion that, 'therein lies the defining character, if there is one, of our contemporary SF' (Baudrillard, 1991: 312). No wonder then that Mitchell's postmodern play with the illusory quality of what we believe to be real in the first four stories of *Cloud Atlas* leads to two central science fiction narratives.

'An Orison of Sonmi~451' adumbrates a potentially dystopian future in which the nation state of Korea has been replaced by the state-corporation Nea So Copros. Taking today's global capitalism and genetic experimentation to its imagined but also logical extreme, the souls of the citizens of Nea So Copros are credited with money which it is then compulsory to spend – hence the mantra, 'A Soul's Value is the Dollars Therein' (*CA*, 341). The story reveals that the entire corporate structure is dependent upon the service of millions of genetically engineered Soap-eating clones called fabricants, who perform all the menial texts that keep the corporate society functioning. The world depicted in 'An Orison of Sonmi~451' could be seen as an illustration of Baudrillard's approach to simulation in which, as Fredric Jameson explains, 'the final stage of commodity reification is famously discovered to be the image, and ultimately the simulacrum. The image indeed abolishes that older distinction between mind and body, between intellectual and manual labor, on which the philosophical humanism of the theory of non-alienated labor was predicted' (Jameson, 2005: 154).

According to Peter Stockwell (2000: 215), 'the end of dystopia is ultimately apocalyptic, either in a personal sense (the death of the character or their sublimation into a collective, or the termination of the role of "reader" in finishing a novel) or in a communal sense (the whole society being destroyed)'. 'Sloosha's Crossin' an' Ev'rythin' After', representing as it does the future of Sonmi's dystopian world, is therefore logically a post-cataclysm narrative, that narrative mode which, according to John Clute and Peter Nicholls (1999: 581), has 'always played a central role in sf, both genre sf and mainstream'. Its presence in a mainstream novel such as Mitchell's is no surprise, since, as Clute and Nicholls (1999: 582) continue, 'the post-holocaust theme, particularly in the UK, has had a strong attraction for mainstream writers, perhaps because it offers such a powerful metaphor for exploring Man's relation with his social structures'. 'Sloosha's Crossin' an' Ev'rythin' After' pictures a preindustrialized and precivilized world and is thus in keeping with a 'post-apocalyptic future ... often envisioned as the resurgence of a pre-modern, pre-industrial past ... [which] is not unrelated to the status of catastrophe as the uncanny, repressed aspect of progress, as "the effaced signal of something which only takes on its value in the future"' (Mousoutzanis, 2009: 459).

In *Cloud Atlas*, the metafictional dimension and the sense of the hyperreal converge to exemplify the fact that in 'postmodernity representation is not conceived as a dilemma but an impossibility, and what can be termed a kind of cynical reason in the realm of art displaces it by way of a multiplicity of images, none of which corresponds to "truth"' (Jameson, 2005: 212). This rhetoric of illusion also leads to the blurring of the sense of identity both within diegesis and without. Implicitly, the reader is also submitted to the fictionalizing process as he shares the position of reader with each new narrator. Thus, the reflexivity we have stressed through the metafictional dimension reappears when we broach notions such as identity and essential selfhood.

Narrators, readers and characters play interchangeable roles, which all point to the idea of a fixed identity as fictitious and to the sense of being as evanescent. Human beings, and the reality that surrounds them (whether fictive or not), seem impossible to grasp.

Postmodernity and the Posthuman

At first sight, one could consider that aspects of postmodernity such as fragmentation and discontinuity prevail in a novel that seems to be of a kaleidoscopic nature.[4] Indeed, as the novel is composed of a succession of stories readers have the feeling that, with each new text, the tube has been rotated and they are presented with a picture different from that they had just viewed. Continuity and connection nevertheless emerge when the reader gradually realizes that each character is indeed a negligible part, but one which fits into a wider pattern.[5] This results from the fact that characters are connected to each other's stories through their reading, viewing or listening to the independent narratives that form the novel. As the second half of each story resumes in turn after its previous arrest, the kaleidoscopic metaphor becomes more appropriately replaced by that of the palindrome that the novel structurally resembles, although the forward movement of each narrative of course prevents it from being literally so. Moreover, the novel revolves on itself as its chiasmic structure grants a central and pivotal position to Zachry's post-cataclysm tale, the only narrative that is given as a whole. This is far from innocent as the central tale is that in which the necessity of a collective vision is reasserted. 'Sloosha's Crossin'' is framed by the narrative taking place in a future posthuman world characterized by an extreme contamination of the virtual and a subjection of individuals. In Sonmi's world, society is not envisaged as a collective entity granting the welfare of its members, it is the exact opposite. The construction of the novel gives the impression that since the end of the eighteenth century humanity has been paving the way to that posthuman dystopia. However, although Sonmi's narrative surrounds the central story it does not lie at the novel's core – even if it proposes a dire perspective on a world where human identity has almost disappeared, at the novel's centre resides a post-cataclysmic narrative in which the return to collective values is asserted.

The temporal dimension is important in *Cloud Atlas* as the independent stories we read also span a period of time. Three turn of the century periods are used as backdrops for specific parts: 'The Pacific Journal' dates back to the turn of the century that follows the first industrial revolution in England; 'Letters from Zedelghem' is set at the beginning of the twentieth century, again following the second industrial revolution; 'Luisa Rey' and 'The Ghastly Ordeal' take place during and after the third industrial revolution, that of computer and biotechnologies. As for 'Sonmi' and 'Sloosha's Crossin'', they also take place before and after a major *peripeteia*, 'The Fall', which implies a different type of rupture. In each story the reader is presented with temporal turning points associated with scientific and technological revolutions that trigger an ontological and epistemological crisis. The repeated use of these ruptures also contributes to the building of a sense of continuity: industrial revolutions provide another thread that weaves the different stories into a wider perspective, which is that of History. Each story is an autonomous star in a system, or an instrument in a piece of music, which is both independent and part of the whole.[6] As Linda Hutcheon writes:

> ... what [postmodernist] novels ... explicitly do is to undermine the ideological assumptions behind what has been accepted as universal and trans-historical in our culture: the humanist notion of Man as a coherent and continuous subject. Like post-structuralist feminist theory and recent historiography, this fiction investigates how, in all these discourses, the subject of history is the subject in history, subject to history and to his story. (Hutcheon, 1988: 177)

The motif of historical recurrence, of revolution as the completion of a circle, or of the eternal return of the same (to use the Nietzschean concept in which Frobisher revels) induces an approach to History that is specific and has both political and philosophical implications. From a political point of view, it annihilates the deterministic view of History as progress and, then, triggers a questioning of the rhetoric of power and dominance voiced by those who control technology and science. From an ontological point of view, it leads to a reappraisal of the 'humanist notion of Man' as a central and essential entity. The political reflection culminates in Sonmi's narrative while the ontological one is embedded in 'Sloosha's Crossin''.

Cloud Atlas shows that the three successive revolutions humanity has undergone since the end of the eighteenth century have gradually shaped contemporary perception of time and of human identity. These epistemological shifts are emphasized through postmodern characteristics omnipresent in the novel. Still, the novel is also suffused with a social and political dimension, a denunciation of how societies can become forces of control and subjection. The first industrial revolution coincides with the rise of the novel which is synonymous with the emergence of the bourgeoisie and the individualistic ethos of capitalism; it is therefore certainly not fortuitous that 'The Pacific Journal' should unfold precisely during that period:

> This age [that of the rise of the novel] – which represented itself as one of Reason and Enlightenment, when an ideology of liberalism stressed the importance of individualism … – is also, crucially, the age which saw the invention of a specific category of primary relevance to character in the novel, for it was during this century that the concept of 'human nature' was invented. (Docherty, 1991: 171).

Frobisher's letters testify to the end of an era after which will emerge an economy of the masses and a consumer society in which power is concentrated in the hands of a few financial tycoons to whom political powers bow down.[7] However, the third industrial revolution is certainly that which Mitchell's novel aims to denounce as the most dangerous threat to the future of humankind. The posthuman world described in Sonmi's narrative leads to a de-humanizing process, which is founded on the annihilation of subjectivity and free will. In order to establish the ruling order's dominance over its subjects, time and History have been eradicated from the clones's environment and the 'purebloods' (*CA*, 191) are described as glued to their 'sonys' (*CA*, 201) or 'AdVs' (*CA*, 201). Human beings and clones alike are fed with images that provide them with a sense of reality that is only virtual but remains established as universally valid and valuable.

In Sonmi's world, temporal perspective has been eradicated, the past does not exist anymore, historical perspective is denied: this is a way to control the minds of individuals; it enables the ruling power to prevent human beings from having access to philosophical and political perspective. Such a feature corresponds to that which Thomas Docherty describes when he tackles the issue of postmodern characterization and links it to the treatment of history:

> This denial of history in earlier theorizations of character is accompanied by a denial of politics ... This reduction of politics to morality is entirely in keeping with a liberalism which operates precisely on the suppression of history (replacing this with eternal, immanent 'truths' of human nature) and the elimination of politics (replaced by 'values'). (Docherty, 1991: 182).

The political dystopia, which seems to be humanity's inevitable fate in Sonmi's narrative, could be seen as an illustration of this reduction of politics to morality. Mitchell uses features of postmodernist writing to deliver a political message: fragmentation can be envisaged as a means of asserting the illusory belief in 'grand narratives' as theorized by Lyotard, and of denouncing the fallacy of the association between time, progress and truth.[8] Linda Hutcheon underlines this refusal to consider history as a narrative that could claim a superior status to that of fiction due to its supposed greater proximity to truth:

> Historiographic metafiction refutes the natural or common-sense methods of distinguishing between historical fact and fiction. It refuses the view that only history has a truth claim, both by questioning the ground of that claim in historiography and by asserting that both history and fiction are discourses, human constructs, signifying systems, and both derive their major claim to truth from that identity. (Hutcheon, 1988: 93)

History and fiction both tend towards a desire to impose 'a global homogeneity, a universal history' (Docherty, 1991: 11), which has important political implications. A single instrumental voice in a piece of music, an isolated cloud in the sky, do not necessarily make sense alone but each acquires meaning when it adds its singularity to the whole in order to form an 'atlas of clouds' or Frobisher's *Cloud Atlas Sextet*.

The postmodern features of the novel serve a specific aim. The novel not only denounces the dangers of a uniformed and universal view of history and man, through claiming the importance of individual stories and subjective perceptions, but also asserts the necessity of connectivity and continuity. The chain of beings formed by the characters whose fundamental link is their common comet-shaped birthmark conveys this sense of continuity; the connection between the characters acquires an essential quality once readers begin to realize that they are linked in spite of the time gaps, which sometimes even prevent them from having had the possibility of knowing one another.[9] Something fundamental in their connectedness emerges as a birthmark points to a very peculiar genetic pool, one that resembles more an essence shared and one which cannot be controlled by any mode of power, be it biotechnological or not: indeed Sonmi, as a 'genomed' clone, should not bear such a birthmark (*CA*, 204). The motif of transmission, of memory and heritage, hence transcends the dislocation otherwise created by the variety of narrative voices the reader encounters. Given their constant interweaving, there is no manichean opposition between the individual and the collective in the novel but rather a warning against the consequences of a social system in which human beings are subjected to modes of power which control thought, knowledge and conscience.

The Resistance of the Human

Throughout his work, Michel Foucault shows how power relations are based on the elaboration of a field of knowledge and this perspective culminates in one of his last series of classes at the Collège de France, that in which he introduces the concept of 'governmentality':[10]

> Exactly as when examining the relations between reason and madness in modern Western societies, we have tried to question the general process of committal and segregation, thus exploring what lies behind asylums, hospitals, therapeutics, classifications, exactly as when dealing with prisons we have tried to underline the general economy of

power, is it possible, when dealing with the State, to operate through the same bypass? Is it possible to explore what lies behind? Is it possible to set the modern State back in a general technology of power which would account for its mutations, its development, its functioning? Can we talk about something like 'governmentality', which would be to the State what segregation techniques were to psychiatry, what discipline techniques were in the penal system, what biopolitics were to medical institutions? (Foucault, 2004: 124)[11]

The connection between power and knowledge applies to the end of the eighteenth century and the organization of capitalism, as well as to the British Empire: the two share a common system of domination.[12] With what we now refer to as the third revolution, that of biotechnology, we have entered an era in which the human body can potentially be turned into a market commodity, as is clearly seen in the Yakuza stolen human organ black market in *number9dream*. Foucault also theorizes the emergence of 'biopower', a term that applies to a power exercising control over the life of populations or classes without taking into account the individual dimension.[13] We find an illustration of it in Sonmi's posthuman world with birth control and the choice over the way a child is genomed (*CA*, 237) or the choice between boy and girl (*CA*, 352).

Sonmi's posthuman world triggers a philosophical reflection on human nature due to the shift from, as François Gros puts it in *L'ingénierie du vivant*, 'l'utilisation de la nature à la fabrique du vivant' (cited in Lecourt, 2003: 9), that is, from the utilization of nature to the production/construction of the living. In Nea So Copros, nature is genetically modified and sterilized:

It had been a brite morning on the plain, but inside the plantation every daylite hour was dank dusk. The only sound was the sterile wind swishing blunted needles. The pollenless tress were genomed to repel bugs and birds; the stagnant air reeked of insecticide. (*CA*, 344)

The fabricants are genomed to become slaves adapted only to the tasks for which they are designed:

> He ... told me those nascents were destined for uranium tunnels un-
> der the Yellow Sea; their eyes were bowl-like. Insanity would ensue if
> xposed to unfiltered daylight for too long. (*CA*, 340)[14]

Similar to the clones in Kazuo Ishiguro's (2005) *Never Let Me Go*, fabricants are not allowed to have souls.[15] However, in Sonmi's world, soul has a very specific meaning: in the socio-economic order imagined by Mitchell, souls are chips used to trace human beings or to be debited when people have to pay for a commodity. Human beings are reduced to consumers genuflecting to the dollar and forced to consume by 'Enrichment Laws' according to which 'consumers have to spend a fixed quota of dollars each month, depending on their strata. Hoarding is an anti-corpocratic crime' (*CA*, 237).

In Mitchell's novel, the human body and soul have entered the exchange circuit, so that, as Jameson (2004: 35) has argued 'the system (now grasped as the free market) is part of human nature'. The process described by Jameson recalls that of the depoliticization and annihilation of the historical dimension of discourse and narrative that Roland Barthes details in *Mythologies* (1972/1991).[16] According to Barthes, the function of the production of myth in bourgeois societies aims at transforming history into nature, and thus avoiding questioning and reflection by establishing a state of things and being as 'true' and immutable:

> It is now possible to complete the semiological definition of myth in a bourgeois society: myth is *depoliticized speech* ... Myth does nor deny things, on the contrary, its function is to talk about them, it makes them innocent, it gives them a natural and eternal justification. In passing from history to nature, myth acts economically: it abolishes the complexity of human acts, it gives them the simplicity of essences, it does away with all dialectics, with any going back beyond what is immediately visible, it organizes a world which is without contradictions because it is without depth, a world wide open and wallowing in the evident, it establishes a blissful clarity: things appear to mean something by themselves. (Barthes, 1972/1991: 142–3)

Myth transforms a socio-economic model into an essence and imposes it as the foundation of human nature. As Barthes phrases it, myth suppresses dialectics of any type, as well as any hindsight beyond what is immediately visible; it generates and organizes a world devoid of contradictions because it is deprived of depth. Jameson adds that once an economic system has been 'naturalized' in that way, only violence can change such a state of things and dictatorship is necessary to maintain such changes against human nature. In Nea So Copros, as in Aldous Huxley's *Brave New World*, History and the past are forbidden areas (*CA*, 243), pre-consumer religions have been abolished, access to knowledge is restricted to dominators, and, according to the end of Sonmi's tale, even her ascension and deviancy were planned to serve the ruling power's propaganda. However, the novel does not doom humankind to such a dehumanizing totally administered society in which capitalist hyperconsumerism has reified beings and transformed most of the planet into dead land.[17] Rather, the novel adumbrates a rupture, a renewal that will occur through an unavoidable environmental disaster, 'The Fall', which paves the way to the novel's core narrative and maybe also to understanding the essence of humanity.

From a structural point of view, the centrality of Zachry's narrative is important as it is the most futuristic tale; it is also the most embedded, as if it were thus protected, nurtured, at the heart the novel. The story it tells, the only one not to be recorded in any written form, preserved, precariously, by oral transmission alone, signifies that essence is both fundamental, but also fragile and evanescent. Connections between Sonmi's posthuman world and that of Zachry's are pervasive and we will not mention all of them here. Let us just stress the important connection that the Abbess represents (especially as she was one of the genuine rebels Sonmi encountered). She is a pivotal character as she claimed in 'An Orison of Sonmi~451' that 'consumers cannot xist without 3D and AdV, but humans used to and still can' (*CA*, 347). The location, 'Ha Why', obviously recalls Xultation and the last trip Papa Song servers are supposed to take towards Paradise on Papa Song's ark. As we know, this is yet another simulacrum as Papa Song's ark is in fact a slaughterhouse where clones are recycled. Eventually, Meronym is connected with Sonmi through the birthmark (*CA*, 319) but also through the preservation of Sonmi's orison; both are voices stressing the necessity of rebellion.

'Sloosha's Crossin'' is also the tale in which the ontogenic and the philogenic perspectives merge. Here, the importance of the tribe gives renewed value to the sense of community that had completely disappeared in the previous tales. The survival of the tribe is at stake in this post-cataclysmic world, which interestingly enough is also a precivilized one.[18] From a historical perspective, we complete a cycle, or a revolution. We move forward to a time that should in fact be located in the far past, the time when man differentiates himself from the animal through his ability to domesticate animality, both within and without:

> So is it better to be savage'n to be civ'lized? ...
> Savages ain't got no laws, I said, but Civ'lizeds got laws.
> *Deeper'n that it's this. The savage sat'fies his needs now. He's hungry, he'll eat. He's angry, he'll knuckly. He's swellin', he'll shoot up a woman. His master is his own will an' if his will say-soes 'Kill' he'll kill. Like fangy animals ...*
> *Now the Civ'lized got the same needs too, but he sees further. He'll eat half his food now, yay, but plant half so he won't go hungry 'morrow. He's angry, he'll stop'n'think why so he won't get angry next time. He's swelling, well, he's got sisses an' daughters what need respectin' so he'll respect his bros' sisses and daughters. His will is his slave an' if his will say-soes, 'Don't!' he won't, nay.* (CA, 318).

Zachry's tribe is built on primitive beliefs akin to animism, together with initiation rites, fetishism, belief in magic, spirits and dreams. The most futuristic community of the novel is a primitive society based on goat-herding, harvesting and bartering. It is hence positioned as the opposite of the posthuman commodity-fetishism model that, in Sonmi's world, was imposed as an essence or a matrix for men who have been turned into dehumanized hyper-consumers. On the contrary, Zachry's tribe takes us back to the genesis of value in labour time, that is to say, to the importance of a straightforward relation between production and consumption. The cash nexus that reigned supreme in Sonmi's world has launched the end of the world it generated and controlled. The primitive society that has then emerged is based on a return to assets such as use value and concrete labour.

The socio-economic system is not however the only thing to which this central tale boils down. Once again, 'The Fall' does not imply a complete rupture between the diegetic past and the diegetic present. In Zachry's tribe, the posthuman world of Sonmi has become a myth that provides the community with an origin both revered and feared. In that sense Meronym plays a pivotal role, that of deconstructing the mythical aura that surrounds the 'Old'Uns'' and the 'Civ'lize Days', and that of showing the way out of false belief.[19] She paves the way towards knowledge, not knowledge used as an instrument of power and domination but a knowledge that would lead to civilized days respecting both humankind and the natural world. According to the character (who could be seen as a voice of the author) the reconstruction of a community based on the respect of human and natural environments is a necessity without which no survival is possible. Meronym and her tribe possess a special 'smart' that *'move magicky ships of steel'*, yet they refuse to interfere with the natural order: *'We Prescients vow not to interfere in no nat'ral order o' things'* (CA, 279–80).

The distinction between belief and knowledge is at the core of Zachry's narrative and it informs the subtle progress of his relationship with Meronym. Linda Hutcheon shows that the attention paid to knowledge in historiographic metafiction is intrinsically connected with historical contextualization within the diegesis. What Meronym tries to convey about past societies and the means they used to impose their authority through the control of knowledge is thus emblematic of the threat looming over humankind:

> Historiographic metafiction is always careful to 'situate' itself in its discursive context, and then uses that situation to problematize the very notion of knowledge – historical, social, ideological. Its use of history is … a questioning of any such authority as the basis of knowledge – and power. (Hutcheon, 1991: 113)

If we come back to the novel as a whole, in *Cloud Atlas* no time is spent on the 'essence' of the characters; the dimension that seems to prevail is the essence of humanity. What connects the characters is

their aspiration or ability to resist politico-ideological systems trying to impose their 'truth' as an immutable model. Human essence
seems to be located beyond temporal and spatial frontiers, in the atlas of clouds or in Frobisher's sextet, in signs or sounds that do not
immediately signify but point to a signified that transcends the here
and now to reach a more universal level. The recurring emphasis on
fiction and fictionalization shows both the aporia of the attempt at
representing reality but also the importance of language and tales as
connectors. Orito Aibagawa, another prisoner of belief from Mitchell's latest novel, voices a similar statement in *The Thousand Autumns
of Jacob de Zoet*:

> It is stories, she believes, that make life in the House of Sisters toler-
> able, stories in all their forms: the Gift's letters, tittle-tattle, recollec-
> tions and tall tales like Hatsune's singing skull. She thinks of myths
> of gods, of Izanami and Izanagi, of Buddha and Jesus; and perhaps
> the Goddess of Mount Shiranui, and wonders whether the same prin-
> ciple is not at work. Orito pictures the human mind as a loom that
> weaves disparate threads of belief, memory and narrative into an en-
> tity whose common name is Self, and which sometimes calls itself
> Perception. (*TA*, 238).

As far as the process of telling is concerned, *Cloud Atlas* gradually
evolves from the written word to the visual and then towards aurality,
especially with the last two tales. Indeed, Sonmi's narrative is a recording of her interview while Sloosha's is fraught with markers of an
audience and presents the narrator as a teller of yarns. We could also
note that along with aurality, the fictive dimension gradually invades
the novel as we begin with the autobiographical mode of a journal and
move towards a narrative the fictitious status of which is recurrently
alluded to: 'Of all my yarnin's, the only'uns I reck'n are truesome mine
an' not'uns I scavved off other Storymen, they're my yarnin's 'bout
her, 'bout Meronym' (*CA*, 260).[20] This movement towards aurality is
in keeping with the postmodernist features Docherty points to:

> postmodernism prioritizes the aural; it is an art which works against
> the specular, and even against theory of speculation in order to re-

install the lost sense of hearing; it shapes itself around the model of the labyrinthine ear. (Docherty, 1993: 15–16)

The sense of hearing is certainly another vector of connectedness in a novel whose title also refers to a piece of music. The novel could then be described as a labyrinth in which readers orientate themselves and build coherence through echoes and recurring notes.

Even though the dangers of a totally virtual-oriented society are clearly stated in Sonmi's tale, Mitchell does not oppose one mode of perception to another but envisages them as complementary. Thus, instead of problematizing visuality and aurality as two opposed dynamics, that is associating modern societies with a move towards the visual while primitive societies would be associated with the aural, Mitchell links them at the end of Zachry's tale: the reader is literally invited to join the tribe, look at Sonmi's orison and listen to the words of a tongue nobody understands anymore but which is akin to soothing music:

Sit down a beat or two.

*

Hold out your hands

*

Look. (*CA*, 325)

The centrality of Zachry's narrative could nevertheless lead us to wonder if the essence of humanity is to be sought for in a precivilized state, a primary stage of development of human tribes in which original mythology is replayed. One could in fact wonder about the use of the term 'the Fall' to refer to the cataclysm that erased posthuman society from the face of the earth. 'The Fall' clearly points to the biblical myth of Adam and Eve's transgression synonymous with access to knowledge. Do we therefore have a re-enactment of that myth at the heart of *Cloud Atlas*? The answer is no. Even if we certainly find in *Cloud Atlas* an emphasis on the fundamental role language has to play in crystallizing community, nevertheless 'Sloosha's Crossin'' should not be considered as advocating the necessity of myth as a purveyor of archetypes that would determine the evolution of a community. On the contrary, the mythical aura of Sonmi is deconstructed in Zachry's narrative, thus presenting narrativity as giving access to knowledge instead of belief; contrary to visuality, which led towards simulacrum, artefacts and the virtual. Thus, the expression 'the Fall' should not be considered as pointing to a recycling of Christian mythology but rather as an ontological experience, a coming to the world that is equated with a coming to language.

Access to language is indeed omnipresent in Sonmi and Zachry's narratives. We have mentioned the fact that rebellion seems to be a red thread running through the novel. Acts of rebellion pave the way to emancipation and the latter is associated with getting access to language. For instance, Sonmi's or any other clones's 'ascension' is synonymous with that access to language: 'The first outward sign of Yoona's ascension was her speech' (*CA*, 191). When Sonmi's ascension occurs she details the successive steps of the process:

> my own ascension had begun. I recognized it from Yoona~939's symptoms ... First, a voice began speaking inside my head ... the voice of sentience ... Second, my language evolved ... I learnt to edit and modify every single word I used. Third, my own curiosity about Outside increased. Fourth, I suffered alienation ... (*CA*, 205–6)

Even though Sonmi's rebellion may have been orchestrated from the beginning, at the end of her narrative she claims that 'the Ascended Cathechisms of *Declarations*, their logic and ethics, denounced at my trial as "the foulest wickedness in the history of social deviancy," were the fruits of *my* mind' (*CA*, 363). She shows that in spite of the manipulation to which she was submitted, access to language leads to conscience and the potential emergence of an independent mind. Seeing language as a primary requisite to thought points to an influence of the modern philosophy of language which, from Saussure's publication of *Course in General Linguistics* (1915) and Walter Benjamin's 'On Language as Such and on the Language of Man' (1916) to Heidegger's *Being and Time* dating back to 1927, claims that precedence. According to the latter, coming to the world equals coming to language (Michaud, 2002) and, in a way, this is what Sonmi's 'ascension' actually means. The linguistic expression of her conscience is then what matters most and this is the reason why her 'Ascended Cathechisms of *Declarations*' had to reach as many human beings as possible whatever the consequences for her own self. Sonmi accepts manipulation and death because her own disappearance is not what is at stake. The evanescence of an individual being is counterbalanced by the continuous flux of beings striving towards a preservation of the essence of humanity:

> **But if you knew about ... conspiracy, why did you cooperate with it?**
>
> Why does any martyr cooperate with his judases? He sees a further endgame.
>
> **What is yours?**
>
> The *Declarations*. Media have flooded Nea So Copros with my Cathechisms. Every schoolchild in Nea So Copros knows my twelve 'blasphemies'. My guards tell me there is even talk of a State-wide 'Vigilance Day' against fabricants who show signs of the *Declarations*. My ideas have been reproduced billionfold.
>
> **But to what end? Some ... future revolution?**
>
> To Corpocracy, to Unanimity, to the Ministry of Testaments, to the Juche and to the Chairman, I quote Seneca's warning to Nero: No matter how many of us you kill, you will never kill your successor. (CA, 364–5)

At the end of his narrative, Zachry ponders the clouds he sees in the sky and compares them to souls:

> I watched clouds awobbly from the floor o'that kayak. Souls cross ages like clouds cross skies, an' tho' a cloud's shape nor hue nor size don't stray the same it's still a cloud an' so is a soul. Who can say where the cloud's blowed from or who the soul'll be 'morrow? Only Sonmi the east an' the west an' the compass an' the atlas, yay, only the atlas o' clouds. (CA, 324)

In this passage, each cloud is seen as evanescent and ephemeral. However, it also connects to the ever-changing atlas of the sky. Contrary to the rational, empirical and determined nature of the map-making process on land (which in passing is a good instance of the double-bind of the quest for knowledge as it both led to the mapping of the world and to colonization), the atlas of clouds defines human beings and humanity as ever-changing and always liable to effacement. In *Cloud Atlas*, Mitchell exposes the frailty of the essence of humanity. From this perspective, the passage from written tales to oral ones is also a means of emphasizing the evanescence of the human. Human essence as seen in Mitchell's text is to be found in what Jean-Luc Nancy sees as characteristic of the human, that is to say its imminent 'effacement':

> The ends of man can be written because in the multiple play of their plural writing man effaces himself, and because it is for him imperative that he should efface himself. And this imperative, this effacement are constitutive of his proper way of being, of that way of being which is not properly a being-which-is, but an *uncanny ethos*. (Crowley, 2005: 27)

From Autua and Adam to Zachry, many characters in *Cloud Atlas* find themselves in danger of being submitted or enslaved, and not only do they have resistance in common but they are also connected through their perception of the human. Effacement is the lot of each human being but through this shared evanescence, they can transcend time and space and reach permanence:

> Working nights on *Cloud Atlas Sextet* … My head is a Roman Candle of invention. Lifetime's music, arriving all at once. Boundaries between noise and sound are conventions, I see now. All boundaries are conventions, national ones too. One may transcend any convention, if only one can conceive of doing so. (*CA*, 479)

Each man is doomed to disappear and, as in Frobisher's case, can be willing to; Frobisher is also profoundly convinced that this effacement is only a temporary one and that 'We do not stay dead long' (*CA*, 490). Whether they mark separations in time, space, countries or beings, boundaries exist only to be crossed over and over again and all the characters that form the novel's atlas of clouds participate in that common aspiration towards a self-effacement which allows for wholeness and completion. It is not surprising that both Zachry, at the very core of the novel, and Adam, whose narrative voice opens and ends it, should strike a common note by using similar metaphors to conclude their narratives. As the first and last narrator puts it at the end of the novel:

> If we *believe* that humanity may transcend tooth & claw, if we *believe* divers races & creeds can share this world as peaceably as the orphans share their candlenut tree, if we *believe* leaders must be just, violence muzzled, power accountable & the riches of the Earth & its Oceans shared equitably, such a world will come to pass. I am not deceived
> ...
> I hear my father-in-law's response ... 'Naïve, dreaming Adam. He who would do battle with the many-headed hydra of human nature must pay a world of pain & his family must pay it along with him! & only as you gasp your dying breath shall you understand, your life amounted to no more than one drop in a limitless ocean!'
> Yet what is any ocean but a multitude of drops? (*CA*, 528–9)

Notes

1 One could more specifically evoke Evelyn Waugh's *Brideshead Revisited* (1945), in which, in a 2010 interview with Harriett Gilbert, Mitchell said he went 'shoplifting' for language and descriptions that were not part of his existing vocabulary.

2 We also encounter a proleptic hint at Sonmi's narrative in 'The Ghastly Ordeal of Timothy Cavendish' when the latter arrives at Aurora House and is threatened to be punished as follows: 'Because you are new I will not have you eat soap powder. This time. Be warned' (*CA*, 175).

3 All the main characters are narrators except for Luisa Rey who is none-theless a focalizer.

4 The image of the kaleidoscope is used by Fredric Jameson about Philip K. Dick's novels, more specifically his eschatological novels: 'In these two works [*Dr Bloodmoney* and *The Simulacra,*], for the first time, there emerges that bewildering and kaleidoscopic plot structure ... both of these works dramatize the utopian purgation of a fallen and historically

corrupted world by some climactic overloading, some ultimate explosion beyond which the outlines of a new and simpler social order emerge' (Jameson, 2005: 349).

5 For further analysis of this trait in *Ghostwritten*, *number9dream*, *Cloud Atlas* and *Black Swan Green*, see Claire Larsonneur (2009) 'Location, location, location' and her discussion of the relation between identity, relation, history, globalia and localia.

6 For an extended discussion of the similar functioning of the stories in *Ghostwritten* in relation to the novelistic whole see Sarah Dillon's (2011) 'Chaotic Narrative', in particular her discussion of autopoeisis.

7 See the way the press reports on the news that the former Energy Secretary Lloyd Hooks becomes head of Seabord Power Inc. (*CA*, 431) and then the way President Ford distances himself from 'his former advisor' (*CA*, 452).

8 'Lyotard has argued that it is becoming increasingly difficult to subscribe to the great – and therapeutically optimistic – metanarratives which once organized our lives. What he has in his sight are totalising metanarratives, great codes which in their abstraction necessarily deny the specificity of the local and traduce it in the interests of a global homogeneity, a universal history' (Docherty, 1993: 11).

9 We learn about these birthmarks very progressively and we begin to identify them as a factor of connectivity even more progressively. In the first half of 'Half Lives', Luisa Rey mentions Robert Frobisher's evocation of his birthmark without relating it to hers (*CA*, 122). Then, Sonmi mentions hers to the archivist (*CA*, 204) presenting it as an anomaly. Next, Zachry notices Meronym's and we are thus given the first description of it: 'a head o' six streaks strandin' off' (*CA*, 319). In the second part of 'The Ghastly Ordeal', Cavendish makes an ironic reference to the birthmark and we incidentally learn he has one as well: 'One or two things will have to go: the insinuation that Luisa Rey is this Frobisher chap reincarnated, for example. Far too hippie-druggy-new age. (I, too, have a birthmark, below my left armpit, but no lover ever compared it to a comet. Georgette nicknamed it Timbo's Turd.)' (*CA*, 373).

10 'A new field of research is opened with that concept: not the history of security techniques anymore, the latter becomes provisionally secondary, but the genealogy of modern state … The aim consists in using the same "point of view" with the state as that which had been adopted, in previous years, in the study of disciplines, when revealing the relations of power

inherent to any institutional or functionalist approach' (Senellart, 2004: 397, my translation).

11 My translation. The page reference is to the French original.

12 'In *Folie et Déraison* Foucault points out that the production of reason is itself dependent upon a primary act of exclusion and incarceration: what reason identifies as its Other – madness – has to be identified and imprisoned in order to enable reason to legitimise itself. Enlightenment reason is in fact a potent weapon in the production of social normativity, driving people towards a conformity with a dominant and centered "norm" of behaviour. Reason, in short, has to produce the "scandal" of its other to keep itself going.' (Docherty, 1993: 14)

13 See Foucault, *La Volonté de savoir* (1976) especially p. 183.

14 We could also mention the example of Wing~027 who is a disasterman: 'We operate in deadlands so infected or radioactive that purebloods perish there like bacteria in bleach' (*CA*, 215).

15 Several aspects point to possible parallelisms between the novels. To read a more thorough analysis of how the two texts can be bridged, see Hélène Machinal (2009) 'From behind the looking-glass' and Hélène Machinal (2010) 'Résistance de l'humain'.

16 The denial of History paving the way to a denial of politics is also exactly what Docherty (1991) describes in 'Postmodern Characterization'.

17 According to Sonmi's orison: 'Nea So Copros is poisoning itself to death. Its soil is polluted, its rivers lifeless, its air toxloaded, its food supplies riddled with rogue genes. The downstrata can't buy the drugs necessary to counter these privations. Melanoma and malaria belts advance northwards at forty kilometers per year. Those Production Zones of Africa and Indonesia that supply Consumer Zones' demands are sixty percent uninhabitable. Plutocracy's legitimacy, its wealth, is drying up; the Juche's Enrichment Laws are mere sticking plasters on haemorrhages and amputations. Its only response is that strategy beloved of all bankrupt ideologues: denial' (*CA*, 341).

18 This is not an uncommon move in post-apocalyptic fiction: one could evoke Hoban's (1980) *Riddley Walker* to which this section is largely indebted as well as Will Self's (2006) *The Book of Dave*, which provides another point of comparison.

19 This deconstruction of myth connects with what I have shown regarding the denial of History leading to a denial of politics paving the way

to the established state of eternal and essential nature, which guarantees stability to the ruling forces in Sonmi's world. It also applies to Ishiguro's (2000) *When We Were Orphans* though the myth deconstructed in that novel is a literary one. See Hélène Machinal (2004) 'The Strange Case of Christopher Banks in Kazuo Ishiguro's *When We Were Orphans*'.

20 We find a direct echo to that quotation in the after-note left by Zachry's son to his narrative: 'Do I b'lief his yarn 'bout the Kona an' his fleein' from Big I? Most yarnin's got a bit o' true, some yarnin's got some true, an' a few yarnin's got a lot o' true. The stuff 'bout Meronym the Prescient was mostly true, I reck'n' (*CA*, 324).

Works Cited

Barthes, Roland (1972/1991) *Mythologies*, trans. Annette Lavers. New York: The Noonday Press.

Baudrillard, Jean (1991) 'Simulacra and Science Fiction', *Science-Fiction Studies* 18(3): 309–13.

Baudrillard, Jean (1994) *Simulacra and Simulation*. Ann Arbor: The University of Michigan Press.

Clute, John and Nicholls, Peter (eds) (1999) *The Encyclopedia of Science Fiction*, 2nd edn. London: Orbit.

Crowley, Martin (2005) 'The Human Without', *The Oxford Literary Review* 27: 67–81.

Deleuze, Gilles (1990) *The Logic of Sense*. New York: Columbia University Press.

Dillon, Sarah (2011) 'Chaotic Narrative: Complexity, Causality, Time and Autopoiesis in David Mitchell's *Ghostwritten*', *Critique: Studies in Contemporary Fiction* 52(2): 1–28.

Docherty, Thomas (1990) *Beyond Theory*. London: Routledge.

Docherty, Thomas (1991) 'Postmodern Characterization: The Ethics of Alterity', in Edmund Smyth (ed.) *Postmodernism and Contemporary Fiction*, pp. 169-88. London: Batsford.

Docherty, Thomas (1993) *Postmodernism, A Reader*. London: Harvester Wheatsheaf.

Foucault, Michel (1976) *La Volonté de savoir*. Paris: Gallimard.

Foucault, Michel (2004) *Sécurité, territoire, population, Cours au Collège de France. 1977–1978*. Paris: Gallimard, Seuil.

Gilbert, Harriett (2010) 'David Mitchell', BBC World Bookclub, 4 June, URL (consulted August 2010): http://www.bbc.co.uk/worldservice/arts/2010/06/100604_wbc_david_mitchell.shtml

Gros, François (1990) *L'Ingénierie du vivant*. Paris: O. Jacob.

Hutcheon, Linda (1988) *A Poetics of Postmodernism*. New York and London: Routledge.

Hutcheon, Linda (1991) 'Discourse, Power, Ideology: Humanism and Postmodernism', in Edmund J. Smyth (ed.) *Postmodernism and Contemporary Fiction*, pp. 105–22. London: Batsford.

Jameson, Fredric (1990) *Signatures of the Visible*. New York: Routledge.

Jameson, Fredric (2004) 'The Politics of Utopia', *New Left Review* 25: 33–54.

Jameson, Fredric (2005) *Archaeologies of the Future: The Desire Called Utopia and Other Science Fictions*. London: Verso.

Larsonneur, Claire (2009) 'Location, location, location', *Etudes Britanniques Contemporaines* 37: 141–9.

Lecourt, Dominique (2003) *Humain, Posthumain*. Paris: Presses Universitaires de France.

McHale, Brian (1987) *Postmodernist Fiction*. New York and London: Routledge.

Machinal, Hélène (2004) 'The Strange Case of Christopher Banks in Kazuo Ishiguro's *When We Were Orphans*', *Etudes Britanniques Contemporaines* 27: 55–66.

Machinal, Hélène (2009) 'From Behind the Looking-Glass: Kazuo Ishiguro's *Never Let Me Go* and Beyond', *Etudes Britanniques Contemporaines* 37: 115–28.

Machinal, Hélène (2010) 'Résistance de l'humain dans *Cloud Atlas* de David Mitchell et *Never Let Me Go* de Kazuo Ishiguro', *L'atelier*, URL (consulted August 2010): http://latelier.u-paris10.fr/index.php/latelier

Michaud, Yves (2002) *Humain, inhumain, trop humain, réflexions philosophiques sur les biotechnologies, la vie et la conservation de soi à partir de l'oeuvre de Peter Sloterdijk*. Paris: Climat.

Mousoutzanis, Aris (2009) 'Apocalyptic sf', in Mark Bould, Andrew M. Butler, Adam Roberts and Sherryl Vint (eds) *The Routledge Companion to Science Fiction*, pp. 458–62. London and New York: Routledge.

Ousby, Ian (1988) *The Cambridge Guide to Literature in English*. Cambridge: Cambridge University Press.

Senellart, Michel (2004) 'Situation des cours', in Michel Foucault, *Sécurité, territoire, population, cours au Collège de France. 1977–1978*, pp. 380–411. Paris: Gallimard, Seuil.

Stevenson, Randall (1991) 'Postmodernism and Contemporary Fiction in Britain', in Edmund J. Smyth (ed.) *Postmodernism and Contemporary Fiction*, pp. 19–35. London: Batsford.
Stockwell, Peter (2000) *The Poetics of Science Fiction*. Harlow: Longman.

7

CLOUD ATLAS AND IF ON A WINTER'S NIGHT A TRAVELLER
Fragmentation and Integrity in the Postmodern Novel

Will McMorran

Introduction

As someone who has worked rather more on the early modern than the postmodern, it may seem that this contributor is rather far from home – perhaps doubly so given that the eighteenth century and its supposed grand narrative of Enlightenment are often represented as all that the postmodern and its fiction are writing against. The truth is that there are clear affinities between the often highly playful experiments conducted in European early modern fiction – before the novel really solidified as the genre it would become in the nineteenth century – and the equally ludic approach to fiction undertaken by postmodern novelists in response to what had since become the settled conventions of the genre. This is not to diminish the achievements of the postmodern as simple or unoriginal repetitions of a remote antecedent: to describe the novels of either Calvino or Mitchell as old-fashioned would be as misguided as the branding of Sterne's *Tristram Shandy* (1759–67) as 'the most modern of eighteenth-century novels' (Anderson, 1980: vii). Such pronouncements offer a misleading shorthand for the more complex truth that if a novel like *Tristram Shandy* seems modern – or even postmodern – it is only because modern and postmodern novelists, for culturally specific reasons of their own, have on occasion engaged in the same kind of

games that writers of the early modern comic tradition had also previously enjoyed for equally specific reasons of *their* own. The affinity
between these fictional experimenters of different periods is striking,
however, and it should therefore come as no surprise that a novelist
like Milan Kundera (1988: 15) should name Sterne's *Tristram Shandy*
and Diderot's *Jacques the Fatalist* (1796) – novels he describes as being 'conceived as grand games' – as his two favourite works of fiction.[1]
Calvino was similarly a great admirer of eighteenth-century fiction,
while Mitchell's *Cloud Atlas* (2004) offers us a globetrotting novel of
ideas that recalls some of the great philosophical fictions of the Enlightenment, such as Voltaire's *Candide* (1759), with its exploration
of optimism, or Diderot's *Jacques the Fatalist*, with its self-conscious
and self-interrupting debate of free will versus determinism. Indeed,
Cloud Atlas opens with a nod to Defoe's *Robinson Crusoe* (1719), as
Ewing discovers 'a trail of recent footprints' (*CA*, 3) on the beach –
left, it transpires, not by a Man Friday but a Dr Goose.

   Both Calvino and Mitchell allude specifically to the earlier tradition of self-conscious fiction inaugurated by Cervantes's *Don Quixote*
(1605–15) within their works. Calvino's Ermes Marana, that most
unreliable of translators, offers a postmodern counterpart to Cervantes's Cid Hamet, while in Mitchell's Luisa Rey segment, a scientist
named Isaac Sachs working at the Seaboard plant confesses he 'once
dated a girl who called her car Rocinante' (*CA*, 134).[2] More significantly, the manner in which Calvino and Mitchell abruptly interrupt
their respective narratives in *If on a winter's night a traveller* (1979)
and *Cloud Atlas*, and the search that ensues within each text for lost
or hidden continuations, strongly recalls Cervantes's novel, which
interrupts the story of Don Quixote at a climactic point when one
manuscript runs out, and continues only when an unreliable translation of an unreliable Arabic version of the story is discovered by
chance. Cervantes's self-conscious problematizing of the art of sus-
taining narrative here is particularly striking in the context of what
he had originally intended as a short story, or *cuento*, that became a
novel by the accumulation of diverse episodes and stories which leave
the ostensible protagonist sidelined or marginalized for considerable
stretches of the novel. Like those early modern comic novels that

found inspiration in Cervantes for their own intercalatory and digressive approaches to the form, *Don Quixote* too could be described as a composite novel in its own right. For reasons beyond the scope of this essay, one senses in many early modern fictions an authorial struggle with, or rejection of, the kind of sustained and unified linear narrative that would rise to prominence in the realist fiction of the nineteenth century – a struggle, or rejection, that would ultimately resurface in postmodern fiction. As the narrator of *If on a winter's night a traveller* observes:

> Long novels written today are perhaps a contradiction: the dimension of time has been shattered, we cannot love or think except in fragments of time each of which goes off along its own trajectory and immediately disappears. We can rediscover the continuity of time only in the novels of that period when time no longer seemed stopped and did not yet seem to have exploded, a period that lasted no more than a hundred years. (Calvino, 1979/1998: 8)

The focus of this essay, however, is neither the influence of early modern fiction on the postmodern novel nor even the influence of the early postmodern (Calvino) on the later postmodern (Mitchell). There is little need to labour the point that Calvino's novel was a formative influence on *Cloud Atlas* – particularly as Mitchell himself has been disarmingly clear about this in various articles and interviews.[3] His openness about this is revealing both of his own self-assurance as an author and of the way postmodern writers of fiction view their relationship to their antecedents. It suggests an attitude towards influence characterized by confidence rather than anxiety – a more positive attitude than has notably always been the case among literary critics.[4] Mary Orr (2003: 83), in her recent work on the history of intertextuality, observes that the error of the New Critics in this regard was to see influence as a repressive hierarchical relationship featuring a recipient '"under the influence of" the forebear or canonical heritage'. She argues persuasively that 'this is only one side of the story. The other, and positive, "influence for" reverses hierarchies or understands influence as complex and plural' (Orr, 2003: 83). Influence, in these terms, may therefore be used to widen the 'cultural frame of reception' (Orr, 2003: 85) of a given text, revealing 'the multiple and often "foreign" differences that make up what appears a single channel of expression' (Orr, 2003: 91).

Mitchell's confidence in talking about his influences in interviews is reflected within *Cloud Atlas*, a novel that continually invites the reader to make intertextual connections with other works of fiction (including Mitchell's own). *Cloud Atlas* celebrates and multiplies these connections, revealing itself to be part of a larger cultural whole that includes an extraordinary range of high cultural and popular cultural sources and resources, from Melville, Conrad, Nietzsche, Huxley, Wilder and Hoban, to airport thrillers, and science fiction films like *Soylent Green* (1973) and *Blade Runner* (1982) to name just a very few of these.[6] Rather than explore *If on a winter's night a traveller* as an intertext or influence for *Cloud Atlas*, therefore, this essay aims to explore what these two novels have to tell us about the place of narrative, and metanarrative, in postmodern fiction.

There is little point in engaging in another debate about the definition of postmodernism. For the purposes of this essay, it is enough to observe that both Calvino and Mitchell are popularly as well as critically identified with the postmodern or postmodernist label. In his seminal essay, 'The Literature of Replenishment', John Barth (1984: 204) famously hailed Calvino as an exemplary postmodernist author while Douwe Fokkema (1984: 37) places Calvino at the 'hard core of Postmodernism'; and, André Brink (1998: 310) is one of many to see *If on a winter's night a traveller* as an 'eminently Postmodernist novel'. Whatever postmodernism is, Calvino apparently has it – and the same may be said of Mitchell. The primary reason for the postmodern epithet in the case of both novels is the formal and structural approach that each novel takes to its storytelling and, in particular, the manner in which each work incorporates multiple narratives within a novelistic frame.

If on a winter's night a traveller

Calvino's *If on a winter's night a traveller* was published in 1979, after six years of an apparently crippling case of writer's block that had afflicted the author since the publication of *The Castle of Crossed Destinies* (1973). All he had published in the meantime was a short essay tellingly entitled 'La Poubelle agréé' or 'The Approved Dustbin' – which itself took two years to write (McLaughlin, 1998: 116). Calvino's way out of this impasse was a novel of beginnings that did not require endings. His novel is often described in slightly misleading terms, however. It is not simply a series of ten novelistic beginnings, or incipits, contained within a storytelling frame. Upon its first publication in English, Calvino stated in an interview that he wanted to write 'a book in which the reader would not be reading the text of a novel but a description of the act of reading *per se*' (du Plessix Grey, 1981: 22). He was referring to his novel as a whole, but this is equally true of the way in which the individual narratives within it are integrated. Calvino does not simply intercalate novelistic samples of various genres, but enacted readings – and writings – of novelistic samples of various genres, as the dazzling opening line of the first of these incipits, itself entitled 'If on a winter's night a traveller', illustrates: 'The novel begins in a railway station, a locomotive huffs, steam from a piston covers the opening of the chapter, a cloud of smoke hides part of the first paragraph' (Calvino, 1979/1998: 10). The scenario that ensues is that of a spy novel, but this is emphatically not a spy novel – just as, in a different way, the Luisa Rey 'Mystery' of *Cloud Atlas* is not quite the corporate espionage thriller it pretends to be. Rather than a spy novel, Calvino narrates an account of a spy novel being read. The narrative that we would like to think of as a framing narrative, of a reader hunting for the continuations of the interrupted novels he begins, does not simply give way to embedded narratives – as is the case in the rich tradition of storytelling collections like *The Canterbury Tales* or *The Decameron*. Instead, this reader, called 'You' (who is emphatically not us, but a third person masquerading as a second person) enters the incipit as his responses to the novel he has picked up in the bookshop are recorded. Thus, the story continues, 'The lights of the station and the sentences you are reading seem to have the job of dissolving more than of indicating the things that surface from a veil of darkness and fog' (Calvino, 1979/1998: 11).

159

If on a winter's night a traveller therefore offers a narrative in which
'The Reader', addressed as 'You', observes a character in a spy thriller
called 'I', where 'I am the man who comes and goes between the bar
and the telephone booth', a character whose autonomy, and that of his
narrative, is immediately undermined: 'Or rather: that man is called
"I" and you know nothing else about him, just as this station is called
only "station" and beyond it there exists nothing except the unan-
swered signal of a telephone ringing in a dark room of a distant city'
(Calvino, 1979/1998: 11). The character named 'I', stuck in a railway
station and unable to leave, offers a double for 'You', lost in a novel
that does not allow him to progress in his reading:

> What you would like is the opening of an abstract and absolute space
> and time in which you could move, following an exact, taut trajectory;
> but when you seem to be succeeding, you realize you are motionless,
> blocked, forced to repeat everything from the beginning. (Calvino,
> 1979/1998: 27)

It is no coincidence that the password the unfortunate spy invokes is
'Zeno of Elea', an allusion to the paradox that asserts the impossibility
of all motion.

The early incipits in the novel, with their continual reference to
their own reception, employ narrators who are both intradiegetic and
extradiegetic, simultaneously and metaleptically inhabiting both the
world of the text and the words of the text. The second incipit, 'Outside the Town of Malbork', begins rather like the first: 'An odor of
frying wafts at the opening of the page, of onion in fact, onion being
fried ... Rape oil, the text specifies' (Calvino, 1979/1998: 34). Other
incipits are less prone to such self-referential interference, and the reader no longer feels his or her reading is so heavily mediated. The third
incipit, 'Leaning from the steep slope,' for example, is told by a first-
person character-narrator who is firmly within his fiction rather than
commentating upon it from a metafictional position; the reader is cor-
respondingly allowed to engage more fully with the story rather than
the storytelling, to feel that he or she is reading these stories at first
hand rather than reading the second-hand account of someone else's
reading of them. Even here our access to the text is problematized:

what the reader of the novel and The Reader *in* the novel encounter are not the same thing. The latter hears, rather than reads the text, as it is translated aloud impromptu from the original Cimmerian by the delightfully named Professor Uzzi-Tuzii, who continually refines his translation, 'going back over every sentence to iron out the syntactical creases, manipulating the phrases until they were not completely rumpled, smoothing them, clipping them' (Calvino, 1979/1998: 68). Once again there is a middleman. In contrast to the previous incipits, The Reader's reception of 'Leaning from the steep slope' is not integrated with the text but deferred until the following chapter, where we discover that our own immersion in this haunting narrative parallels his own: 'Now, around you, there is no longer the room of the department, the shelves, the professor: you have entered the novel, you see that Nordic beach, you follow the footsteps of the delicate gentleman' (Calvino, 1979/1998: 69). As the novel progresses, the incipits increasingly refer self-consciously to their own composition rather than their own reception. 'In a network of lines that intersect' refers to its own 'plot' as if the narrator were no longer the protagonist but the author: 'I must not neglect to insert every so often, at the point at which the plot becomes thickest, some quotations from an ancient text' (Calvino, 1979/1998: 165).

Calvino's novel insists throughout on the fictional status of its various narratives – he does not just tell stories, but tells us he is telling stories in little phrases such as 'The novel begins' (Calvino, 1979/1998: 10), 'the text specifies' (Calvino, 1979/1998: 34), and repeated references to whatever 'the story' is doing at any particular moment. It is the postmodern counterpart to the games that Cervantes also plays with his readers in *Don Quixote* when he includes throughout references to what 'Cid Hamet relates' just to remind the reader that the story is always being mediated. The effect of this can be interpreted in different, even contradictory, ways. At times it seems that Calvino's novel is a narrative that exists on a single plane, in which all that happens, happens to the character called 'You' – his unfolding love story, and the interrupted novels he encounters on the way, all forming part of the same overarching plot. The boundary that would separate the internal stories from the frame narrative is porous and prone to meta-

lepses that undermine the solidity of the different levels we would like
to map onto the text. At other times, it seems that *If on a winter's night
a traveller* is composed neither of one level, nor of two, but of three,
four or even more: the level of You's love story with Ludmilla; the
level of the events related in the incipits; and, the additional levels
such as the level on which the incipits refer to themselves as texts – an
intermediary level somewhere between the framing narrative and its
embedded stories.

Calvino's novel reminds us that the narratological mapping of narrative – according to spatial models of levels, frames, borders and
thresholds – is not quite the objective scientific process that narratologists would like it to be. Metalepsis and *mise en abyme* abound
and destabilize the narrative models of framing and containment that
we are used to in storytelling collections. The eighth chapter, which
comprises the diary of Silas Flannery, offers a series of moments in
which we are both inside and outside the fiction simultaneously – or
rather, in which the inside and the outside of the fiction are reduced
to the same single level. Flannery writes:

> I have had the idea of writing a novel composed only of beginnings
> of novels. The protagonist could be a Reader who is continually inter-
> rupted. The Reader buys the new novel A by the author Z. But it is a
> defective copy, he can't go beyond the beginning .... He returns to the
> bookshop to have the volume exchanged ....
> I could write it all in the second person ... (Calvino, 1979/1998:
> 197–8)

It is striking that when Calvino comes to the *Arabian Nights* (in the
essay 'Levels of Reality in Literature', which he first published while
he was writing *If on a winter's night a traveller*) he notes the ways in
which the same text can be one in which the 'stories are like boxes
within boxes' (Calvino, 1989: 116) and then writes 'but to my reading, at least in the only way we can read them, these tales all appear to
be on the same plane' (Calvino, 1989: 117).

Cloud Atlas

Despite the obvious structural differences from Calvino's novel (and the absence of a frame narrative in particular), Mitchell's *Cloud Atlas* is similarly resistant to the spatial mapping of its various narratives in relation to each other. A number of critics and reviewers have alluded to the matryoshka doll structure of the novel – an image or model that the novel repeatedly invokes. Isaac Sachs, for example, writes the following in a notebook shortly before his death:

- *Q: Is there a meaningful distinction between one simulacrum of smoke, mirrors + shadows – the actual past – from another such simulacrum – the actual future?*

- *One model of time: an infinite matrioshka doll of painted moments, each 'shell' (the present) encased inside a nest of 'shells' (previous presents) I call the actual past but which we perceive as the virtual past. The doll of 'now' likewise encases a nest of presents yet to be, which I call the actual future but which we perceive as the virtual future.*

- *Proposition: I have fallen in love with Luisa Rey. (CA, 409)*

This may work as a temporal model, according to which the past encases the present, and the present encases the future – although it is a bleakly deterministic model. It works less well as a narrative model for the novel, since it implies a process of framing, or mothering, in which each successive segment is contained within the previous segments, so that Adam Ewing's story is the mother of Frobisher's, which in turn is the mother of Luisa Rey's and so on. If this were translated into a Genettian narratological model, it would produce a model according to which each narrative were extradiegetic to the one that followed it, when this is precisely the opposite of what actually happens. Each segment enjoys an extradiegetic relationship to the *preceding* one, commenting upon it, questioning it, and so seeming to master and contain it. Each narrative seems more like the child of the one that follows it, rather than the mother – making the outermost shell, or ultimate mother, of the novel 'Sloosha's Crossin'' not Ewing's journal. There is indeed a moment in the second part of 'An Orison of Sonmi~451' when Sonmi observes a sign for a troubling freakshow that reads, 'Gaze upon Madame Matryoshka and her Pregnant Embryo' (*CA*, 353).[7] The effect here can be read as a simple *mise en abyme* in which the reproduction of the child extends ad infinitum, but it also hints at the possibility of a kind of reverse matryoshka effect in which the embryo is the mother of the baby, and so on ever backwards. The same effect of texts within texts asserting authority over the texts that embed them also strikingly occurs in microcosm within some of the individual narratives of the novel – when, for example, Luisa Rey reads a newspaper report in the *Western Messenger* that refers to her exposé as a 'libellous fantasy culled from a spy novel and wholly unworthy of a serious response' (*CA*, 452). Such comments, like the excerpts from Silas Flannery's diary in Calvino's *If on a winter's night a traveller*, are simultaneously both within and without the text, a fiction within the fiction in formal terms, and a metafiction in affective terms in their dialogic relationship to the reader.

Perhaps the attempt to 'structuralize' the novel as a narrative of mothering, or embedding, is misleading – might the novel be better described as a linear narrative that goes forwards then backwards while remaining throughout on the same level or plane (as Calvino's novel can also be read)? The problem here is the manner in which the Luisa Rey narrative is integrated with the rest of the novel. While Adam Ewing's journal and Frobisher's letters are ostensibly, within the terms of the novel, historical documents (although Frobisher does playfully question the status of the Ewing text), the Luisa Rey narrative is explicitly fictional: 'The First Luisa Rey Mystery' – the first of what one imagines will be a series of thrillers featuring the intrepid reporter. Cavendish's narrative also confirms its status as a fiction, it is by an author named 'Hilary Hush'. In making Luisa Rey a fiction within the Cavendish section, a baby of the mothering narrative that follows it, Mitchell turns those previously 'real' sections that preceded it, the Ewing and Frobisher narratives, into fictions within the fiction of the Luisa Rey story. The Luisa Rey mystery thus retrospectively frames as fictional the earlier narratives within it – the matryoshka effect in reverse once again – not to mention what it does to Mitchell's first novel, *Ghostwritten*, in which Luisa Rey first appears. The explicitly fictional status of Luisa Rey within the context of the novel works like a virus or a parasite – not unlike the other, equally fictional, parasite that afflicts Ewing.

If matryoshka dolls do not offer a satisfactory model for the structuring of *Cloud Atlas*, a peculiarly apt alternative is suggested in the final section of the novel – the second instalment of Adam Ewing's journal. Irritated by the cockroaches in his cabin, Ewing writes:

> I complained to Finbar, who urged me to pay a dollar for a specially-trained 'roach-rat.' Later, doubtless, he will want to sell me a 'rat-cat' to subdue the roach-rat, then I will need a cat-hound & who knows where it will all end? (*CA*, 514)

Or, put in another way, 'There was an old lady who swallowed a fly, I don't know why she swallowed a fly, perhaps she'll die. She swallowed a spider to catch the fly … '.[8] A metaphor of narratological consumption and predacity fits the themes as well as the structure of *Cloud Atlas* well – each tale is consumed by the next to come along, and, depending on one's point of view, Mitchell, or the novel overall, is the old lady.[9]

The spatial terms according to which readers and narratologists seek to map fiction – with its levels and frames and embedded stories – seem ultimately inadequate to a novel like *Cloud Atlas*. Is 'Sloosha's Crossin'' a frame, or is Adam Ewing's journal the frame? While we begin and end with Ewing as readers in terms of the chronology of our reading of the novel (he has both the first word and the last word), the framing situation, the fictional reality that embraces all the previous fictional realities, is Zachry's (and he too, in an important sense, could be said to have the last word). Although even this is an inadequate simplification, as Mitchell's structure allows Ewing's narrative to look back on the future as well as the past: the discussion of 'the rises & falls of civilizations' (*CA*, 527) that concludes the novel offers a commentary of its own on the future through which the reader has travelled. *Cloud Atlas* thus reminds us that the act of framing is a matter of subjective interpretation rather than objective identification – how we map the novel in our minds will ultimately rest upon whether we privilege Ewing's fragile optimism or the bleak post-apocalyptic world of 'Sloosha's Crossin'' as the ultimate message of the novel.

On Narratives and Grand Narratives

Most accounts of postmodern fiction tend to describe a form of storytelling in which the fragmentary, and the local, is privileged, in
marked contrast to the unifying and totalizing narratives of the nineteenth-century realist tradition. While David Lodge (1977: 220–45)
explores the disruptive strategies of postmodernist writing (contradiction, discontinuity, randomness, excess, the short circuit), Mihály
Szegedy-Maszák (1987: 46) argues that the loss of teleology is 'a distinguishing feature of postmodernist fiction'. Steven Connor (2004:
75) identifies the '(non)cohering collection' of fictions as a particularly postmodernist arrangement, because it displays connectedness
without completeness. Arguably the most influential definition of the
postmodern, however, remains that of Lyotard:

> Simplifying to the extreme, I define postmodern as incredulity to-
> ward metanarratives. This incredulity is undoubtedly a product of
> progress in the sciences: but that progress in turn presupposes it. To
> the obsolescence of the metanarrative apparatus of legitimation cor-
> responds, most notably, the crisis of metaphysical philosophy and of
> the university institution which in the past relied on it. The narrative
> function is losing its functors, its great hero, its great dangers, its great
> voyages, its great goal. It is being dispersed in clouds of narrative lan-
> guage elements – narrative, but also denotative, prescriptive, descrip-
> tive, and so on ... Where, after the metanarratives, can legitimacy
> reside? (Lyotard, 1984: xxiv–xxv)

(Note the reference to clouds here that in this context recalls both
those obscuring the first paragraph of Calvino's first incipit, and those
of Mitchell's atlas.) Calvino seems in tune with Lyotard when he too
admits the artificiality of the grand narratives through which we see
both the world we inhabit and the fictions we read, alluding to

> the Third Person necessary for the novel to be a novel, for something
> to happen between that male Second Person and the female Third, for
> something to take form, develop, or deteriorate according to the phas-
> es of human events. Or, rather to follow the mental models through
> which we live our human events. Or, rather, to follow the mental

models through which we attribute to human events the meanings that allow them to be lived. (Calvino, 1979/1998: 141)

But if Calvino admits their artificiality on the one hand, he also admits their necessity to the way we construct meaning from the world. It is telling that Lyotard describes metanarratives as fictions – as novels or odysseys – because fictions themselves continue to institute their own metanarratives (as the great voyages and epic sweep of *Cloud Atlas* amply illustrate). Linda Hutcheon (1988: 6), following Lyotard, argues that postmodernism 'refuses to posit any structure or, what Lyotard calls, master narrative – such as art or myth – which, for such modernists, would have been consolatory'. Despite all our expectations of what postmodern fiction is and does, Calvino and Mitchell both construct master-narratives for their fictions. While the incipits of *If on a winter's night a traveller* share little beyond the occasional repetition of a name, or certain recurring topoi (such as the triangular relationships to which he refers in the earlier quotation), Calvino houses his fragments in a classic, teleologically driven love story that ends in the marriage of his two fictive readers. As self-conscious as this adoption of a classic storytelling structure is, the self-consciousness does not undermine so much as celebrate both the artifice and the sentiment that drives it. The frequently quoted observation of another Italian postmodernist, Umberto Eco, is pertinent here:

> I think of the postmodern attitude as that of a man who loves a very cultivated woman and knows that he cannot say to her, 'I love you madly,' because he knows that she knows (and that she knows he knows) that these words have already been written by Barbara Cartland. Still there is a solution. He can say, 'As Barbara Cartland would put it, I love you madly.' At this point, having avoided false innocence, having said clearly it is no longer possible to talk innocently, he will nevertheless say what he wanted to say to the woman: that he loves her in an age of lost innocence. If the woman goes along with this, she will have received a declaration of love all the same. (Eco, 1985: 67–8)

The innocence of expression may be lost, Eco suggests, but not the force of feeling behind it. Equally, for all its self-consciousness, *If on a winter's night a traveller* remains, after all is said and done, a love story.

While Calvino's novel nods to classical precedents by its storytelling frame and ten embedded stories, Mitchell's novel in some ways may seem more radical in that it does away with the frame entirely, leaving only the stories. Conversely, *Cloud Atlas* may seem more conservative than its predecessor in its contrasting insistence on the cohesion and connectedness of its constituent parts. The comet-shaped birthmark offers a symbol for the connectivity that binds together and transcends the individual stories to make of the novel a unified whole. The birthmark is the author's signature – a sign of the author's hand, and a sign that the novel is a novel, rather than a collection of short stories; it thus has the same function within the text as the paratextual naming of the title 'Cloud Atlas' on the front cover. Like Calvino's love story, the use of the birthmark to suggest a transcendent narrative does not escape self-conscious critique within the novel – Cavendish, the editor, thoroughly disapproves of the motif: 'One or two things will have to go: the insinuation that Luisa Rey is this Robert Frobisher chap reincarnated, for example. Far too hippie-druggy-new age. (I, too, have a birthmark, below my left armpit, but no lover ever compared it to a comet. Georgette nicknamed it Timbo's Turd.)' (*CA*, 373). Cavendish's criticism operates according to Eco's model of the postmodern attitude. Following Eco, we may say that Mitchell avoids 'false innocence' by admitting the artifice of his birthmark, and the interconnectedness it represents, but, having done so, writes the novel that he wants to write. Consequently, when we read *Cloud Atlas* we may on one innocent level read an individual section as if no other section existed, but on another, less innocent and more knowing level, we will know we are not turning these fragments into a novel of our own, but uncovering the underlying novel already made by an author from these fragments. The birthmark is moreover just a symbol of an interconnectedness that goes much further with all those 'backflashes, foreshadowings and tricksy devices' that Cavendish contemptuously dismisses as belonging 'in the 1980s with MAs in Postmodernism and Chaos Theory' (*CA*, 152).[10] *Cloud Atlas* thus resembles *If on a winter's night a traveller* in repeatedly engaging the reader in its own construction as well as reception.

For all their postmodern pyrotechnics, *If on a winter's night a traveller* and *Cloud Atlas* ultimately both reflect the extent to which a classical aesthetic continues to inform our values as both authors and readers of novels. Mitchell's expressed desire to see a version of Calvino's novel in which the interrupted stories would be concluded is just one example of this.[11] Even (or perhaps especially) in a composite novel, we continue to look for a unity that entails completion, for reassurance that the text we are reading is not going to be 'just' a collection of stories. And, inevitably, the more difficult this unity is to find the more the reader desires and searches for it – the influence of a classical aesthetic lingers still, even in a postmodern age. In contrast to Calvino's approach to *If on a winter's night a traveller*, Mitchell is forever at pains to underline the connectedness rather than the separateness of the stories that comprise his novel. Ultimately, the disruptions and interruptions to which *Cloud Atlas* is subject reaffirm rather than undermine the importance of narrative cohesion to novelistic practice and reception. Although John Barth famously stated, 'the old analogy between Author and God, novel and world, can no longer be employed unless deliberately as a false analogy' (Barth, 1967: 125), the reader continues to expect the author to be master of his or her fictional universe. Part of the pleasure of reading novels continues to be that of discovering a design: we want to read in the knowledge that the pieces of the puzzle will fit together, that there is still a link between the artist and the artisan. Mitchell goes further than most in this regard: not satisfied with weaving connections between the individual sections of one novel, he weaves connections between individual novels too. The most obvious precedent for this practice is Balzac, who used the technique of recurring characters across his fictions to offer a *comédie humaine* of nineteenth-century society, to be a human zoologist of social species.[12] In a sense what Mitchell does is create a *comédie humaine* of his own, in which characters like Luisa Rey, Cavendish and Eva van Crommelynck may move beyond a single narrative and erase the formal borders that separate one novel from another.

In Mitchell's most recent novel, *The Thousand Autumns of Jacob de Zoet* (2010), Doctor Marinus, a benevolent if cantankerous man of science, reflects upon the growing impact of science on the globe in a learned gathering at the Shirandô academy:

> Had a man fallen asleep two centuries ago … and awoken this morning, he should recognise this world unchanged in essence … But were the same fellow to fall asleep tonight and sleep for a hundred years, or eighty, or sixty, on waking he shall not recognise the planet for the transformations wrought upon it by Science. (*TA*, 206–7)

When a geographer, Yoshida Hayato, asks, 'when the doctor's imagined Sleeper awakens in the year 1899, shall the world most closely resemble Paradise or the Inferno?', Marinus responds 'I shan't know it until I see it' (*TA*, 207). Although *The Thousand Autumns of Jacob de Zoet* is not populated with any characters from Mitchell's previous novels, it engages with the same questions that are at the heart of *Cloud Atlas* – it features a hero, in fact, who watches as 'West to East, the sky rolls and unrolls its atlas of clouds' (*TA*, 340). For all Cavendish's talk of 'tricksy devices', Mitchell's approach to narrative is inseparable from his engagement with the grand narratives of western civilization. The formal tension between the individual sections and the novel as a whole translate to a thematic tension between the local and the universal. At the end of the novel, Adam Ewing argues for the constructedness of metanarratives when he asserts:

> Scholars discern motions in history & formulate these motions into rules that govern the rises & falls of civilizations. My belief runs contrary, however. To wit: history admits no rules; only outcomes.
>
> What precipitates outcomes? Vicious acts & virtuous acts. (*CA*, 527–8)

Ewing then concludes his journal, and the novel, by asking the question:

> Is this entropy written within our nature?
> If we *believe* that humanity may transcend tooth & claw, if we *believe* divers races & creeds can share this world as peaceably as the orphans share their candlenut tree, if we *believe* leaders must be just, violence

muzzled, power accountable & riches of the Earth and its oceans shared equitably, such a world will come to pass. I am not deceived. It is the hardest of worlds to make real. (*CA*, 528)

Ewing insists on the individual and the local – the 'multitude of drops' – rather than the universal 'ocean', and demands an act of faith that rests on an inescapable 'if'. To use another natural metaphor, however, one could argue that Ewing cannot see the wood for the trees. While he asserts that disintegration is not inevitable but a matter of local and individual choices, the pessimism of the novel resides in the way that the virtuous acts within the novel, such as Autua's rescue of Ewing himself, are unable to staunch the flow of predacity from which they briefly distract us. Although there is no shortage of internal happy endings or virtuous characters in *Cloud Atlas*, the novel as a whole makes these seem like sideshows to an overwhelming master narrative of predacity leading inexorably to the disintegration of civilization. Just as each narrative metaphorically consumes the previous one, so the novel offers one proof after another of Henry Goose's 'First Law': 'The Weak are Meat the Strong do Eat' (*CA*, 508). If Mitchell debunks an Enlightenment grand narrative of civilizing progress, another equally grand, but far darker Enlightenment narrative takes its place that chimes with Theodor Adorno and Max Horkheimer's *Dialectic of Enlightenment* (1947/1979) in which 'the fully enlightened earth radiates disaster triumphant' (Adorno and Horkheimer, 1947/1979: 3). While 'Sloosha's Crossin'' can only end with the hope that this metanarrative will be cyclical – that a fall can in turn lead to another rise – the apocalyptic trajectory of the novel seems, ultimately, to offer little cause for optimism.

At the end of *Cloud Atlas* we are therefore left with a choice – a pessimistic Enlightenment grand narrative according to which predacity leads inexorably to the disintegration of civilization, or a more Romantic insistence on the power of the individual to effect and shape the world around him. When questioned on the tension between the novel's optimistic moments and its pessimistic trajectory, Mitchell has been reluctant to align himself with either side of the argument: 'Mondays, Wednesdays, and Fridays I view the world in a bleak way.

Tuesdays, Thursdays and Saturdays I view it in an optimistic way. And Sundays I take the day off' (Mullan, 2010). He has, however, wryly admitted that 'Probably in the long run we're kind of doomed. All things end and probably our civilization will ... But I could be wrong!' (Naughtie, 2007). At the end of the novel one senses Mitchell resisting his own grand narrative, and taking refuge with Ewing in the 'multitude of drops'. Whether the reader follows him in this respect may in the end be a matter of temperament: *Cloud Atlas* offers the ultimate philosophical litmus test for its readers, a means of separating the optimists from the pessimists. When all is said and done, it is left to the reader to choose where to end –with Adam or with Zachry – the first man or the last.

Notes

1 Kundera (1988: 15) laments that 'Afterward, the novel got itself tied to the imperative of verisimilitude, to realistic settings, to chronological order.'

2 This allusion to Don Quixote's horse has American as well as Spanish resonance –John Steinbeck named the truck in which he travelled across the United States in 1960 'Rocinante', an admission of the quixotic nature of his enterprise. (Steinbeck's journey is related in *Travels with Charley* [1961].)

3 Mitchell refers to Calvino's influence in a BBC Radio 4 'Bookclub' interview (3 June 2007), and also cites *If on a winter's night a traveller* as one of three important sources for *Cloud Atlas* in an interview with *The Washington Post*: 'I wondered what a novel might look like if a mirror were placed at the end of a book like Calvino's so that the stories would be resolved in reverse.' (*Washington Post*, 2004). Upon the publication of *Cloud Atlas*, Mitchell also offers a timely account of his reading and re-reading of Calvino's novel (Mitchell, 2004).

4 In a different way, the same confidence is equally striking in Kathy Acker's engagement with, and appropriation of, canonical texts in her own *Great Expectations* (1983) and *Don Quixote* (1986).

5 The character of Luisa Rey, for example, simultaneously connects both to Thornton Wilder's novel, *The Bridge of San Luis Rey* (1927), and Mitchell's first novel, *Ghostwritten* (1999), where Luisa makes her first brief appearance as a caller on a radio show.

6 A. S. Byatt (2004) touches on many of these influences and intertexts in her review of *Cloud Atlas* for the *Guardian*.

7 Mitchell offers a Japanese variation on this image in *The Thousand Autumns of Jacob de Zoet* (2010) when Orito is imprisoned in the House of Sisters: 'The Goddess is disrobed for the Annunciation of Engifting: her exposed breasts are ample with milk; and her belly, devoid of a navel, is swollen with a female foetus so fertile, according to Abbess Izu, that the foetus's own tiny womb encloses a still smaller female foetus, which is, in turn, impregnated with a still smaller daughter ... and so on, to infinity' (*TA*, 208).

8 These lines come from a children's song written by the Canadian folk singer, Alan Mills, with lyrics by Rose Bonne. The song was made popular by the American singer and actor, Burl Ives, in the 1950s who recorded it for his album of 'Folk Songs Dramatic and Humorous' (1953).

9 Mitchell himself, in an interview with the *Washington Post* (2004), uses a similarly predatory analogy: 'Each block of narrative is subsumed by the next, like a row of ever-bigger fish eating the one in front'.

10 These are too numerous to catalogue here but there are recurring topoi (such as the sea), recurring characters (such as Sixsmith), and recurring names (the taxi-driver who takes Cavendish to Aurora House asks for 'Sick teen-squid Zachary' [*CA*, 174], while Zachry's brother is called Adam [*CA*, 249]). Many of these connections are related to the eternally recurring soul that links the protagonists, with Frobisher dreaming he is in a pit (recalling Adam Ewing's experience of 'Conical Tor' [*CA*, 19–20]), and Sonmi of 'seeing Hawaii over the turquoise waves' (*CA*, 451).

11 'I wondered what a novel might look like if a mirror were placed at the end of a book like Calvino's so that the stories would be resolved in reverse' (*Washington Post*, 2004). Mitchell has also revealed his frustration at the inconclusiveness of Calvino's approach: 'knowing that the endings stay untold meant I didn't invest any emotional capital in the stories' (Mitchell, 2004).

12 Balzac dedicates his *Père Goriot* (1834) to Geoffroy Saint-Hilaire, celebrated naturalist and curator of the first Parisian zoo. The apocalyptic conclusion of Mitchell's *Ghostwritten* memorably features the figure of a zookeeper who has lost control of the animals.

Works Cited

Adorno, Theodor W. and Horkheimer, Max (1979) *Dialectic of Enlightenment*, trans. John Cumming. London: Verso.

Anderson, Howard (1980) 'Preface', in Lawrence Sterne, *The Life and Opinions of Tristram Shandy, Gentleman*, pp. vii–viii. New York: Norton.

Barth, John (1967) 'The Literature of Exhaustion', *Atlantic Monthly* 220: 29–34.

Barth, John (1984) *The Friday Book: Essays and Other Nonfiction*. Baltimore, MA: Johns Hopkins University Press.

Brink, André (1998) *The Novel: Language and Narrative from Cervantes to Calvino*. London: Palgrave Macmillan.

Byatt, A.S. (2004) 'Overlapping Lives', *Guardian*, 6 March, URL (consulted June 2010): http://www.guardian.co.uk/books/2004/mar/06/fiction.asbyatt

Calvino, Italo (1989) *The Uses of Literature*, trans. P. Creagh. San Diego, CA: Harcourt Brace Jovanovich.

Calvino, Italo (1979/1998) *If on a winter's night a traveller*, trans. William Weaver. London: Vintage.

Connor, Steven (2004) 'Postmodernism in Literature', in Steven Connor (ed.) *The Cambridge Companion to Postmodernism*, pp. 62–81. Cambridge: Cambridge University Press.

du Plessix Gray, Francine (1981) 'Visiting Italo Calvino', *New York Times Book Review* (21 June).

Eco, Umberto (1985) *Reflections on The Name of the Rose*, trans. William Weaver. London: Secker & Warburg.

Fokkema, Douwe W. (1984) *Literary History, Modernism, and Postmodernism*. Amsterdam and Philadelphia, PA: John Benjamins.

Hutcheon, Linda (1988) *A Poetics of Postmodernism: History, Theory, Fiction*. London: Routledge.

Kundera, Milan (1988) *The Art of the Novel*, trans. Linda Asher. London: Faber and Faber.

Lodge, David (1977) *The Modes of Modern Writing: Metaphor, Metonymy, and the Typology of Modern Literature*. Ithaca, NY: Cornell University Press.

Lyotard, Jean-François (1984) *The Postmodern Condition: A Report on Knowledge*, trans. Geoffrey Bennington and Brian Massumi. Manchester: Manchester University Press.

McLaughlin, Martin L. (1998) *Italo Calvino*. Edinburgh: Edinburgh University Press.

Mitchell, David (2004) 'Enter the Maze', *Guardian*, 22 May, URL (consulted August 2010): http://www.guardian.co.uk/books/2004/may/22/fiction.italocalvino

Mullan, John (2010) '*Guardian* Book Club: John Mullan Meets David Mitchell', *Guardian*, 28 June, URL (consulted August 2010): http://www.guardian.co.uk/books/audio/2010/jun/16/david-mitchell-guardian-book-club

Naughtie, James (2007) '*Cloud Atlas* – David Mitchell', BBC Radio 4 Bookclub, 3 June, URL (consulted June 2010): http://www.bbc.co.uk/radio4/arts/bookclub/ram/bookclub_20070603.ram

Orr, Mary (2003) *Intertextuality: Debates and Contexts*. Cambridge: Polity.

Szegedy-Maszák, Mihály (1987) 'Teleology in Postmodern Fiction', in Matei Calinescu and Douwe Fokkema (eds) *Exploring Postmodernism: Selected Papers Presented at a Workshop on Postmodernism at the Xith International Comparative Literature Congress*, pp. 41–57. Amsterdam and Philadelphia, PA: John Benjamins.

Washington Post (2004) 'Q&A: Book World Talks with David Mitchell', 22 August, URL (consulted June 2010): http://www.washingtonpost.com/wp-dyn/articles/A17231-2004Aug19.html

8

'Strange Transactions'
Utopia, Transmigration and Time in *Ghostwritten* and *Cloud Atlas*

Caroline Edwards

After the Second World War and throughout the 1950s, totalitarian communist regimes were seen by many academics and commentators as exhibiting a conflation of utopian idealism with brutally repressive collectivist ideologies. Russell Jacoby (2005: 13) notes that eminent Anglo-American and Western European scholars subsequently '[threw] communism, Nazism, and utopia into one tub', persuasively arguing that 'utopia leads to totalitarianism and mass murder'. At the time, utopia was understood as the restoration of some lost, broken unity – a monastic order of dull, static completion. Such perfection endangered what the liberal philosopher Isaiah Berlin (1959/1990: 46) called the society of 'open texture'. In *The Crooked Timber of Humanity*, Berlin (1959/1990: 45) wrote that utopia consequently favoured 'trying to foist an artificial order on a reluctant humanity ... trying to fit human beings, like bricks, into a preconceived structure'.

The discourse of anti-utopianism – which gained so much rhetorical force through the works of Jewish liberal refugees from fascism, such as Isaiah Berlin, Karl Popper, Norman Cohn and Hannah Arendt – developed with the radical generation of the 1960s into a forceful denunciation of systemic thinking and a protracted lexis of political disillusion; what Jean-François Lyotard (1997: 81) called 'the nostalgia of the whole and the one'. However, over the last few decades, defendants of utopian thinking have laboured to differentiate between 'traditional' (systemic) and 'post-traditional' (processual) concepts of utopia. According to this deconstruction of the Soviet myth, *traditional* literary utopias are identified as programmatic blueprints expounding a monotheistic and static perfectionism. In contrast, *post-traditional* utopian imaginaries introduce a mode of utopian thinking that is flexible, pluralized, heterogeneous and dialectical. As with all dichotomies, this is a caricatured opposition. If we return to Karl Popper's *The Open Society and Its Enemies, Vol. 1: The Spell of Plato* (1945/1966) – one of the most renowned critiques of utopia – we are reminded that Popper (1945/1966: 162) differentiates 'piecemeal' or small-scale reform from the complete overhaul of society associated with 'utopian' engineering. Despite his strong aversion to wholesale political restructuring, Popper's critique of utopia cannot be said to denounce a non-systemic understanding of utopian possibility.

New Utopian Imaginaries

This question of the diminished *scale* of utopian possibility – of the piecemeal experimental dialogue that fosters not static perfectionism but heterogeneity and difference within society – was addressed by H. G. Wells as early as 1905 in *The Modern Utopia*. Wells (1905/2005: 11) argued that utopia 'must be not static but kinetic, must shape not as a permanent state but as a hopeful stage leading to a long ascent of stages'. Wells's fictional reflections on the limits of the utopian imagination offer a useful point from which to approach David Mitchell's aesthetic project in his novels *Ghostwritten* (1999) and *Cloud Atlas* (2004). Both novels interrogate utopian literary and analytical concerns with the relationships between individuals and communities at voluntaristic as well imposed levels: from the recurrent struggle of characters against corporate or colonial structures of power and exploitation in the recent historical past, through the globalized interconnectedness of Mitchell's fictional present, into distant hypercapitalist and post-civilized projected futures. Mitchell's aesthetic ingenuity has earned him critical acclaim: John Freeman (2004) signals his literary importance, stating that 'Mitchell is already being called his generation's Pynchon'; while Berthold Schoene (2009: 97) has recently written that Mitchell's novels 'pioneer a new cosmopolitan modus operandi for twenty-first-century British fiction'. Schoene's analysis of *Ghostwritten* and *Cloud Atlas* in his recent study *The Cosmopolitan Novel* (2009) offers one of the first academic investigations into Mitchell's complex narrative structures, his engagement with the apocalyptic limitations of our contemporary systems of production and consumption, and his experimentation with various stylistic modes: from appropriating the aesthetic lexicons of such 'genre' elements as science fiction, pulp thrillers and mystery, to pastiching nineteenth-century diary forms as well as post-apocalyptic dialect. Perhaps most importantly, Schoene (2009: 102–3) argues that Mitchell's various narrative temporalities and spatialities construct what he calls a 'cosmopolitan vision [that] never deteriorates into facile utopianism'.

Schoene touches here on a crucial trend not only in David Mitchell's aesthetic output but also central to the work of many other contemporary novelists. Mitchell's optimistic, humanist aesthetic can be identified as expressing a new direction in contemporary British fiction in which a host of established as well as emerging novelists are turning to (non-'facile') utopian imaginaries to question social values and political assumptions, as well as to expose apocalyptic, ecological futures in ways that move beyond mere dystopian catastrophes. Considered alongside writers like Jim Crace, Doris Lessing, Jeanette Winterson and Maggie Gee, David Mitchell's novels can be seen to posit the continuation of some form of utopian alternative to our globalized, neoliberal present.[1] Crucially, these utopian impulses remain provisional rather than absolute, fluxional rather than static, and heterogeneously multi-voiced rather than authoritarian. This essay argues that a utopian mode of literary analysis is essential to understanding the interrogation of social, political and ecological ways of being found in Mitchell's fiction. Such an analytical mode needs to offer some way of imagining the connection between an infinite series of fragmented utopian 'moments' appearing with ever-increasing, self-reflexive frequency in the works of contemporary British writers. This approach foregrounds the ways in which contemporary novelists like David Mitchell are moving beyond the crippling passivity of domestic individualism towards a reformulated vision of community, solidarity and political alternatives. Formally, this indicates a rejuvenation of speculative fiction. Conceptually, it signifies a shift towards a revised version of humanism as it is being played out through the spatially- and temporally-disjunct coordinates of unevenly expanding globalization, with its emerging cosmopolitan identities.

Deconstructing the Totalitarian Utopia

Mitchell's first step towards offering a differently conceived utopian imaginary composed of scaled-down, networked moments of radical otherness is outlined in his aesthetic response to the anti-utopian consensus of the second half of the twentieth century. *Ghostwritten*, in particular, constructs an explicitly foregrounded deconstruction of totalitarian utopianism that utilizes Maoist and Stalinist communism, Islamic fundamentalism and exploitative capitalist globalization to shape a recognizably familiar historical landscape. One illustration of the dangers of so-called grand or totalizing utopian projects is articulated through Mitchell's depiction of the cultish millenarianism underpinning a terrorist network in Tokyo – with its allegorical overcoding of present-day Islamic fundamentalism – in which the utopia of a 'New Earth' will cleanse the sinful, westernized, capitalist world through suicide bombs. Following his gas attack on the Tokyo subway system the narrator-bomber, Quasar, fantasizes about the New Earth and its White Nights:

> There will be no bullying. No victimising. All the selfish, petty, unbelieving unclean, they will fry in the fat of their ignorance. We will eat papayas, cashew nuts and mangos, and learn how to make traditional instruments and beautiful pottery. (*G*, 25)

Quasar's 'doomsday cult' – with its worship of a transmigratory Boddhisatva divinity, belief in astral telepathic systems of communication and its post-materialist, teleological prophecies – is revealed to be a form of brainwashing. One woman angrily criticizes Quasar's beloved astral Fellowship of spirit, arguing that it is offering its foot-soldiers false visions of a blissful afterlife in return for the renunciation of personal conscience and social responsibility. This false ideology perpetuates itself, she argues, because people:

> need shinier myths that will never be soiled by becoming true. The handing over of one's will is a small price to pay, for the believers. They aren't going to need a will in their New Earth. (*G*, 23)

This criticism of the 'shinier myths' of Quasar's New Earth echoes those vehement critiques of Stalinist communism made by such distinguished refugees from fascism as Hannah Arendt, Norman Cohn, and Isaiah Berlin. 'Never has our future been more unpredictable', writes Hannah Arendt in *The Origins of Totalitarianism* (1958): 'Desperate hope and desperate fear often seem closer to the center of such events than balanced judgment and measured insight' (Arendt, 1958: vii). Meanwhile, in the 'Tokyo' section of *Ghostwritten* Satoru's quotation from Flaubert's *Madame Bovary* (1857) reinforces the impossible perfection such utopian regimes attempt to implement politically through idolization: "*One should be wary of touching one's idols, for the gilt comes off on one's fingers*" (*G*, 53).

Mitchell's deconstruction of totalitarian utopianism continues with a fictional interrogation of Mao's communist modernization in rural China and the brutal oppression of the Chinese communist State in the chapter 'The Holy Mountain'. Narrated by an elderly proprietress of a dilapidated teashack in the foothills of the Holy Mountain (conjectured to be Mount Emei, one of the Four Sacred Buddhist Mountains of China in the Sichuan province) (Brown, 2007), the chapter stretches from the Second Sino-Japanese war in the late 1930s, through the period of regional warlords, and the Communist Party's split from the Kuomintang, to Mao's revolutionary cultural projects, including the Five Year Plan, the Great Leap Forward and the distribution of his Little Red Book. Mao's Five Year Plan is recollected by the Teashack Lady as being as deluded and programmatic as Quasar's millenarian New Earth, basking under the alpha rays of its transmigratory figurehead, His Serendipity:

A New China was emerging from somewhere called Feudalism, and the New China would lead the New Earth. It would be here in five years' time, because the international revolution of the proletariat was a historical inevitability ... 'Your leaders must know powerful magic.'

'Yes,' said one of the women. 'The magic is called Marx, Stalin, Lenin, and Class Dialectics.'

It didn't sound very convincing magic to me. (G, 127)

Meanwhile, Communist agrarian policy leads to widespread famine as the disenfranchisement of peasant labourers working under poor centralized planning means that '[n]obody owned the land, so nobody made sure it was respected' (G, 130). Finally, the totalitarianism of programmatic utopian social engineering is also revealed in the 'Petersburg' section of *Ghostwritten* where Margot Latunsky, the deluded ex-lover of a communist official, recalls the former Soviet Union:

what was this Union of Socialist Soviet Republics, really? *Republics* need real elections and I never saw any of those, I damn well never heard of any *Soviets* – I'm not even sure what one is. *Socialism* means the common people own the country, and all my mother ever owned was her intestinal parasites. (G, 212)

Like the Teashack Lady's hapless suffering at the hands of the various political factions operating on behalf of Mao's communist China, Margot's personal history embodies the national trajectory of Soviet Russia and the gaping chasm between political idealism and the casual violence engendered by its social implementation.

Mitchell's critique of political utopianism is not limited to institutionalized communism or socialism. What George Soros (1998: xx) has called 'market fundamentalism' – the untrammelled regime of aggressively expansionist laissez-faire capitalism across the world – is often referred to as a neoliberal or rightwing utopia and Mitchell offers as trenchant a critique of this mode of utopianism as he does of communist state totalitarianism. Margot, for instance, reveals Russia's newly capitalist economy to be a repeat of the corruption of the former Party-led socialist oligarchy:

nothing's changed. You used to pay off your local Party thug, now you pay off your local mafia thug. The old Party used to lie, and lie, and lie some more. Now our democratically elected government lies, and lies, and lies some more ... Where's the difference? (*G*, 213)

The deconstruction of capitalist, free-market utopianism is continued in *Cloud Atlas* through Mitchell's projection of the dystopian hyper-capitalist colonialism of twenty-second-century Korea, known as Nea So Copros.[2] In this violently exploitative and rigidly striated society, citizens ('consumers') are monitored at every second through ID chips in their fingertips ('soul rings'), and have to adhere to Enrichment Laws in which they must spend a fixed number of dollars each month according to their social status. All menial labour is performed by genetically-modified ('genomed') clones or fabricants. The narrator, a fabricant called Sonmi~451, works in an underground restaurant where the fabricants are kept in slavery through their addiction to 'Soap', their genetically-modified stupidity and passive natures, as well as their religious devotion to a hologram, which tells them they will be released into 'Xultation' after 12 years of devoted service. This turns out to be a cruel fabrication and 'Xultation' is revealed to be a slaughtership where they are killed like cattle, rather than released into the paradisal Hawaii they were promised.

Sonmi becomes unwittingly involved in a government programme to stage a show-trial branding fabricants as dangerous and subversive, facilitating the passing of a Fabricant Containment Act intended to crush the revolutionary, abolitionist Union movement. In the course of her activities, she is shown the dark underbelly that sustains this hyper-capitalist corpocracy, and the uncontainable tensions that are destabilizing its apparent regime of harmonious perfection:

> Nea So Copros is poisoning itself to death. Its soil is polluted, its rivers lifeless, its air toxloaded, its food and supplies riddled with rogue genes ... Plutocracy's legitimacy, its wealth, is drying up; the Juche's Enrichment Laws are mere sticking plasters on haemorrhages and amputations. Its only other response is that strategy beloved of all bankrupt ideologues: denial. (*CA*, 341)

The biotechnological corpocracy of Nea So Copros, then, is suffering from the same violent contradictions that underpin our own era of free market capitalism. Moreover, far from embodying the tenets of 'equitable commerce' the regime reveals, as Sonmi describes in her universal *Declaration* of rights, 'a cycle as old as tribalism' (*CA*, 360).

In *Cloud Atlas*, Mitchell unequivocally couples the so-called 'progress' of various civilizations – from the savage racism that legitimizes the colonial projects of Victorian-Christian Missionaries to the ecological catastrophe of market fundamentalism's futuristic manifestation in Nea So Copros – with barbaric acts of exploitation, violence and subjugation. For instance, the nineteenth-century American notary, Adam Ewing, is confronted by Henry Goose with the racism and brutality of colonialists's ideological distinctions between 'civilization' and 'savagery':

> Why tinker with the plain truth that we hurry the darker races to their graves in order to take their land & its riches? Wolves don't sit in their caves, concocting crapulous theories of race to justify devouring a flock of sheep! (*CA*, 509).

Similarly, an inhabitant of Chatham Island, Mr D'Arnoq, relates the destruction of the native Moriori way of life by newly settled Maori colonizers, brought to the island during British whale trading. He suggests that the Moriori had a way of life more peacefully utopian than American and European national constitutionalism: 'Who can deny Old Rēkohu lay closer to More's Utopia than our States of Progress governed by war-hungry princelings in Versailles & Vienna, Washington & Westminster?' (*CA*, 12). It is not colonial modernization that embodies utopian principles here, but the peaceful coexistence with nature practised by the Moriori. This deconstruction of the expansionist logic of capitalism thus reveals Mitchell's suggestion that an alternative mode of living has been squandered in our contemporary world; a pacifist, utopian way of life that acts as a foil to our current predicament of excessive consumption, extraction of surplus value through polluting industrial production, and the unequal distribution of power between nations.

Beyond the Bucolic Utopia: Mitchell's Minor Utopian 'moments of possibility'

While David Mitchell explores the dangers of what Susan Buck-Morss (2002: x) has categorized as utopian 'mass dreamworlds' in the fictional worlds of *Ghostwritten* and *Cloud Atlas* – inaugurating engineered societal totalities – he does not renounce the utopian possibilities of what Adam Ewing calls 'the hardest of worlds to make real' (*CA*, 528). Instead, the characters of these two novels reveal the 'minor' scale at which utopian moments are possible: fleeting instances of sympathy and connection between strangers momentarily flung together in chance encounters; moments when individuals are able to transcend the reifying alienation of their multiple, compartmentalized selves; and episodes of social fulfilment within small-scale alternative political communities. In this way, Mitchell's novels parallel the scaling-down from the totalitarian dreamworlds of mass utopianism to what Jay Winter (2006: 2) calls in *Dreams of Peace and Freedom* utopian 'moments of possibility'. Winter (2006: 2) defines such 'moments of possibility' as small-scale 'imaginings of liberation', brief instances of 'hopes and dreams rarely realized, but rarely forgotten as well'. Crucially, minor utopian visions are distinguished from major utopian systems of 'collective violence' (Winter, 2006: 5) because they 'frequently carry within their thinking the very contradictions they seek to supersede' (Winter, 2006: 7).

The utopian moments of solidarity articulated in *Ghostwritten* and *Cloud Atlas* do not offer alternative societies *in totem* but, rather, offer fugacious expressions of non-alienated life in which the 'naturalization of man and the humanization of nature' that Marx (1971: 271) outlined as the goal of Communism in the *Economic and Philosophic Manuscripts* can be momentarily achieved. The dying, diabetic, criminal corporate lawyer Neal Bose in the 'Hong Kong' section of *Ghostwritten*, for instance, illustrates Mitchell's interest in exploring the dangerous effects of capitalism's system of alienated social and productive relations. Late for work one morning commuting from Lantau Island to the commercial district on Hong Kong Island, Neal decides on an impulse not to catch the ferry and walks in a daze along the shore, eventually climbing the mountain to reach the island's bronze Giant Buddha statue. Along the way he flings his briefcase and mobile phone into the sea, and deposits his office clothes and Rolex watch in the bushes, letting nature absorb the accoutrements of his excessively unhealthy and insecure lifestyle, and offering – through escapism – the briefest glimpse of an alternative mode of being and relating within the contemporary world.

Meanwhile, Mitchell's description of the small community of political exiles Sonmi encounters in her revolutionary Union activities in *Cloud Atlas* offers us a utopian instance of political opposition to the consumerist dictatorship of Nea So Copros. Underneath the shadow of a massive Siddhartha rock carving lives a micro-community of dissidents who have chosen to renounce the regime's exploitative, corpocratic social hierarchies and accompanying benefits of electricity, shopping gallerias, fabricant service and entertainment franchises to live in a fifteen-century-old abbey. Mitchell's interest in a utopian alternative to the corpocracy is represented not as a statically perfected utopian community but as a struggling group of squabbling individuals. As Sonmi notes:

> It was no bucolic Utopia. Yes, winters are severe; rainy seasons are relentless; crops are prey to disease; the caves are susceptible to vermin, and few colonists live as long as upstrata consumers. Yes, the colonists bicker and grieve as people will. But they do it in a community. Nea So Copros has no communities; it only has the state. (*CA*, 347)

This resistant, illegitimate community conforms to what I have elsewhere defined as a 'microtopian' community: it self-reflexively reveals the limitations of the 'traditional' utopian narrative synthesis in the manner of what Tom Moylan calls the 'critical utopia' (Edwards, 2009: 775–6). 'Critical utopias', writes Moylan (1986: 211), 'still describe alternative societies, but they are careful to consider the flaws and insufficiencies of these systems'. The scale of such literary utopian communities is diminished in an aesthetic trend that appears to be paralleling Jay Winter's political analysis of 'minor' utopian moments in twentieth-century history. Crucially, this community is not articulated in ontological terms but, rather, is composed of multiple irreducible individuals: 'Each colonist had a different story' (*CA*, 346).

Mitchell's microtopian community of political exiles thus actuates an aesthetic encounter with what political theorists have conceptualized as 'the multitude'. Rather than occupying a position of 'ontological centrality' (Laclau and Mouffe, 2001: 2) attributed to previous subjects of agency – the working class, for instance – the multitude, write Hardt and Negri,

> is composed of innumerable internal differences that can never be reduced to a unity or a single identity – different cultures, races, ethnicities, genders, and sexual orientations; different forms of labor; different ways of living; different views of the world; and different desires. The multitude is a multiplicity of all these singular differences. (Hardt and Negri, 2005: xiv)

Hardt and Negri use the Internet as a metaphor for understanding the globally communicating and producing multitude, brought together through a 'common cycle of struggles' against capitalist exploitation.[3] This offers a useful way of reading Mitchell's own networked microtopian communities. Mitchell has said in interview that writing 'is a strange business transaction, which occurs largely between the imaginations of complete strangers who will stay complete strangers' (McWeeney, 2000). However, the most salient theme throughout his novels is the connection between characters who *do not* remain complete strangers. Sonmi's post-bucolic microtopian community offers an alternative model of utopian collectivity that is directly opposed to totalitarian social engineering through its small scale, politically marginalized position, and its non-homogeneous and internally contradictory nature. This utopian moment thus reveals the scale at which utopian collectivities are operating within contemporary British novels; what Ian McEwan calls in *Saturday* 'a utopian community briefly realised', 'tantalisingly conjured before fading away' (McEwan, 2006: 171–2).

Transmigration: Networking 'our brief time with the historical time we cannot live'

The representation of a globally-connecting, familiarized community is rendered with extraordinary formal ingenuity by Mitchell. Building on isolated utopian moments in which individual characters overcome their self-alienation and microtopian alternative communities are suggested, Mitchell develops a narrative world in which all his characters become networked through accident or chance, and in which a transmigration of souls occurs across various historical temporalities. Central to *Ghostwritten* and *Cloud Atlas* are metaphors of connection and fate, the synthesis of electrons as understood through the lens of quantum physics, and the networking of different historical locales through noncorporeal characters parasitically transmigrating into human 'host' bodies, as well as characters that are reincarnated, repeating their actions in different centuries. As Mo Muntervary argues in *Ghostwritten*, 'Nothing exists that cannot be synthesised' (*G*, 344):

> However far away they are: between John and me, between Okinawa and Clear Island, or between the Milky Way and Andromeda: if one of the particles is spinning down, then you know that that other is spinning up ... Phenomena are interconnected regardless of distance, in a holistic ocean more voodoo than Newton. (*G*, 375)

This 'holistic ocean' reveals the uncanny interconnectedness of Mitchell's characters as they encounter one another in a meticulously plotted concatenation of coincidences. Through the lexis of quantum physics, Mo Muntervary continually reflects on the relationship between predestination and unknowable futurity that informs her mediation of the world; for her, the utopian synthesis that binds the world together is love. However, Mo's utopian networking of the universe's constituent components within a momentarily totalizing narrative of unity and connectedness offers a problematic instance of narrative association. Mo's unity of all electrons, protons and neutrons through the love that binds her nuclear family together in fact delineates an instance of individualist escapism rather than a convincing expression of political or utopian communal alternatives. It is Adam Ewing who most successfully connects what the utopian philosopher Ernst Bloch (2000: 257) calls the 'pathetic brevity of our existence' with the 'broad, historical life granted to "humanity" as a whole'; and, who establishes the importance of networking his individuality within a community or multitude that stretches across history. Ewing contemplates his life – what he calls 'one drop in a limitless ocean' of humanity (*CA*, 529) – not with despair at the limitations of what he can achieve but with energetic optimism at the thought of the individuals that compose each civilization, asking: 'what is any ocean but a multitude of drops?' (*CA*, 529). As Jean-Luc Nancy (1991: xxxviii) writes in *The Inoperative Community*, 'the thinking of community as essence – is in effect the closure of the political'. Mitchell effectively de-essentializes his networked communities in *Ghostwritten* and *Cloud Atlas*, insisting on the importance of each individual so that his characters maintain their agency and do not become subsumed within the larger historical ambit of any generalized transmigration of humanity and its constellation of vastly disjunct historical temporalities.

The connection between utopian imaginaries and transmigration is explored by Mitchell at various points in *Ghostwritten* and *Cloud Atlas*: a lonely transmigratory spirit (*noncorpum*) wanders the earth in the 'Mongolia' section of *Ghostwritten*, while another non-corporeal, transmigratory being named Arupadhatu converses with a sentient, machinic world peacekeeping AI known as Zookeeper through radio transmissions in 'Night Train'. However, it is the human transmigrations in the two novels that offer a utopianized mode of community that networks globalized spaces and historical times. This theme is introduced through Luisa Rey in *Cloud Atlas* (herself a character in a manuscript given to another of Mitchell's protagonists appearing in *Ghostwritten* and *Cloud Atlas*, Timothy Cavendish), as she senses a reincarnated connection with Robert Frobisher through his letters:

> It is not the unflattering light they shed on a pliable young Rufus Six-
> smith that bothers Luisa, but the dizzying vividness of the images of

> places and people that the letters have unlocked. Images so vivid she can only call them memories. (*CA*, 121)

Mitchell, however, also self-reflexively refers to Luisa's reincarnated connection with Frobisher – and, indeed, the connection between several of the novel's characters as reincarnated versions of the same self (Naughtie, 2007) – as a ludicrous expression of New Age spiritual cultism. Timothy Cavendish, the publisher who is reading the Luisa Rey manuscript, meanwhile calls the insinuation that Luisa is Robert Frobisher reincarnated, '[f]ar too hippie-druggy-new age' (*CA*, 373).

Despite Mitchell's self-reflexive criticism of reincarnation, his use of transmigration can be identified as offering a loosely-structured community of individual characters throughout history, networked into correlation with one another without losing their indissoluble individuality. Such a project offers a fictional parallel to such contemporary political theories of de-essentialized agency as Hardt and Negri's 'multitude', or Jean-Luc Nancy's 'inoperative community'. What is particularly interesting for a utopian reading is that Mitchell's innovative experimentation with the novel form through his 'matryoshka doll' structure (more on this later) is expressed explicitly using the lexicon of utopian temporality. Luisa's birthmark, for instance throbs: 'She grasps for the ends of this elastic moment, but they disappear into the past and the future' (*CA*, 448). The throbbing of her birthmark connects Luisa not only with the other characters of *Cloud Atlas* but, more importantly, with the other historical temporalities within the novel, stretching from the nineteenth century right through to the distant, post-civilized future. This mediation between one individual and history *in totem* is actuated through the powerfully inscribed metaphor of the transmigration of souls which, as Ernst Bloch (2000: 262) writes, reconciles the pathetically small individual subject within a '*cosmic process of self-recognition*' (emphasis in original):

> The doctrine of the transmigration of souls, this penetrating application of the certainty of the We to the improvident course of this world, should have proved itself as the strongest antidote to the contradiction between our brief time and the historical time we cannot live. (Bloch, 2000: 263)

This historical time that we as individuals cannot live is thus achieved metaphorically through the metonymic narrative vehicle of transmigration-as-universal struggle, which threads together those disparately shifting moments of individual agency, striving for political democratization in the various worlds of Mitchell's novels.

However, Mitchell's aesthetic figuration of the multitude also enacts a critique of Bloch's conception of transmigration at this point. Mitchell does not utilize transmigration merely to represent the same human being who appears in different centuries; crucially, it is the connections between different characters throughout various historical times that constructs a trans-historical community whose different resistances to colonial power construct a forceful, oppositional agency in *Ghostwritten* and *Cloud Atlas*. The 'elastic moment' in which Luisa's birthmark throbs reveals the inherent connectedness between her battle against the violent avarice of American corporate self-interest and the struggles of the novel's other characters against different modes of violent societal predation: from Adam Ewing's realization of the horrors of naturalized colonial ideology, to Sonmi~451's political opposition to the biotechnological-totalitarian state of Nea So Copros, as well as the Darwinistic struggle for survival between Zachry's peaceful Valleysmen and the barbaric cruelty of the bloodthirsty Kona tribe. These moments of fragile, anti-imperial resistance are networked together through the symbolic figure of transmigration. In Mitchell's hands, transmigration becomes more than just the *'dispersal of our self across all of history'* (emphasis in original) in what Ernst Bloch (2000: 264) called *'the soul's various historical existences'* (emphasis in original). Rather, transmigration becomes a utopianized literary strategy in which a post-individual mode of community and political agency can be posited at a symbolic level.

Mitchell's use of transmigration – not a common trope in twentieth- and twenty-first-century literature – can also be found in two other recent novels: Jeanette Winterson's *The PowerBook* (2000) and Marina Warner's *The Leto Bundle* (2001).[4] The engagements of these novels with the 'contradiction between our brief time and the historical time we cannot live' pose some provocative questions about how we conceive historical time in twenty-first-century literature. For instance, are we finally able to move beyond literary postmodernism's inability to reflect on any historical representation that is not spatialized, flattened out, pastiched and shorn of original context? Do these novels represent the beginnings of a new generation of fiction that can address our loss of faith in any meaningful collective life? The narrative present of *Cloud Atlas* enacts its utopian critique of contemporary neoliberalism by connecting the world of Mitchell's readership with various historical and futural projects of aggressive imperialism. Meanwhile the resistant actions of individuals and small communities to such corpocratic violence expand their limited possibilities for agency and resistance through transmigratory networks that stretch across various temporalities, positing a dislocated utopian time of *immediacy* (processual critique within the present) rather than *deferral* (futural perfection). In *Specters of Marx* (1994), Jacques Derrida calls for a conception of time that can accommodate what he calls the '*non-contemporaneity with itself of the living present*' (Derrida, 1996: xviii, emphasis in original), or, an immanent present time that is, as Hamlet observes, 'out of joint': off its hinges and bearing a debt both to 'those who are no longer or who are not yet *present and living*' (Derrida, 1996: 114, emphasis in original). Through his use of the symbolic figure of transmigration, Mitchell thus offers us a non-contemporaneous narrative present, which reveals its utopian critique – implicitly demanding political change – through various dystopian pasts and futural projections of the globalized capitalist world of his readership, as well as its utopian counterparts of anti-imperial resistance.

In *Cloud Atlas*, Isaac Sachs sketches this plastic understanding of time, offering a temporal model that incorporates the virtual future (our utopian hopes) as well as the virtual past (the redemption of the failed utopian struggles of the past). Sachs calls this:

> *an infinite matrioshka doll of painted moments, each 'shell' (the present) encased inside a nest of 'shells' (previous presents) I call the actual past but which we* perceive *as the virtual past. The doll of 'now' likewise encases a nest of presents yet to be, which I call the actual future but which we* perceive *as the virtual future.* (CA, 409)

The virtual past is the past we remember, 'landscaped' or mediated by power through mythologization, blotting out the past as it actually occurred so that it becomes as unrealizable as utopia: '*Like Utopia*', writes Sachs, '*the actual future + the actual past exist only in the hazy distance, where they are no good to anyone*' (*CA*, 409). Sachs's bifurcation of the past *as it really happened* (the 'actual' past) and the past *as we perceive it through historical documentation* (the 'virtual' past) can usefully be explored with reference to Walter Benjamin's redemptive, monadological reading of history as arrested dialectical image. For Benjamin, the materialist historian's task is the rupturing of nineteenth-century triumphalist bourgeois narratives that totalize history and portray it as an inevitable and eternally recurring cycle of technological progress and modernization.[5] This cyclical recurrence is invoked by Mitchell in *Cloud Atlas* as the Nietzschean eternal return, encoded both positively and negatively: positively, because the individual can transcend death through his or her transmigrational connection with other individuals in different times and places; negatively, because the struggle against those violently rapacious forces underpinning any dominant mode of civilization will continually reappear. As Robert Frobisher writes:

> Rome'll decline and fall again, Cortazar'll sail again and, later, Ewing will too, Adrian'll be blown to pieces again, you and I'll sleep under Corsican stars again ... Nietzsche's gramophone record. When it ends, the Old One plays it again, for an eternity of eternities.
> Time cannot permeate this sabbatical. We do not stay dead long.
> (*CA*, 490)

Mitchell unambiguously couples our conceptions of temporality – as applied to historical events as well as to the unknowable future – with structures of power, revealing the struggle for historical remembrance and futural projections of hope as a struggle between corporate interests and the actions of individuals or small communities. Microtopian temporalities are thus pitted against the grand utopian times of totalizing and totalitarian regimes, as revealed in a conversation between the investigative journalist Luisa Rey and her neighbour, Javi:

'If you could *see* the future, like you can see the end of 16th Street from the top of Kilroy's department store, that means it's already there. If it's already there, that means it isn't a thing you can change.'

'Yes, but what's at the end of 16th Street isn't made by what *you* do. It's pretty much fixed, by planners, architects, designers, unless you go and blow a building up or something. What happens in a minute's time *is* made by what you do.' (*CA*, 418)

Luisa distinguishes between the future as enacted by individual or small-scale agency and the future as a predestined programming imposed by state institutions on ordinary people. This temporal opposition is at the heart of Mitchell's narrative imaginary in both *Ghostwritten* and *Cloud Atlas*: the struggle for individuals to overcome predestined futures, 'ghostwritten' by forces far exceeding their control; their confrontations with happenstance, or what Marco in *Ghostwritten* calls 'the cocktail of genetics and upbringing fixed for [us] by the blind barman Chance' (*G*, 273); and, the fight against a crippling passivity in the face of violent corporate structures.

Finally, Adam Ewing's resounding faith in humanity at the end of *Cloud Atlas* reveals Mitchell's unambiguously optimistic message concerning individual agency: a utopian imaginary is essential if we are to transcend the eternally recurring cycle of causality that gives rise to the supremacy of exploitation, brutality and greed in the various civilizations depicted in *Cloud Atlas*. Such an imaginary retains the possibility that a cyclically recurring pattern of history might be overturned by the actuation of one of the many alternative possible futurities that Mo Muntervary hinted at in *Ghostwritten* when she asked 'what happens to the other universes where electrons follow other paths, where thoughts and mutations and actions differ?' (*G*, 377). The agency possible within those 'minor' utopian futurities that Mo Muntervary, Adam Ewing or Luisa Rey consider remain, however, at a strikingly minimalist scale. Such moments can therefore only build towards a concrete utopian future if they can be successfully networked with other similar instances of small-scale resistance. Although such mobilization is not fully constructed in either *Ghostwritten* or *Cloud Atlas*, the novels do offer strikingly resilient instances of hope in the face of desperate violence and exploitation. As Mitchell has said in interview:

> You only need a small amount of hope – it works as a trace element. Of course, it's best if you've got loads and it can translate into the political sphere. But in the mean time, trace elements will do. (Edwards, 2010a)

This 'trace element' of hope is present throughout *Cloud Atlas*, despite the overwhelmingly bleak experience of Mitchell's characters in the face of oppressive 'mass' temporalities. Adam Ewing's resounding faith in humanity at the end of the novel can thus be said to balance the struggle between violent, large-scale social predation and hopeful, small-scale peace and freedom in the favour of the latter. Pledging himself to the Abolitionist cause on his return to San Francisco, Ewing concludes that hope and faith can transform exploitative historical situations into movements of emancipation:

> If we *believe* humanity is a ladder of tribes, a colosseum of confrontation, exploitation & bestiality, such a humanity is surely brought into being ... [But] one fine day, a purely predatory world *shall* consume itself. (*CA*, 528)

Ewing's 'one fine day' contains the beginnings of a concrete utopian anticipation capable of mobilizing progressive social change. 'If we *believe* that humanity may transcend tooth & claw', Ewing reflects, 'such a world will come to pass' (*CA*, 528).

Concluding Remarks

In 2000, the literary critic Elaine Showalter complained that English novelists were 'afraid to tackle big subjects', writing about 'love instead of money, about sex instead of power, about the past instead of the future'. In contrast, Mitchell's utopian 'moments of possibility' reveal a narrative strategy in which politicized demands for something better are being *articulated in common* by globally dispersed characters, networked together through transmigratory temporalities that encompass unknown, speculated futures as well as contested pasts.

While Mitchell's aesthetic universe can be identified as speculative or utopian in the commonly understood sense that it estranges the world of his readership in order to critique it, it is also utopian in a different way. This second utopian function reveals the emergence of a processual, scaled-down utopian imaginary that is expressed through the networking of variously disjunct temporalities all acting within the 'present'. Ruth Levitas (2005: 44) calls utopias 'exercises in joined-up thinking', and it is my argument that Mitchell's overcoding of predestination on to the actions of his characters as they struggle against societal and historical forces reveals, paradoxically, how they cannot help but be connected to each other. That is, Mitchell's characters achieve a mode of communal solidarity not always through their own individual and collective agency but because chance encounters network them into an intricately structured, yet beneficent chain of causality, connecting them both within and between his novels.

In this way, Mitchell's utopian moments of collectivity in *Ghostwritten* and *Cloud Atlas* actuate a de-essentialized mode of globalized community that effects transmigrational mediations between vastly disparate historical temporalities in what Bloch called the 'contradiction between our brief time and the historical time we cannot live'. However, the problematic nature of these utopian temporal moments is revealed by Mitchell's own playful, self-reflexive attitude as expressed by Timothy Cavendish who asserts: 'As an experienced editor I disapprove of backflashes, foreshadowings and tricksy devices, they belong in the 1980s with MAs in Postmodernism and Chaos Theory' (*CA*, 152). This postmodernist narratorial self-reflexivity is echoed in Frobisher's comments concerning the structure of the overlapping soloist components of his eponymous *Cloud Atlas Sextet*: 'Revolutionary or gimmicky? Shan't know until it's finished, and by then it'll be too late' (*CA*, 463). The explicit utopianism of Frobisher's atlas of clouds is revealed by Cavendish's yearning for the 'Joyous Isles' he encountered briefly in his youth: 'What wouldn't I give now for a never-changing map of the ever-constant ineffable?' (*CA*, 389).

Mitchell's narrative experimentation with dystopian and apocalyptic futures, his borrowing from 'genre' elements – among them, pulp thrillers, science fiction and mystery (Q&A)[6] – thus creates an ambitiously conceived aesthetic world in which not only are the various protagonists connected at the level of *content* but, moreover, the various pastiched, stylistic vocabularies are networked together at the level of *form* into a many-voiced, contradictory and heterogeneous whole. Herbert Marcuse calls this the 'critical function of art' in *The Aesthetic Dimension* (1978/2003):

> The critical function of art, its contribution to the struggle for liberation, resides in the aesthetic form. A work of art is authentic or true not by virtue of its content (i.e. the 'correct' representation of social conditions), nor by its 'pure' form, but by *the content having become the form*. (Marcuse, 1978/2003: 8, emphasis added)

Thus, Mitchell's thematic preoccupation with networking between globally and historically dispersed characters *becomes* the aesthetic form he uses to structure his narratives. Mitchell educates us, therefore, into a new way of understanding how transnational and historically discrete communities can successfully be delineated in the contemporary novel form. More importantly, *Ghostwritten* and *Cloud Atlas* reveal how aesthetic form can shape a reconceptualizing of contemporary modes of being and relating through a self-reflexive interrogation of utopian values. In Mitchell's work, utopian possibility lies not in any totalizing political ideology, but in those processual, scaled-down instances of social collaboration networked together across space and time.

Acknowledgements

I would like to thank Professor Peter Brooker for his generous comments in response to an earlier draft of this essay.

Notes

1 See, for instance, Doris Lessing's *Mara and Dann: An Adventure* (1999) and *The Story of General Dann and Mara's Daughter, Griot and the Snow Dog* (2005), Maggie Gee's *The Ice People* (1999) and *The Flood* (2004), David Mitchell's *Cloud Atlas* (2004), Kazuo Ishiguro's *Never Let Me Go* (2005), Will Self's *The Book of Dave* (2006), Jeanette Winterson's *The Stone Gods* (2007), Jim Crace's *The Pesthouse* (2007), Nick Harkaway's

The Gone-Away World (2008), and Sam Taylor's *The Island at the End of the World* (2009).

2 Mitchell has admitted that the name Nea So Copros is an acronym for 'New East Asian Sphere of Co-Prosperity', alluding to the Japanese Empire's self-appellation of the East Asian Sphere of Co-Prosperity during the Second World War (Edwards, 2010b).

3 Hardt and Negri (2005: 215) include within this 'common cycle of struggles': the indigenous Mexican Zapatista National Liberation Army (EZLN), which uses the Internet to construct solidarity with other anti-globalization movements; the globally dispersed WTO protestors meeting in Seattle in 1999 and at the World Social Forum in Porto Alegre, Brazil in 2005; and the Palestinian Intifada.

4 Virginia Woolf offers a strong literary precedent for the theme of characters existing across different centuries in *Orlando* (1928).

5 See, for instance, Benjamin's critique of the bourgeois concept of historical time as the perpetuation of the 'always new' in *The Arcades Project*. The period's triumphalist idea of itself is, for Benjamin, a dream from which we must awake if we are to uncover any genuine historical experience and rupture the 'dream formation of events as "the eternal return of the same"' (Benjamin, 2002: 546). 'The dreaming collective', writes Benjamin (2002: 546), thus 'knows no history. Events pass before it as always identical and always new'.

6 Mitchell has said in interview that he pastiched Herman Melville, Christopher Isherwood, generic 'airport thriller[s],' 'gossip magazines' and Russell Hoban's post-nuclear novel *Riddley Walker* (1980) for the different narrative voices in *Cloud Atlas* (*Washington Post*, 2004).

Works Cited

Arendt, Hannah (1958) *The Origins of Totalitarianism*. London: George Allen and Unwin.

Benjamin, Walter (2002) *The Arcades Project*, trans. Howard Eiland and Kevin McLaughlin. Cambridge, MA: The Belknap Press of Harvard University Press.

Berlin, Isaiah (1959/1990) *The Crooked Timber of Humanity: Chapters in the History of Ideas*. London: John Murray.

Bloch, Ernst (2000) *The Spirit of Utopia*, trans. Anthony A. Nassar. Stanford, CA: Stanford University Press.

Brown, Jonathan (2007) 'Sichuan: Tourists are Now Welcomed in the Chinese Province where Ancient Collides with Modern', *Independent*, 11 August, URL (consulted August 2009): http://www.independent.co.uk/travel/asia/sichuan-tourists-are-now-welcomed-in-the-chinese-province-where-ancient-collides-withmodern-461025.html

Buck-Morss, Susan (2002) *Dreamworld and Catastrophe: The Passing of Mass Utopia in East and West*. Cambridge, MA: The MIT Press.

Derrida, Jacques (1996) *Specters of Marx: The State of the Debt, the Work of Mourning and the New International*, trans. Peggy Kamuf. New York: Routledge.

Edwards, Caroline (2009) 'Microtopias: The Post-Apocalyptic Communities of Jim Crace's *The Pesthouse*', *Textual Practice* 23(5): 763–86

Edwards, Caroline (2010a) 'The Books Interview: David Mitchell', *New Statesman*, 11 August, URL (consulted August 2010): http://www.newstatesman.com/books/2010/08/japan-novels-exploitation-life

Edwards, Caroline (2010b) Extended interview with David Mitchell, unpublished (25 March).

Freeman, Jonathan (2004) 'A Six-stranded, Psychedelic Blend of Genres, Settings', *Boston Globe*, 29 August, URL (consulted August 2009): http://www.boston.com/ae/books/articles/2004/08/29/a_six_stranded_psychedelic_blend_of_genres_settings/?page=2

Hardt, Michael and Negri, Antonio (2005) *Multitude: War and Democracy in the Age of Empire*. London: Penguin Books.

Jacoby, Russell (2005) *Picture Imperfect: Utopian Thought for an Anti-Utopian Age*. New York: Columbia University Press.

Laclau, Ernesto and Mouffe, Chantal (2001) *Hegemony and Socialist Strategy: Towards a Radical Democratic Politics*. London: Verso.

Levitas, Ruth (2005) 'Utopia Matters?', in Fátima Vieira and Marinela Freitas (eds) *Utopia Matters: Theory, Politics, Literature and the Arts*. Porto: Universidade do Porto.

Lyotard, Jean-François (1997) *The Postmodern Condition: A Report on Knowledge*, trans. Geoffrey Bennington and Brian Massumi. Manchester: Manchester University Press.

McEwan, Ian (2006) *Saturday*. London: Vintage Books.

McWeeney, Caroline (2000) 'Interview with David Mitchell', *Bold Type* 4(7), URL (consulted February 2009): http://www.randomhouse.com/boldtype/1100/mitchell/interview.html

Marcuse, Herbert (1978/2003) *The Aesthetic Dimension: Toward a Critique of Marxist Aesthetics,* trans. Herbert Marcuse and Erica Sherover. Boston, MA: Beacon Press.

Marx, Karl (1971) *Economic and Philosophic Manuscripts of 1844,* in Karl Marx and Frederick Engels, *Collected Works, Vol. 3.* New York: International Publishers.

Moylan, Tom (1986) *Demand the Impossible: Science Fiction and the Utopian Imagination.* New York: Methuen.

Nancy, Jean-Luc (1991) *The Inoperative Community,* trans. Peter Connor, Lisa Garbus, Michael Holland and Simona Sawhney. Minneapolis: University of Minnesota Press.

Naughtie, James (2007) '*Cloud Atlas* – David Mitchell', BBC Radio 4 Bookclub, 3 June, URL (consulted June 2010): http://www.bbc.co.uk/radio4/arts/bookclub/ram/bookclub_20070603.ram

Popper, Karl (1945/1966) *The Open Society and Its Enemies, Vol. 1: The Spell of Plato.* London: Routledge and Kegan Paul.

Schoene, Berthold (2009) *The Cosmopolitan Novel.* Edinburgh: Edinburgh University Press.

Showalter, Elaine (2000) 'Eternal Triangles: Jeanette Winterson's *The Power-Book* is Lost in Cyberspace', *Guardian,* 2 September, URL (consulted October 2009): http://www.guardian.co.uk/books/2000/sep/02/fiction.jeanettewinterson1

Soros, George (1998) *The Crisis of Global Capitalism: Open Society Endangered.* London: Little, Brown.

Washington Post (2004) 'Q&A: Book World Talks with David Mitchell', 22 August, URL (consulted June 2010): http://www.washingtonpost.com/wp-dyn/articles/A17231–2004Aug19.html

Wells, H. G. (1905/2005) *A Modern Utopia.* London: Penguin.

Winter, Jay (2006) *Dreams of Peace and Freedom: Utopian Moments in the 20th Century.* London: Yale University Press.

9

SPECULATIVE FICTION AS POSTCOLONIAL CRITIQUE IN *GHOSTWRITTEN* AND *CLOUD ATLAS*

Nicholas Dunlop

One of the aspects of David Mitchell's fiction that has been eagerly seized upon by critics and readers alike is its tendency towards an inclusive and technically adventurous generic bricolage. Justine Jordan (2004), in her review of *Cloud Atlas* in the *Guardian*, refers to the 'genre-busting' author whose work 'knits together science fiction, political thriller and historical pastiche with musical virtuosity and linguistic exuberance'. Theo Tait (1999) in reviewing *Ghostwritten* for the *Telegraph* describes Mitchell as an 'alarmingly versatile writer' whose 'virtuoso performance is deeply impressive'. Tait also emphasizes how *Ghostwritten* 'effectively pastich[es] everything from Victorian travelogue to corporate kill-speak to airport thriller'. As these reviews indicate, Mitchell's work frequently oscillates between disparate narrative modes and conventions, among them the *Bildungsroman*, the conspiracy thriller, the epistolary novel, the ghost story, science fiction, magic realism, fantasy and realist autobiography. This formal ludicism firmly situates Mitchell's work within the realm of the postmodern, conflating as it does a panoramic range of cultural influences and various mediating strategies of apprehension and representation.

The privileging of the postmodern eclecticism of his work, incorporating and recalibrating a range of intertextual self-reflexive strategies, and its concomitant polyvalency of perspectives, means that it is tempting to assume an affiliation with those aspects of postmodernism which are most often criticized by the likes of Jameson and Habermas: namely, the relativistic ahistorical and apolitical aspects of the postmodern historical moment of late capitalism. Following this line of argument, Linda Hutcheon (1991: 168) contends that post-modernism is often 'politically ambivalent' and that any implied cri-tique of the prevailing historical and social conditions must paradoxi-cally 'coexist with an equally real and equally powerful complicity with the cultural dominants within which it inescapably exists'. In contrast, I want to suggest that while Mitchell's undoubted technical achieve-ment and its postmodern implications are indeed a central part of any discussion of his fiction, such a unilateral perspective runs the risk of sidelining Mitchell's imaginative dialogue with the politics of post-coloniality by overlooking the oppositional politicized engagement that his technique enables. Through a discussion of speculative fiction tropes in *Cloud Atlas* and *Ghostwritten*, this essay explores this often-overlooked political element of Mitchell's work.

Science Fiction and Fantasy as Subversive Modes

Speculative fiction is a contested term that has been taken to include such disparate narrative modes as science fiction, genre fantasy, hor-ror fiction, alternate history and magic realism. If literary realism, in its strictly mimetic form, is perceived to be inherently limited in its potential for subversion, speculative fiction can be seen to offer greater scope for the interrogation and reimagining of dominant po-litical ideologies. Characteristic of its postmodern appropriation of different narrative genres, Mitchell's work incorporates a hybridized form of speculative fiction that employs, but is not constrained by, both the conventions and narrative strategies of science fiction, and the techniques of the literary fantastic. The literary fantastic, as Lucie Armitt usefully summarizes, is a term originating in the work of Tz-vetan Todorov that describes:

> a mode of writing distinct from genre fantasy in two main ways. First, where genre fantasy deals in enclosed worlds, the literary fantastic deals in disruptive impulses. Second, where genre fantasy implies complicity on the part of readers, the literary fantastic actively seeks out reader hesitancy as a means of building in competing readings of the text. (Armitt, 2005: 7–8)

Echoing Armitt's choice of terminology in relation to the fantastic, Farah Mendlesohn (2003: 2) asserts that science fiction is also 'a discussion or a mode, and not a genre'. My analysis of Mitchell's novels is premised on this notion that both science fiction and the fantastic may most usefully be categorized not as genres, but as modes or 'discussions'. This position is one adopted by influential critics of each mode, particularly Rosemary Jackson in the case of fantasy, and Damien Broderick and Brian Aldiss with regard to science fiction.[1] Rather than prescriptive formal templates, the labels 'science fiction' and 'the fantastic' are instead best viewed as ideological orientations based on the interrogation of dominant cultural forms. This process is enabled by, and most clearly evident in, each mode's capacity for articulating and extending what Samuel R. Delany (2009: 10) calls 'subjunctivity' – a term usefully glossed by Brooks Landon (2002: 8) as 'the tension between the words of ... [a] story and their referents'. Accordingly, productive politicized analyses of these modes tend to focus on this semiotic tension and its interrogative aspect rather than placing a decontextualized emphasis on structural characteristics.

The fantastic and the science-fictional are discrete modes that resist simplistic efforts towards conflation, and generate the crucial semiotic hesitation alluded to earlier in distinct ways. Making this point, Darko Suvin (1979: 4) suggests that in direct opposition to the 'cognitive estrangement' of science fiction, the fantastic is an 'anti-cognitive' (Suvin, 1979: 8) metaphysical mode that lacks rigour and is therefore unsuitable for extrapolation. For Suvin, what characterizes science fiction is the novum – the diachronically-displaced point of discontinuity, often technological but never supernatural, which marks out the narrative space as profoundly distinct from the implied reader's immediate experiential environment. The fantastic, Suvin (1979: 8) proposes, in allowing the intervention of the unscientific and supernatural, is 'committed to the interposition of anti-cognitive laws into the empirical environment'. Through this process it 'causes a grotesque tension between arbitrary supernatural phenomena and the empirical norms they infiltrate' (Suvin, 1979: 8). Reorienting and elaborating upon Suvin's argument, I want to suggest that this very 'tension', though taking different forms, is in fact what embodies the fundamental affiliation between the modes of science fiction and the fantastic.

It is apparent that the means of articulating disruption of these empirical norms within fantasy and science fiction may differ (as Suvin suggests with his emphasis on the cognitive possibility of the novum), but it can be argued that they share an originating impulse – both are based on the principle of hesitation, and this principle may be considered a key element in the radical potential of each. Todorov (1975: 25), as outlined earlier, foregrounds the concept of hesitancy as crucial, and defines the fantastic as 'that hesitation experienced by a person who knows only the laws of nature, confronting an apparently supernatural event'. Echoing this, Istvan Csicsery-Ronay (1991: 387) defines science fiction as not a coherent 'generic effects engine', but rather a 'mode of awareness, characterized by two linked forms of hesitation, a pair of gaps'. The first of these gaps relates to the space 'between the conceivability of future transformations and the possibility of their actualization' (Csicsery-Ronay, 1991: 387). The second, and perhaps more theoretically significant, hesitation embodies the oscillation between the plausibility of the novum – the (often technological) point of discontinuity that characterizes the narrative as science fiction – and the ethical and sociological implications of its creation and manipulation. Csicsery-Ronay writes of science fiction that,

> [it] names the gap between, on the one hand, belief in the immanent possibility (and perhaps inexorable necessity) of those transformations, and, on the other, reflection about their possible ethical, social, and spiritual interpretations (i.e. about their embeddedness in a web of social-historical relations). (Csicsery-Ronay, 1991: 388)

If we extend this theoretical formulation to incorporate the literature of fantasy as well, it is apparent that the antagonism towards, and consequent rejection and recalibration of, realist norms mean each mode has great radical or subversive potential. This is because they offer the disruptive potential for literalization of metaphor. The mechanics of the discontinuity such literalization facilitates – whether that discontinuity is the 'plausible' novum or the inexplicable fantastic

'tension' whereof Suvin speaks – and its subsequent enabling of critical reimaginings, is crucial in constructing meaningful social and cultural interventions.

Jackson, as the title of her seminal study *Fantasy: The Literature of
Subversion* indicates, proposes that fantasy is the ultimate subversive
literature in its potential for reorienting our perspective on empirical social experience, while Teresa de Lauretis (1980: 170) argues
with reference to science fiction that, 'the construction of a possible
world ... entails a conceptual reorganization of semantic space and
therefore of material and social relations, and makes for an expanded
cognitive horizon, an epic vision of our present social reality'. This
last phrase is most resonant in the context of my own argument, as I
wish to sideline considerations of technique *qua* technique, focusing
instead on the deployment of modal conventions to generate a range
of possible imagined futures. Mitchell subtly yet consciously embeds
postcolonial critiques in his fiction, using these imbricating strategies
not simply to knowingly reflect what Elleke Boehmer (2005: 238)
characterizes as postmodernism's celebratory concern with 'all things
parodied, piebald, dual, mimicked, always-already borrowed, and
ironically secondhand', but also to adopt a more humanistic, empath-
ic and engaged perspective that eschews the postmodern tendency
towards politically anaesthetized or otherwise complicit texts, articulating instead a persuasively subversive reading of the history, present
and projected future of colonialism and its associated ideologies.

'Realism' and Neo/Postcolonialism in *Ghostwritten* and *Cloud Atlas*

Mitchell draws upon a range of conventions from both the fantastic
and science-fictional modes to great effect to interrogate and renego-
tiate a particular set of material and social relations – the discourses of
colonialism in its overtly ideological initial phase and its more insidious neo-colonial guise. *Ghostwritten* and *Cloud Atlas* repeatedly allude
to the discourses of power in relation to notions of race and culture,
and their various ideological and physical manifestations. These allusions are not limited to the speculative modules of the novels, but

constitute notable elements of what may be termed the mimetic or putatively realistic sections as well. These non-speculative modules frequently evoke Hutcheon's (1991: 169) category of 'historiographic metafiction', in their ironic initiation of what she terms a 'dialogue with history', which can be read as part of a recalibratory postcolonial strategy.

In *Cloud Atlas*, for example, the opening (and closing) narrative of 'The Pacific Journal of Adam Ewing' engages with the installation and maintenance of European imperial authority in its expansive phase in the mid-nineteenth century. References to 'the dark arts of colonization' (*CA*, 14) and pseudo-scientific analyses of racial difference and cultural hierarchization abound throughout the narrative and Adam Ewing himself, when faced with the claims to prominence of an exiled Englishman who seeks to elevate his status within the colonial context by exaggerating his metropolitan achievements, tellingly reveals that 'I am versed enough in Antipodese etiquette to let such unlikely truths lie' (*CA*, 4). Such asides, seemingly incidental to the narrative thrust of the novel, in actuality articulate a persuasively knowing reconstruction of the imperial project as a narcissistic fantasy of aggrandisement, motivated by a desire for a coherent Self rather than the purported aim of civilizing and assimilating the Other within imperialistic discourse. When the ideologically synecdochic Preacher Horrox delivers his risible sermon on the teleological necessity of 'Progress' and the essentialist racial politics of what he terms 'Civilization's Ladder' (*CA*, 506), this may profitably be read as Mitchell's evocation of the critical possibilities of the conflation of the postmodern and the postcolonial aesthetics. Horrox's speech engenders the twin responses of: first, an ironic rejection, recalling Lyotard, of the kinds of overarching narratives that underpin and facilitate the enactment of colonization and cultural exploitation; and, second, by emphasizing the ideological contradictions inherent in the emptily benign rhetoric of colonization, the enactment of a parodic negotiation of 'the once tyrannical weight of colonial history' (Hutcheon, 1991: 169).

In addition to this perhaps somewhat obvious engagement with the European colonial projects of the past, Mitchell's work in its 'realist' guise takes its critique beyond the simplistic and historically static binary model of colonialism, which posits an unproblematic and hierarchized relationship between the Oriental object and Occidental subject, to argue the need for a more nuanced set of culturally specific responses. In the 'Holy Mountain' narrative segment of *Ghostwritten*, for instance, there are ironic allusions to the universality of the colonizing impulse, with the Tea Shack of the narrator's father being 'requisitioned by His Imperial Egg of Japan' (*G*, 120) during her childhood. The obfuscatory discourse of appropriation is revealed to be not simply the historical residue of European hegemony, but rather a continually self-replicating means of regulating and erasing resistance and/or difference, as evidenced by the quasi-religious performative statement of the soldiers. This simultaneously assigns and withholds subjectivity from the narrator and her family: 'The Holy Mountain now belongs to the Asian Sphere of Co-prosperity. We are here to percolate our Sick Mother China from the evil of the European imperialists' (*G*, 120). Predation and economic exploitation under the rhetoric of nationalistic enlightenment and cultural authenticity are for Mitchell clearly part of what David Punter (2000: 3) characterizes in *Postcolonial Imaginings* as the violently assertive 'new world order' of late capitalism. Embedded within Mitchell's analysis of this ongoing process, however, remains a tantalizing if marginalized hint of resistance and reconfiguration of the homogenizing impulse of cultural neo-colonialism. In the 'Tokyo' narrative of *Ghostwritten*, for instance, the protagonist suggests this potential when he sardonically describes Japanese counter-culture's mimicry and mockingly knowing reverse colonization of western forms:

> Then one of them asked why Japanese kids try to ape American kids? The clothes, the rap music, the skateboards, the hair. I wanted to say it's not America they're aping, it's the Japan of their parents that they're rejecting. And since there's no home-grown counter-culture, they just take hold of the nearest one to hand, which happens to be American. But it's not American culture exploiting us. It's us exploiting it. (*G*, 44)

Crucially, the final phrase here is 'lost in translation' by Satoru's friend, hinting at the preservation of cultural difference and the possibility of appropriating and subverting the discourses of the dominant neo-colonizing culture.

Ghostwritten and Postcolonial Haunting

Non-speculative strategies of postcolonial interrogation in *Ghostwritten* and *Cloud Atlas* are effective and frequently persuasive. But the two novels most successfully manifest their destabilizing potential in the different and perhaps more thought-provoking responses by the two speculative modes. In their deployment of science fictional and fantastic conventions both novels suggest a symbolic grammar for articulating and exploring what J. P. Telotte (1990: 152) has usefully categorized as 'a space of desire', an unbounded place within the self where we can imaginatively experience a kind of otherness, and speculate about alternative modes of being and the tantalizing possibility of transcendence. This space is fluid, nebulous, open and transitory; its modal mutability offers a range of potential responses, unconstrained by temporal or spatial boundaries.

The literary fantastic in *Ghostwritten* is a suitably ghostly presence throughout the novel, hovering in a phantasmic way on the edges of the narrative even in the non-speculative episodes. The presence of this potentially disruptive perspective, an ideologically subversive polyphony of marginalized discourses of racial and cultural displacement, is proleptically alluded to in the novel's title. Even the opening line – 'Who was blowing on the nape of my neck?' (*G*, 3) – is aimed at unsettling the implied reader and generating hesitancy in a manner that recalls Edgar Allan Poe or M. R. James.[2] Most effectively, however, in the 'Hong Kong' narrative, Mitchell presents a profoundly metafictional postmodern ghost story of sorts, in that the episode literalizes and traces the ambiguity between the real and the imagined that Todorov theorizes. The narrative is superficially a tale of a failed marriage, corporate greed and neo-colonial financial exploitation, but Mitchell introduces and begins to work through the uncanny psychological processes characteristic of the fantastic experience when Neal

Brose, the protagonist, encounters what appears to be the ghost of a little girl. Narrated in the first person, the ambivalence in his initial response is startling in its blatant paradoxicality: 'I knew she was there, and I knew there was no such child' (*G*, 83). Brose experiences the dialogue between the real and the imagined which characterizes the experience of Todorov's protagonist and, by extension, the implied reader, as defined in *The Fantastic*:

> In a world which is indeed our world ... there occurs an event which cannot be explained by the laws of this same familiar world. The person who experiences the event must opt for one of two possible solutions: either he is the victim of an illusion of the senses, of a product of the imagination – and the laws of the world then remain what they are; or else the event has indeed taken place, it is an integral part of reality – but then this reality is controlled by laws unknown to us. (Todorov, 1975: 25)

The intrusion of the possibility that the apparition of the child may be real, embodied in Brose's initial cognitive response 'Fear breathed on the nape of my neck' (*G*, 83), is offset at first by Brose's rational appeal to the likelihood of temporary illusion – 'Reason entered, brandishing its warrant. It ordered that I behave as though nothing untoward was happening' (*G*, 83). This internal dialogue between conflicting interpretations of the uncanny event then becomes more heated, with more seemingly at stake: '*There's a fucking ghost in your apartment! A fucking ghost, you hear me?*' (*G*, 83). 'Nobody, and nothing. *See?* said Reason, smugly ... Behind my back I heard her giggle. *Fuck you,* said Fear to Reason' (*G*, 83–4). In giving full rein to his fear, Brose's narrative enacts an initial rejection of the Todorovian imaginary in favour of the 'real'. However, despite this apparent decisiveness, there remains a fundamental ambivalence at play throughout this section of the narrative.

The epistemological ambiguities of Brose's perspective ensure that the 'Hong Kong' module resists authoritative classification as regards the literary-fantastic mode that the narrative employs. Todorov makes a systematic distinction between what he delineates as neighbouring modes of the fantastic: the uncanny and the marvellous. The uncanny, classifies events that are ultimately explainable by science, which may be readily accounted for by the laws of reason, but which are, in one way or another, incredible, extraordinary, shocking, singular, disturbing or unexpected, and which thereby provoke in the character and in the reader a reaction similar to that which works of the fantastic have made familiar. (Todorov, 1975: 46)

The other, the marvellous, classifies events as genuinely supernatural and inexplicable. The former interpretation of Brose's experience is hinted at, with the possibility that the child may be merely a hallucination brought about by his diabetic condition. A more convincing reading involves invoking the concept of postcolonial haunting as a process of reparation and renegotiation. As David Punter (2000: vi) writes, 'the process of postcolonial abjection is ... one that confronts us every day in the ambiguous form of a series of uncanny returns'. Mitchell's adoption of the speculative mode of the fantastic enables him to ambiguously literalize this metaphor of postcolonial haunting in the figure of the ghostly girl in the apartment.

Brose seems to be a prime candidate for precisely this kind of phantasmic return of the repressed colonial voice. As Justin D. Edwards (2008: 121) writes, 'to be haunted is to be called upon ... for the phantom presence returns to collect an unpaid debt'. Brose's complicity in the economic exploitation of what he significantly terms 'the colonies. Well, the ex-colonies' (G, 85) is immediately apparent. As a financial lawyer, Brose is, like Preacher Horrox in Cloud Atlas, a synecdochic figure of imperial complicity, representing one branch of the ideological state apparatuses that operates primarily to maintain and replicate the ideological structures of late capitalism and its neo-colonial aspects. It is revealing that Brose is watching Die Hard 3 (1995), a key signifier of western cultural production, dubbed into Cantonese when the ghost first appears. The ghost's 'voicing' of the physical and psychological violence of the colonial past fantastically mirrors the intrusion of the marginalized colonial voice into the discourse of western culture; the figure of the ghost can be decoded as the postcolonial Gothic manifestation of Neal's guilt regarding his role in an ongoing process of displacement, manipulation and exploitation.

Brose is all too clearly aware of the historic inequities of colonial-ism, as he makes clear when he traces the history of the colonial space he currently inhabits:

> How about this? Hong Kong had been appropriated by British drug pushers in the 1840s ... When the Chinese understandably objected to this arrangement, we kicked the fuck out of them, set up a pup-pet government ... and occupied this corner of their country as an import base. Fucking godawful behaviour, when you think about it. (*G*, 107–8)

Thus, the ghost articulates the necessary confrontation of the postco-lonial subject with the traces of the past – in Edwards's (2008: 121) words, the debt called upon by such ghostly figures 'refers back to the imperial dominance and territorial appropriation that forces the voice of the colonized into the unconscious of the imperial subject and thus haunts the colonizer across generations, time and space'. Mitchell's novel, however, characteristically moves beyond the narrow historical moment of European imperialism to encompass the contemporary sense of climactic and repressed guilt concerning globalized capitalism and its exploitation of geographic and cultural specificity in an age that is putatively 'post'-colonial. The categorization of Hong Kong as a nebulous, fluid space where the rigid moral and legal stric-tures of the west cease to apply gestures towards the contradictorily coherent hegemony of neo-colonialism: 'Now in London, New York, everyone knows what's what. The playing field is even, the goalposts are fixed. But Asia is the last wild frontier, eh? ... Regulators? Forget 'em! Paid off. Every last man ... I'm talking about originality in cap-ital-manipulation! About reinterpretation!' (*G*, 106). The hypocrisy, ideological myopia, and ongoing enactment of economic and social relations of dependency and control implicated in this 'reinterpreta-tion' (or renegotiation) manifest in Brose's psyche.

This interrogation of narrowly appropriative and exploitative epis-temologies is further developed in the 'Mongolia' narrative in *Ghost-written*. Typically, Mitchell's fiction is postmodern in its rejection of simplistic allegorical and directly metaphorical strategies. This fantas-tic segment can usefully be read as both a parable of anxieties about the human body as a potential site of appropriation and exploitation by a powerful external agency, and as the literal working out of some of the implications of the conceptualization of colonialism as a process of contagion and contamination. Once again, the narrative mode deployed is ambiguous: the narration of the '*noncorpum*' seems to oscillate continually between (in Todorovian terms) fantastic-uncanny and fantastic-marvellous, prolonging the ontological hesitation on the part of the reader and perpetually deferring the possibility of a definitive meaning. This process of deferral is particularly apparent in the description of the process by which the *noncorpum* switches between human bodies:

> Once or twice I've tried to describe transmigration to the more imaginative of my human hosts. It's impossible. I know eleven languages, but there are some tunes that language cannot play ... When another human touches my host, I can transmigrate. The ease of the transfer depends on the mind I am transmigrating into, and whether negative emotions are blocking me. The fact that touch is a requisite provides a clue that I exist on some physical plane, however sub-cellular or bio-electrical. (*G*, 165)

A range of postcolonial anxieties converge and are interrogated in this passage. This ambiguous process cannot be seamlessly assimilated within westernized scientific discourse. Even the quasi-scientific name assigned to this process seems calculatedly opaque, the tautological redundancy of its component parts serving to obfuscate rather than clarify meaning. The semantic hesitation evident in the term 'transmigrating' – which, in invoking both a 'physical plane' and 'negative emotions', seems to oscillate between absorption within the discursive structures of western epistemology and resistance towards those structures – suggests both a Lyotardian scepticism toward the monolithic metanarrative of scientific explanation, and an awareness of the limitations of the mediating discourse of language itself. In its attempt at ontological self-definition, the *noncorpum* can provide only clues and hints rather than the Euclidean scientific proof necessary for immutable meaning.

This disparity between discursive codes and empirical experience, then, encodes a critique of the claims to authority of colonial discourse – in the Lacanian sense that power is the ability to limit and restrict meaning, objective scientist colonial discourse suppresses 'deviant' epistemologies, and *Ghostwritten* tentatively proposes, with its references to 'imagination' and 'emotions', alternative approaches to perceiving and experiencing the world that privilege individual experience and cultural specificity. When the *noncorpum* states that 'it was good to transmigrate out of a Westernised head' (*G*, 166), the narrative displaces the monolithic status of Eurocentric epistemology, emphasizing instead a profound, yet marginalized, variety of epistemological systems. By so doing, *Ghostwritten* posits a potential shift towards a hybridized, fluid mode of knowledge not constrained (or embodied) by static formulations. Like the 'Hong Kong' narrative, the fantastic in this case offers a subversive means of vocalizing and, in Spivak's (1988: 280) term, partially ameliorating the 'epistemic violence' endemic in neo-colonialism.

In 'Mongolia', the narrator's corporeal colonization of European tourists may also be read as another means of textual resistance in its metaphorical enactment of an ironically inverted cultural contamination and the insidious assimilatory strategies characteristic of neo-colonialism – the *noncorpum*, despite its marginalized status, displaces and ultimately overinscribes the subjectivity and agency of its host, invading and manipulating body and memory in a way that deliberately invokes the physical and cultural reorganization of cultural discourses performed by colonialism and its ideological successors. The *noncorpum* is, like the Hong Kong ghost, a usefully liminal presence in the narrative, eschewing a single authoritative perspective in favour of a polyphony of fluid micronarratives. By operating simultaneously as a colonizing agent and as a radically displaced entity seeking its own originary myth, the *noncorpum*'s subversive ambiguity enables Mitchell to construct and articulate his sophisticated analysis of the politics of neo-colonialism.

In the 'Clear Island' segment, the narrative adopts a more directly science-fictional mode imbricated within a Crichton-esque techno-thriller format. The island narrative marks a bridge between the earlier emphasis on the interplay between the fantastic and the realistic, charting a shift towards the extrapolated cognitive future of the 'Night Train' module. The shift from Todorovian hesitation and the synchronic speculation of the fantastic gives way to the diachronic extrapolations of science fiction as, through the figure of the ethical scientist Mo Muntervary, we witness the origins and early development of the artificial intelligence that will eventually become the sentient 'Zookeeper' in the climactic segment of the novel. References to colonial resistance are studded throughout the near-future narrative of 'Night Train' and a number of clues indicate the continuing existence of the neo-colonial mechanisms of late capitalism. One of the callers to the talk radio show, for instance, explicitly delivers a manifesto for exposing and resisting neo-colonial hypocrisy and its transparent rhetoric of postcolonialism. It is what Punter (2000: 124) terms an alibi for this new world order:

> For centuries the West has bound us in chains. When iron shackles became too embarrassing for their sensibilities, they replaced them with chains of debt. When we chose rulers who tried to resist, the West shot these rulers down and replaced them with pliable tyrants. (*G*, 408)

The fantastic and science fictional modes are intertwined into a fittingly hybridized narrative form in the apocalyptic climax to the novel, as the two 'entities' – one a rigidly cognitive Suvinian novum, the other a fluid manifestation of the Todorovian fantastic-marvellous – engage in a dialogue of ontological equivalence, with the *noncorpum* mockingly asking, 'How could a being with your resources believe yourself to be the only non-corporeal sentient intelligence wandering the surface of creation?' (*G*, 422). Ultimately, although the narrative seems to suggest the ontological triumph of the rational cognitive over the multivocalic fantastic – the Zookeeper appears to eliminate the *noncorpum* in a burst of electronic noise – *Ghostwritten* leaves much of its generated hesitation unresolved and, with its tantalizing hints of a transformed future, leaves the reader asking questions about the distributions and flows of power within both a colonial and neo-colonial context.

Cloud Atlas and Dystopia

In *Cloud Atlas*, Mitchell deploys the tropes of speculative fiction alongside realist generic pastiches to elaborate upon the apocalyptic implications of unequal socio-economic relations first proposed in *Ghostwritten*. The narrative segment 'An Orison of Sonmi~451' eschews the ambiguity of Todorovian hesitation entirely, focusing instead primarily upon a diachronically-displaced technological novum. In inscribing contemporary anxieties pertaining to race and colonialism onto the ambivalent figure of Sonmi, the narrative literalizes Jameson's conception of science fiction as a 'structurally unique method for apprehending the present as history' (Jameson, 2005: 288), in order to unmask and work through the ideological contradictions of our own historical moment.[3]

The extrapolated future environment of Nea So Copros is a world where all potential sites of physical and ideological dissent and difference are eradicated, marginalized or flattened, reflecting the diagnoses of contemporary urban culture by Jameson in *Postmodernism, or the Cultural Logic of Late Capitalism* and Punter in *Postcolonial Imaginings*. As such, Nea So Copros operates as what Constance Penley (1990: 117) usefully terms a 'critical dystopia', namely an imagined dystopic future that progresses beyond mere description of symptoms to actively engage with the potential causes of social dysfunction. Some of these sites of dissent and fragmentation throughout the history of colonialism are alluded to in the narrative's inversion of established binaries of western dominance; for instance, Nea So Copros, encoded as the vibrant centre of human achievement, is located in what is contemporary Korea, and there are knowing references to the 'Californian Boat-people solution' (*CA*, 224), suggesting a catastrophic reordering of the circulation of global power structures in the near future. However, if as Robert Scholes (1975: 22) argues, the primary purpose of science fiction is to confront the ideological schisms of our contemporary world 'in some cognitive way', then it soon becomes apparent that the novum itself – the troublesome and menacing figure of the fabricant – is precisely the locus of that confrontation.

'An Orison of Sonmi~451' constitutes a meditation upon a complex intersection of anxieties concerning identity, authenticity and technology, each of which has a (post) and (neo) colonial aspect. The narrative draws upon the radical potential of science fiction by literalizing a set of critical metaphors; in this case, both Haraway's (1991) evocative conception of the cyborg as a model for scrutinizing the cultural construction of the self and, more persuasively, the embodiment of what Adam Roberts (2006a: 118) calls 'the alterity of the machine, the paranoid sense of the inorganic come to life'. The ontological status of the fabricant, though articulated as cognitively coherent and definitively Other, is nonetheless perpetually unsettled in the narrative, oscillating between organic and inorganic, simultaneously manifesting properties of the machine, the human, the clone and the cyborg. Sonmi is the science-fictional (cognitive) *alter ego* of the disembodied *noncorpum* of *Ghostwritten*, embodied in this case in an empirically realized but socially marginalized corpum that is engineered as Other at the genetic level. Both physically and ideologically, Sonmi is, in Bhabha's well-worn phrase, 'almost the same, but not quite' (*CA*, 84), the product of a profoundly flawed mimesis where to be a fabricant is emphatically not to be human. Decoding the postcolonial politics of the novel, Sonmi's ontological instability invokes that which is described by LeiLani Nishime (2005: 34) in her analysis of the 'mulatto cyborg' as an analogue for the displaced and racially hybrid postcolonial subject. Nishime (2005: 35) observes that it is a small step to interpret 'anxieties about the incoherence of the body of the cyborg as a parallel to the confusion and concern that centers on the body of the multiracial human'. It is thus fitting that the body of the fabricant is the site upon which Mitchell focuses his postcolonial critique.

As Scott Bukatman (1993: 19) notes, science fiction 'obsessively substitutes the rational for the corporeal, the technological for the organic'. Bukatman identifies here the unsettled and frequently anxious engagement of SF with the simultaneous attraction and threat of technology and its intrusion upon the physical and cognitive boundaries of the human. This engagement – a central feature of much science fiction, from Mary Shelley's *Frankenstein* (1818) to Philip K. Dick's

Do Androids Dream of Electric Sheep? (1968) – recalls and crystallizes the ontological uncertainties inherent in Martin Heidegger's distinction, in 'The Question Concerning Technology' (1978), between *types* of existence; namely the fundamental ontological rupture between the existence of a being with agency and subjectivity – what he terms *Dasein* – and the lesser existence of the 'technical object', which we categorize purely in terms of its utility (*Zuhandenheit*). As Adam Roberts (2006b: 12) has usefully observed, '[o]ne of the key themes of SF for the last half-century has been precisely to delineate and explore the place where the technical object achieves *Dasein*, a Being-in-the-World and a Being-Towards-Death'. The 'Sonmi' narrative is the quest of the technical object – the enslaved fabricant – for access to precisely this kind of authentic Being-in-the-World, suggesting a newly hybridized mode of existence that collapses established boundaries. 'Myself xcepted, fabricants are the ultimate organic machinery' (*CA*, 341–2).

This Heideggerian uncertainty is extended in the future society of *Cloud Atlas* and imbricated with the ambivalent discourse of colonialism, which consistently manifests the same self-conscious uncertainties about the dismantling of the epistemological categories of identity, authenticity and ontological certainty. By literally embodying these anxieties, Sonmi enacts and enables the return of the repressed colonial Other – the marginalized and enslaved technical object of colonialism – in her manifestation as 'an emphatic, techno-organic reconstruction of the flesh' (Bukatman, 1993: 19). Like the ghostly little girl and the *noncorpum* of *Ghostwritten*, the figure of Sonmi, by enacting this cognitive mode of technological haunting, provides an outlet for exposing displaced colonial complicity in both its historical and contemporary phases – as Sonmi challenges her interviewer (and, by extension, the reader), 'do you still maintain there are no slaves in Nea So Copros?' (*CA*, 342).

Sonmi's potential for physical metamorphosis is a more directly unsettling form of Bhabhaian mimicry. In exploiting scientific progress in order to subversively disguise herself as human, Sonmi performs a profoundly transgressive action which, in its infiltration of the colonial symbolic, reveals contradictory anxieties about the linked discourses of (neo)-colonialism and technology. The 'facescaping' technology may be profitably understood as the literalization of the colonial metaphor of difference. It is significant that Sonmi is corporeally altered by technological means to 'pass' as human by altering her genetically-encoded physical signifiers of otherness, her homogenous yet uncanny 'server's features'.[4] She states that 'my ivory irises were hazelized, my eyes lengthened and my hair follicles ebonized' (CA, 337–8). It is only by committing to this physical transformation that Sonmi can begin to access authentic Being, since fabricants are actively denied agency and differentiation within this society.

The fabricants's genetic Otherness is inculcated and further internalized through an Althusserian process of perpetual interpellation, reinforced by the quasi-religious discourse of Papa Song. It is apt, then, that Sonmi's initially superficial mimicry of the colonizing body is mirrored and reinforced by the rebellious fabricant Yoona, whose own consciously resistant strategy of mimicry focuses on manipulating and recalibrating the performance and discursive practices of dominance: 'Yoona-939 mimicked the consumer. When we mopped the diners' hygiener, Yoona pretended to be an ill-mannered pureblood. She yawned, chewed, sneezed, burped and acted drunk. She hummed Papa Song's Psalm in absurd deviations' (CA, 191–2). The process of 'ascension' clearly has a subversive linguistic element, with Yoona's parodic rearticulation of the discourse of authority serving to foreground the imbrication of language and power within the discursive structures of colonialism and late capitalism. Yoona's acts of subversion manifest the expressive potential of the subject that is ideologically denied to the colonized subject. Her strategy of imitating becomes ever more sophisticated until the fundamental signifiers of difference and inferiority are placed under erasure: 'Yoona's language grew more complex ... [her] speech was filled with blanks the rest of us could not register. She sounded pureblood' (CA, 191). As with Sonmi – whose physical transformation marks the onset of an ideological and political metamorphosis – Yoona's exaggerated parody of consumer discourse is 'at once resemblance and menace' (Bhabha, 1994: 86).

In different ways, the resistant behaviours of Yoona and Sonmi enact precisely that uncannily destabilizing mimicry which engenders the 'double vision which in disclosing the ambivalence of colonial discourse also disrupts its authority' (Bhabha, 1994: 88). Bhabha's well-known formulation is a critical metaphor of mimesis and its destabilizing potential, and its metaphorical impact is successfully appropriated and literalized by Mitchell within his narrative: 'Try this: fabricants are mirrors held up to purebloods' consciences; what purebloods see therein sickens them. So they blame the mirrors' (*CA*, 231). The threat posed by the resemblance of the fabricants to the purebloods is a persuasive analogue for that posed to colonial discourse, foregrounding and questioning its myopic construction and articulation of the other as a means of formulating a stable identity of the Self. Ultimately, Sonmi and Yoona represent the omnipresent yet repressed possibility of disruption and inversion inherent within that discourse.

As in *Ghostwritten*, the narrative of Sonmi eschews easy answers, with both figures of resistance meeting violent ends and the status quo remaining apparently intact.[5] This ambivalence is entirely in keeping with Jameson's (1991: 288) assertion that science fiction is about forcing a critical perspective on the present, 'regardless of the "optimism" or "pessimism" of the imaginary future world which is the pretext for that defamiliarization'. In a revelatory move, *Cloud Atlas* juxtaposes an extrapolated apocalyptic future with its dialectical opposite: the ultimate social breakdown outlined in "Sloosha's Crossin'" may well lie at the centre, and the farthest future, of the novel, but the novel's structure denies it any status of historical inevitability; rather, the novel beings and ends with the contrastingly optimitic humanism, albeit in the distant past, of Adam Ewing.[6] Mitchell's speculative critique thereby eschews the metanarrative of historical inevitability and instead suggests infinite choice and multiple alternative 'futures'. In doing so, the novel reinforces an interventionist and resistant perspective, emphasizing and imaginatively tracing a plurality of potential outcomes to the ideological forces of the present.

Conclusion

Neither *Ghostwritten* nor *Cloud Atlas* are texts that produce answers or solutions to the problematics of postcolonial and neo-colonial discourse; rather, each asks significant questions and offers some potentially alternative modes of thinking about the world and re-structuring its mechanisms of dominance and exploitation. This resistant potential is most effectively rendered by Mitchell's deployment of the twin speculative modes of the fantastic and science fiction. As Jameson (1991: 286) argues, science fiction enables us to register diachronic 'fantasies about the future'. Mitchell's work demonstrates that the cognitive emphasis of science fiction may function effectively alongside the synchronic emphasis and ontological ambivalence of the literary fantastic in order to provide a bifocal critical perspective on the ideological contradictions of the present. Mitchell uses speculative modes alongside the realistic, but not to posit an immutable and inevitable dystopic future rooted in a doomed present. Rather, these technically adventurous texts persuasively diagnose contemporary and historical systems of colonial dominance. They satirize the discursive formations and empirical practices that enable and reinforce that dominance and, ultimately, propose a multivocal and open-ended range of potential responses to the problematic past and possible futures of colonialism.

Notes

1 See Rosemary Jackson's *Fantasy: The Literature of Subversion* (1981), Brian W. Aldiss and David Wingrove's *Trillion Year Spree* (1986) and Damien Broderick's *Reading by Starlight: Postmodern Science Fiction* (1995).

2 See, for instance, M. R. James's *Ghost Stories* (1904/1994) and Edgar Allan Poe's *Tales of Mystery and Imagination* (1908/2008).

3 It is worth noting that the modular narrative structure of *Cloud Atlas* as a whole literally seeks to re-present the 'present as history', as each module explicitly re-presents the events of the previous module as petrified historical artefact – for instance, Rufus Sixsmith reads Adam Ewing's journal, Sonmi watches the motion picture of the Ghastly Ordeal of Timothy Cavendish, and, most obviously, the holographic testament of Sonmi her-

self is a central feature of the 'final' post-apocalyptic narrative 'Sloosha's Crossin' an' Ev'rythin' After'.

4 Ironically, Sonmi is aware that the homogeneity of fabricant faces is in fact purely a matter of myopic hegemonic perception. Her assertion that 'all fabricants, even same-stem fabricants, are singular as snowflakes. Pureblood eyes cannot discern these differences, but they exist' (*CA*, 191) is a further subtle interrogation of the essentialist Othering of racial discourse.

5 Sonmi, like many robotic or cyborg figures in science fiction, from Asimov's 'Bicentennial Man' to Roy Batty in *Blade Runner* (1982), seems only to finally attain that Heideggerian Being-Towards-Death characteristic of 'humanity' when facing her own extinction.

6 Interestingly, the imagined dystopia of 'Sloosha's Crossin'' seems to be pessimistic proof of Jameson's belief that the innate ideological contradictions of the present necessarily result in 'our inability to imagine' (Jameson, 1991: 288) a desirable or utopian future.

Works Cited

Aldiss, Brian W. and Wingrove, David (1986) *Trillion Year Spree: The History of Science Fiction*. London: Victor Gollancz.

Armitt, Lucy (2005) *Fantasy Fiction: An Introduction*. New York and London: Continuum.

Bhabha, Homi (1994) *The Location of Culture*. London and New York: Routledge.

Boehmer, Elleke (2005) *Colonial and Postcolonial Literature: Migrant Metaphors*. Oxford: Oxford University Press.

Broderick, Damien (1995) *Reading By Starlight: Postmodern Science Fiction*. London and New York: Routledge.

Bukatman, Scott (1993) *Terminal Identity: The Virtual Subject in Postmodern Science Fiction*. Durham, NC and London: Duke University Press.

Csicsery-Ronay, Istvan (1991) 'The SF of Theory: Baudrillard and Haraway', *Science Fiction Studies* 18: 387–404.

Delany, Samuel R. (2009) *The Jewel-Hinged Jaw: Notes on the Language of Science Fiction*. Middletown, CT: Wesleyan University Press.

De Lauretis, Teresa (1980) 'Signs of Wo/ander', in Teresa De Lauretis, Andreas Huyssen and Kathleen Woodward (eds) *The Technological Imagination: Theories and Fictions*, pp. 159–74. Madison, WI: Coda Press.

Edwards, Justin D. (2008) *Postcolonial Literature*. Basingstoke: Palgrave.

Haraway, Donna (1991) *Simians, Cyborgs and Women: The Reinvention of Nature*. London and New York: Routledge.

Heidegger, Martin (1978) 'The Question Concerning Technology', in *Basic Writings*, pp. 283–318. London and Henley: Routledge & Kegan Paul.

Hutcheon, Linda (1991) 'Circling the Downspout of Empire', in Ian Adam and Helen Tiffin (eds) *Past the Last Post: Theorising Post-colonialism and Post-modernism*, pp. 167–90. Hemel Hempstead: Harvester Wheatsheaf.

Jackson, Rosemary (1981) *Fantasy: The Literature of Subversion*. London and New York: Methuen.

James, M. R. (1904/1994) *Ghost Stories*. Harmondsworth: Penguin Popular Classics.

Jameson, Fredric (1991) *Postmodernism, or The Cultural Logic of Late Capitalism*. London: Verso.

Jameson, Fredric (2005) *Archaeologies of the Future: The Desire Called Utopia and Other Science Fictions*. London: Verso.

Jordan, Justine (2003) 'Seconds Out', *Guardian*, 27 December, URL (consulted November 2009): http://www.guardian.co.uk/books/2003/dec/27/featuresreviews.guardianreview9

Landon, Brooks (2002) *Science Fiction After 1900: From the Steam Man to the Stars*. London and New York: Routledge.

Lyotard, Jean-François (1984) *The Postmodern Condition: A Report on Knowledge*, trans. Geoff Bennington and Brian Massumi. Manchester: Manchester University Press.

Mendlesohn, Farah (2003) 'Introduction: Reading Science Fiction', in Edward James and Farah Mendlesohn (eds) *The Cambridge Companion to Science Fiction*, pp. 1–12. Cambridge: Cambridge University Press.

Nishime, LeiLani (2005) 'The Mulatto Cyborg: Imagining a Multiracial Future', *Cinema Journal* 44(2): 34–49.

Penley, Constance (1990) 'Time Travel, Primal Scene and the Critical Dystopia', in Annette Kuhn (ed.) *Alien Zone: Cultural Theory and Science Fiction Cinema*, pp. 116–27. London and New York: Verso.

Poe, Edgar Allan (1908/2008) *Tales of Mystery and Imagination*. London: Arcturus Publishing.

Punter, David (2000) *Postcolonial Imaginings: Fictions of a New World Order*. Edinburgh: Edinburgh University Press.

Roberts, Adam (2006a) *Science Fiction*. London and New York: Routledge.

Roberts, Adam (2006b) *The History of Science Fiction*. Basingstoke: Palgrave.

Scholes, Robert (1975) *Structural Fabulation: An Essay on the Fiction of the Future*. Bloomington, IN: Indiana University Press.

Spivak, Gayatri Chakravorty (1988) 'Can the Subaltern Speak?', in Cary Nelson and Lawrence Grossberg (eds) *Marxism and the Interpretation of Culture*, pp. 271–313. Urbana, IL: University of Illinois Press.

Suvin, Darko (1979) *Metamorphoses of Science Fiction: On the Poetics and History of a Literary Genre*. New Haven, CT: Yale University Press.

Tait, Theo (2004) 'From Victorian Travelogue to Airport Thriller', *Telegraph*, 1 March, URL (consulted November 2009): http://www.telegraph.co.uk/culture/books/3613044/From-Victorian-travelogue-to-airport-thriller.html

Telotte, J. P. (1990) 'The Doubles of Fantasy and the Space of Desire', in Annette Kuhn (ed.) *Alien Zone: Cultural Theory and Science Fiction Cinema*, pp. 152–s9. London and New York: Verso.

Todorov, Tzvetan (1975) *The Fantastic: A Structural Approach to a Literary Genre*. Ithaca, NY: Cornell University Press.

10

'Moonlight bright as a UFO abduction'
Science Fiction, Present-Future Alienation and Cognitive Mapping

William Stephenson

Near the beginning of David Mitchell's second novel, *number9dream* (2001), the protagonist Eiji Miyake sits in a Tokyo coffee bar, imagining his journey into the towering office block opposite, where he plans to confront the lawyer Akiko Kato and discover the identity of his long-vanished father. His daydream begins with a disconcertingly high-tech encounter with the office receptionist, an 'ice maiden' who is communicating with him via a screen: 'I wonder how human she is. These are the days when computers humanize and humans computerize' (*n9d*, 6). When she frowns, he thinks, 'Excellent. She's only human' (*n9d*, 6). Eiji deviates from the figurative usage of 'only human' common in today's colloquial speech, as a means, usually expressed in the third person, of excusing someone's flaws (he or she is only human, after all). She's 'only human' instead, meaning *literally* so in the futuristic narrative that Eiji is evolving in his head.

Mitchell thus presents his audience with the key device of all science fiction: a novum, meaning a thing not found in the world of the reader. In Darko Suvin's definition, 'a novum or cognitive innovation is a totalizing phenomenon or relationship deviating from the author's and implied reader's norm of reality' (Suvin, 1979: 64). Suvin uses 'totalizing' to mean that the novum changes the character of the *world* of the science fiction text: it is never just an incidental object but lays down the unfamiliar norms on which the narrative world is based and establishes the SF text's distance from the reader's reality. In Eiji's fantasy, his reaction to the Ice Maiden proves that companies can employ robotic or digital receptionists. Eiji quickly realizes that the Ice Maiden is *not* a robot or computer program, but it is her ambiguous appearance, leading to his initial doubt, which points to the novum that such virtual people are commonplace. More nova are to follow. After Eiji tricks his way into the building, he confronts his father's lawyer, Ms Kato, then shoots her with a tranquillizer gun and begins rooting through her files. Unfortunately, he has only shot a decoy in the form of a convincingly human-looking robot: a mere 'bioborg, dummy! A replicant!' as the real Ms Kato tells him, menacing him with her gun (*n9d*, 11).

Replicants, bioborgs, virtual receptionists – this looks like a comic but conventional SF world, an ironic re-run of Ridley Scott's *Blade Runner* (1982), itself an adaptation of Philip K. Dick's *Do Androids Dream of Electric Sheep?* (1968).[1] This impression is immediately confirmed when Ms Kato sarcastically adds, 'You never watched *Bladerunner?*' (*n9d*, 11–12). This sub-Dickian episode appears marginalized within the novel, because it is merely Eiji's daydream, and is clearly a parody. Thus, the reader might believe that they are still in a realist text and that the world-changing potential of Suvin's totalizing SF novum has been successfully contained. Mitchell appears to be poking fun not only at the overused SF trope of 'artificial constructs masquerading as humans' (Dick, 1995: 185) but also at the retrograde orientation of much SF from the 1990s onwards, that 'responds to the intensification and global extension of technological modernity not with new forms, but rather with ones lifted from the genre's venerable past' (Luckhurst, 2005: 221).

However, the parodic, generic surface of the episode is deceptive. A substratum of Eiji's fantasy is mimetic. His statement 'These are the days when computers humanize' *does* actually apply to the real twenty-first-century world; since human-like robots are currently being developed, such as Repliee Q1, an android designed to resemble a human woman, which was shown at the 2005 World Expo in Tokyo. The resemblance is strong enough to disturb some viewers and exalt others, but is not yet convincing.[2] Although a witness remarked 'the robot is so lifelike that roboticists may want to start working on a *Bladerunner*-style Voight-Kampf test [to distinguish it from a human] now' (Christensen, 2005: 1) the remark was intended as a hyperbolic compliment to Repliee Q1's designers. More importantly, for some decades, computers have become increasingly humanized in the way they think and act, rather than how they look. This was in evidence as early as 1972, according to *number9dream*'s main SF source, Philip K. Dick:

> suppose a study of ourselves, our own nature, enables us to gain insight into the now extraordinary complex functioning and malfunctioning of mechanical and electronic constructs? ... Machines are becoming more human, so to speak ... The constructs do not mimic humans: they are, in many deep ways, *actually* human already. (Dick, 1995: 184–5)[3]

So the brief appearance of a seemingly digital receptionist and of a quasi-human replicant early in *number9dream* helps build a new, altered world for a short period – thus enabling a self-contained segment of SF narrative – but also reaches implicitly beyond the moment of its deployment to connect the novel to the twenty-first century's rapidly developing, technology-driven environment in which the everyday 'real' world appears increasingly inhabited by what were, and still are, the tropes of SF. These tropes are not only technological, embedded in objects, as in the Dickian example earlier, but also psychological, embedded in the subjective: the deployment of SF imagery in *number9dream* is partly a response to what Roger Luckhurst (2005: 238) has called 'the felt sense of intermittent or gapped subjectivity in the 1990s'. Something Luckhurst links specifically to *The X-Files* and the popularity in the millennial period of the theme of abduction by aliens. And, in one of his memories of his dead sister Anju, Eiji describes 'Moonlight bright as a UFO abduction' around her (*n9d*, 57). Thus, Eiji's attempt to compensate for the greatest gap in his subjectivity, the absence of his sister, is framed in terms of a popular SF novum involving extraterrestrial intervention, body theft and enforced amnesia.

Through such SF devices and allusions, Mitchell's novels create their own distinctive form of cognition, meaning the recognition of the resemblance between the fictional world of the novum and the reader's reality that Darko Suvin argues is a fundamental part of the process of reading SF. As the reader progresses through an SF text, its imaginary world is fleshed out through the accumulation of nova, each of which estranges the reader, but at the same time suggests cognitive links to his experience. Estrangement involves 'a point of view or look implying a new set of norms' and Suvin derives it from the Russian formalist concept of *ostranenie* or defamiliarization developed by Viktor Shklovsky and others (Suvin, 1979: 6). Cognition is the recognition by the reader of similarities to his world, but with a certain reflexive charge, so that 'this term implies not only a reflecting *of* but also *on* reality' (Suvin, 1979: 10). Hence cognition, which generally follows estrangement in SF, enables the reader to see either that his own world can be changed, or that it might differ from his preconceptions.

Estrangement and cognition operate continuously when SF is read. When all the cognitive operations made by the reader are added together, a picture of the SF world is built up. Suvin argues that the imaginary worlds of SF may be regarded as complex, high-grade metaphors that differ from the ordinary or low-grade metaphors found in realist fiction or most poetry by virtue of their coherence, richness and novelty (Suvin, 1988: 190–1).[4] That is to say, a successful SF world must be logically self-consistent, be worked out in considerable depth and detail and contain one or more nova. Adam Roberts suggests that the richness of the Suvinian high-grade metaphor is more important to SF than its coherence or novelty; citing Samuel Delany, he argues that SF operates through a 'psychological, poetic surplus' (Delany, 1994: 174 cited in Roberts, 2006: 139), whereby the metaphor exceeds its basic function of commenting on or revealing a referent; it goes further by engaging the reader through its surplus connotative power. This is achieved through 'the infusoria of detail' (Roberts, 2006: 139) of alien worlds and races, technology and so on. Consequently, SF is closer to poetry than to realist fiction; it is a symbolist discourse that, like poetry or religious thought, is characterized by its '*hospitality to otherness*' (Roberts, 2006: 148, emphasis in original).

David Mitchell's novels are very hospitable to otherness but at most are only partly science fiction. *Ghostwritten* and *Cloud Atlas*, in particular, confront the reader with a bewildering alterity of widely di-

vergent narrative voices in often estranging contexts. The very plurality of these voices, and the complex and sometimes abrupt movements
between them, are evidence of Mitchell's willingness to eschew linear
chronology and subvert mimetic plausibility, such as when Adam Ewing's nineteenth-century Pacific journal ends in mid-sentence and the
reader is launched immediately into the mind of an ambitious young
musician in 1930s Belgium (*CA*, 39–43); but as this example shows,
SF is not necessary to achieve these effects. *Cloud Atlas, Ghostwritten*
and *number9dream* employ SF tropes, but only as part of larger wholes;
Mitchell uses SF devices and metaphors to enrich his polyphonic,
plural, unpredictable worlds. These worlds are enhanced by their labyrinthine webs of spatio-temporal coincidence that lift the novels above
mere mimesis by implying, but never fully revealing, a self-contained
alternative universe, a high-grade metaphor of the sort outlined by
Suvin. However, this metaphor is unfolded to the reader in a largely
non-SF context: most of the time, Mitchell's fiction takes place not on
other planets or in the far future, but on something approximating the
present or the past, even if that approximation is a conventionalized
textual construct, a generic stylized matrix for representing reality,
such as the gritty surface realism of the thriller or the quotidian factu-
ality of the historical journal.

But even in Mitchell's non-SF chapters, nova catalyse the imagined worlds of his first three novels.[5] They are fundamental to the
surplus of detail that gives Mitchell's work the symbolic resonance
and hospitality to otherness shared by poetry and SF. Mitchell has
said, 'I want to smudge the pencil lines somewhat between sci-fi and
non-sci-fi' (Wood, 2010: 32). The deployment of nova in a non-SF
context is one means of doing this. It allows Mitchell to move beyond
any single genre and to avoid reductive categorization. There are several reasons why Mitchell's work exists in such complex multi-generic
forms. These forms help Mitchell's novels to describe and negotiate
the interconnected, globalized world that has existed since the end
of the Cold War. At the same time, they help to articulate on a symbolic level a future that is unknown yet which, due to the pace of
technological change and the increasingly estranged basis of everyday
experience, appears paradoxically already to be here. In Mitchell, this

sense of the presence of the future does not lead to a threatened, re-actionary response, based on what Fredric Jameson has disparagingly called 'Nostalgia for the Present' (Jameson, 1991: 279) or 'the logic of "future shock"' (Jameson, 1991: 377). Rather, it causes what might be termed present-future alienation, a sense of estrangement brought about by the paradoxical coexistence of accepted present-time data along with objects (or tropes or events) that seem rightly to belong to an imagined or foreseen future. This paradox of presence and futurity occurs because Mitchell's fictions imply that the hard distinction between the novum (new thing) and datum (fact) accepted by SF *and* realist fiction is breaking down. In the twenty-first century, and in Mitchell's novels, something that appears to belong in the realm of SF may in fact be part of everyday reality; and, something that is received as a novum in one subjective world or cultural context may be a datum in another.

'The waitresses all had the same face': The Challenges Posed by Mitchell's Nova

In conventional SF, nova are at first alienating but are soon assimilated by the reader as tools of orientation: he or she uses them to work out what the world of the SF text is like. In realist fiction, the equivalents are data: pieces of information that locate the characters within the real world. Tom Shippey (2005: 12) defines a datum as 'a discrete fact stated or implied' that usually leads the reader to a conclusion about the real world as imitated in a realist novel, for instance the social positions or psychological anxieties of the main characters.[6] The novum is a somewhat more challenging beast. Shippey (2005: 13–14) argues that rather than inviting recognition, or confirming the reader's view of the world, the novum serves as 'the basic building-block of science fiction ... a discrete piece of information recognizable as not-true, but also not-unlike true, not-flatly-(in the current state of knowledge)-impossible'. Unlike the datum, the novum cannot be unconsciously absorbed. It requires the knowing agreement of the receiver: the implied reader of SF is required to legitimize the new thing by recognizing that it is outside his conception of the real, but is nevertheless plausible within the universe of the novel. This universe is enriched and simultaneously reordered for the reader as he assimilates the new facts or events. The 'essential tension of SF' is between the reader and 'the encompassing and at least equipollent Unknown or Other introduced by the novum' (Suvin, 1979: 64). The encounter with the novum, then, is a world-changing encounter with Otherness.

In Mitchell, this convention is adapted and revitalized. Like the replicants encountered in Eiji Miyake's daydream, the nova in *Ghost-written* or *Cloud Atlas* do not in fact cause 'a change of the whole universe of the tale' (Suvin, 1979: 64). This is because the universe of either of these novels extends beyond the chapter or intercalated story, or the subjective world of the narrator. Mitchell's nova do not permit an encounter with Otherness that is all-encompassing or world-altering. This does not mean that Mitchell limits the impact of his nova by imprisoning them within a secondary genre or marginalized interior discourse. Instead, the reader is offered a reflection on a 'real' world that is already, in a sense, science fictional: it is based on narrative, on ideology, consensus reality and semiotics; on science, technology and the virtual fabrication of the real; and, it is estranging, through encounters with new and complex technology, or unpredictable flows of mediated information. This represents a movement beyond Jean Baudrillard's fourth stage of the image that informs his theory of hyperreality. In this stage, the image 'has no relation to any reality whatsoever: it is its own pure simulacrum' (Baudrillard, 1994: 6). Mitchell is not simply asserting a triumph of the virtual over the real. Rather, in his first three novels, the manifold images (meaning scenes, characters, intercalated narratives, as well as nova) become interconnected building blocks for a new reality, based on a complex blend of a chaotic present and a symbolically articulated future that is in the process of being realized.

This means that the sort of cognition Mitchell's narratives produce is different both from that achieved by conventional SF through nova and that achieved by realist fiction through data. Mitchell's novels, unlike others of either genre, produce a distinctive version of what Carl Freedman (2000: 18) has called 'the *cognition effect*' meaning 'the attitude *of the text itself* to the kinds of estrangements being performed' (emphasis in original).[7] Mitchell's work offers an 'attitude' to its own data and nova that deliberately confuses the distinctions between the imaginary and the real that are made by realism and by SF. Put at its most simple, Mitchell's data are sometimes nova and vice versa; reading his novels reveals that the reader's 'real' world to which the novel's facts and events are cognitively related is as complex and as strange as that of the narrative.

In 'Hard Reading: The Challenges of Science Fiction', Shippey makes the powerful argument that SF is not only the most intellectually challenging genre, but also the most emotionally challenging, as the estranging encounter with nova breaks the reader's cosy certainties. SF nova discomfort the reader by positing a world, say, in which the USA does not exist, or humanity is enslaved by aliens; 'The corollary of *Things do not have to be the way they are* is that *Nothing is sacred*' (Shippey, 2005: 18, emphasis in original). The reader's ideologies and prejudices are unstable and can be demolished by SF on a visceral, affective level as well as through reason. However, the emotional estrangement proposed by Shippey (2005: 11) begins to look weak when one set of certainties is disrupted by an SF text, only for another to be enforced; for instance where the invading aliens turn out to be mere allegories for enemies in the real world.[8] The challenge of SF is also diluted where the text includes only nova that are so clichéd as not to be nova at all (the retro-styled starships and robots of the *Star Wars* universe, say). Indeed, Shippey (2005: 11) makes clear the limitations of a view that considers *Star Wars* or *Star Trek* to be definitive of SF.

Mitchell's novels pose new emotional and ideological problems. They recognize both the strengths and weaknesses of SF; they exploit the genre's potential while not allowing the SF world to become a place of comforting certainty. They lay down for the reader many of the same intellectual and affective gauntlets as conventional SF, but never allow the genre to offer a comfort zone or place of escape. The second point applies because in Mitchell the novum no longer totalizes, as Suvin would wish. It only changes part of the world of the text part of the time. Mitchell's work refuses to allow its SF sections to establish a dominant view of the future, one that could risk becoming a reassuringly deep and self-consistent fantasy world that is sustained throughout the entire novel.

Such escapist reassurance is possible in SF because it normally positions its nova in the service of one reality, however carefully concealed from the reader. Nova appear and gradually establish what the imaginary world is going to be like, sometimes after some initial pleasurable disorientation, where the reader may be confused but relies on the unstated premise that the world's laws will be revealed and will make sense. In *Ghostwritten* and *Cloud Atlas*, all the subjective realities of the characters are instead provisional; the high-tech future in which Sonmi~451 lives, for instance, is just one of a number of interrelated worlds within *Cloud Atlas* and, in a further future, is only a recording viewed, and misunderstood, by Zachry and his fellows. Thus, the seemingly totalizing hold of Sonmi's dystopia is weakened by her world's partiality; the grim relentlessness of the oppressive regimes of Orwell, Huxley and Zamyatin is avoided, as is the solid sense of certainty that each earlier novelist brings to his protagonist's world.[9] Instead, the oppressed Sonmi will become the god of the Valleysmen in another more distant future (*CA*, 254) and she herself treats Timothy Cavendish's *Ghastly Ordeal* as a classic film, 'a picaresque ... from the early twenty-first century' (*CA*, 243): somehow, Cavendish's story has survived and been reinterpreted. Vyvyan Ayrs dreams of the music in a 'nightmarish café' of the future, where 'the waitresses all had the same face' (*CA*, 80). He transcribes the haunting, cyclic tune and presents it to Frobisher, who in turn appropriates it as the basis of the *Sextet*. Ayrs's dream is Sonmi's reality, and the realistic narrative of Ayrs and Frobisher is not privileged over the SF one of Sonmi; no single ontology is dominant. The genres of *Cloud Atlas* (post-apocalyptic and dystopian SF, comedy, airport thriller, epistolary fiction and historical journal) are voices that can be adopted and can work together, like Frobisher's musical voices, in complex polyphony.

'Nearing the speed of light, time buckled': Forging the Links

Part of the distinctive pleasure of engaging with Mitchell's writing lies in linking these voices and their respective genres together and establishing the connections between them. For instance, the reader can dystopianize the non-SF contemporary world of Timothy Cavendish by linking the oppressive conditions at Aurora House to the nightmare future that Sonmi inhabits: Sonmi's interviewer, when told of the old people's homes of Cavendish's time, says 'It all sounds grimly dystopian' (*CA*, 244). The interviewer's comment unintentionally echoes the reader's likely reaction to Sonmi's world, implying that dystopia is a matter of perception, and thus we may well be blind to the dystopias we inhabit. Aurora House and Papa Song's diner are both, in fact, dystopian prisons. Neither set of inhabitants is allowed to leave, although they are nominally free, and the old people and fabricants alike are addressed in childish language: 'Everyone's visited by the Glum Family at first' (*CA*, 181); 'A gas called evil xists in the world, Papa Song said. When purebloods breathe in this gas, they change' (*CA*, 203).[10]

Sections, sentences and ideas in Mitchell that appear to have no basis in SF become virally infected by the SF content that comes from around and outside them. Mo Muntervary, on a plane fleeing her job at Light Box, thinks of orthodox Einsteinian physics, and then of her work: her fellow passengers 'don't know how our Boeing 747's velocity increases our mass and slows time ... None has heard of quantum cognition' (*G*, 337). This is a brilliant deployment of a novum, achieved by situating it among known science to render it more plausible. Mo says time stretches according to velocity: this is not science fiction but early twentieth-century physics, however weird it may seem to the uninitiated. However, she then links people's ignorance of this to their ignorance of quantum cognition – the artificial intelligence she is building – which *is* science fiction. This can be compared with the preceding 'London' section, in which the narrator, the drummer and ghostwriter Marco, is betting in a casino. He aims to pay a debt and thus save his drums and his livelihood as a musician. Down to his last stake on the roulette table, feeling intense anxiety, he thinks: 'Nearing the speed of light, time buckled' (*G*, 314). Later, having won enough money, he proposes marriage to his girlfriend. As he awaits her reply, his extreme anxiety means that to him, time seems to have become solid: 'the few moments that passed had more mass than ordinary time, because a possible lifetime was compressed into them' (G, 318). On a routine level, these references to time are descriptions of Marco's emotional state; images that illustrate his feelings. And yet, we are also in the universe of the 'Clear Island' section that follows where, as Mo Muntervary points out, velocity, mass and time *are* all interrelated variables but people act as if they were entirely separate, quantities. Hence Marco's world is also that of Mo's, where time can *literally* slow down, and of quantum cognition. So in Mitchell, the datum is no longer distinct from the novum as a means of clarifying a single 'real' world, as opposed to a mere SF world. Instead, data and nova interbreed, mutate and mix.

A novum can, in some circumstances, become a datum. For Bat Segundo, unlike Mo, superhuman machine intelligences are merely a science fiction concept until he actually encounters one, the Zookeeper, who is a virtual entity limited only by four laws. They are very like Isaac Asimov's Three Laws of Robotics, a clear SF allusion.[11] The Zookeeper is far less restrained than Asimov's creations: it has the power to disable more primitive computer systems and take over any technology seemingly at will. It is an example of the superhuman machine intelligence predicted by the science fiction writer and mathematician Vernor Vinge. The ascension of this machine consciousness is termed the singularity, defined as 'the imminent creation by technology of entities with greater than human intelligence' (Vinge, 1993). Perhaps fortunately for him, Bat Segundo does not read much science fiction; he appears never to have heard of the singularity, even though he lives in the period between 2005 and 2030 when Vinge predicts the singularity will occur (Vinge, 1993). Unlike Bat, Mo Muntervary can foresee the possibility of such intelligences, as she is helping to design one, but she has no idea of another novum: that at some point she has been inhabited by a *noncorpum* or disembodied spirit who styles himself 'the fallen angel' (G, 422) and who raised her intelligence to enable her to think beyond the limitations of other scientists (G, 421).

The *noncorpa* of *Ghostwritten* sometimes communicate with their human hosts 'via external objects that function as projectional surfaces' (Griffiths, 2004: 86), such as the tree that the narrator thinks is talking to her in the 'Holy Mountain' section, and that promises that she will see her daughter again (*G*, 122). In much the same way, Mitchell's fictions communicate through the projectional surfaces of objects and ideas that are ambiguously data and/or nova. This can be seen when a datum is repeated, so that it reappears in a new context, as a novum, in another section. The orison that we encounter as the 'silver egg-shaped device' introduced by the archivist at the start of Sonmi's testimony (*CA*, 187) reappears in the following section 'Sloosha's Crossin'' as something 'most wondersome' (*CA*, 276) to Zachry: 'One big silv'ry egg it was, sized a babbit's head, with dents 'n' markin's on it what fingers rested in. Its fat weight was eery an' it wouldn't roll' (*CA*, 276). To Sonmi, the orison simply needs to be explained; she can then get on and use it; only its function is mysterious to her, and then briefly. But to Zachry, the very form of the orison is wondrous even though he instinctively knows the indentations in it are for fingers.[12]

The orison has a dual function; not only is it a datum then a novum, it also creates a communicative link between worlds. Meronym and the other Prescients in the far future are using the same device handed down to them from the higher-tech world of Sonmi's Korea. Zachry watches Sonmi's interviews but has no idea who or what he is seeing, which is ironic, given that he worships Sonmi as a god (*CA*, 277). At the end of his story, the orison reappears as a toy, and the narrator of the closing section of 'Sloosha's Crossin'', Zachry's son or daughter, invites his listener(s) to sit down and hold it:

Sit down a beat or two.

*

Hold out your hands.

*

Look. (*CA*, 325)

The implication is that the narrator is retelling Zachry's story to one or more members of his or her community, but the invitation to look is equally addressed to the reader. The narrator's call draws the reader, and thus the 'real' world he/she inhabits, into the complex of linked worlds signified by the orison. It is without coincidence that exactly at this point the reader is plunged back into the second halves of all the stories, and *Cloud Atlas* begins to solve the mysteries its structure has created; the reader is drawn further into the novel's ontological eco-system, in which 'Souls cross ages like clouds cross skies' (*CA*, 324).

On one level, the deployment of the orison as an object the reader is invited to hold is simply a cognitive device; the reader's world be-comes closer to the SF world as a connection is drawn between them. However, the final paragraphs of 'Sloosha's Crossin'' are also estrang-ing, because they throw into relief the possibility that the 'real' world may not be as immutable as the typical western reader might think it is. Even such phenomena as metempsychosis – souls crossing ages like floating clouds, as Mitchell's narrator says – may be possible. This is not quite as far-fetched as it sounds, because thought may be more substantial than the material world. The Copenhagen Interpretation of Quantum Mechanics

> says that what we perceive to be physical reality is actually our cog-nitive construction of it. This cognitive construction may appear to be substantive, but the Copenhagen Interpretation of Quantum Me-chanics leads directly to the conclusion that the physical world itself is not.
>
> This claim at first appears so preposterous and remote from experi-ence that our inclination is to discard it as the foolish product of clois-tered intellectuals. However ... physicists are not the only people who view the world this way. They are only the newest members of a sizeable group; most Hindus and Buddhists also hold similar views. (Zukav, 1991: 105)

The Copenhagen Interpretation, along with the Many Worlds In-terpretation, which posits multiple universes, is a 'respectable minority view' (Gribbin, 1991: 235) among physicists. Mitchell sometimes treats sceptically the more spiritually orientated responses to quantum theory: Marco and Katie Forbes discuss 'the old quantum physics equals eastern religion bollocks' as a chat-up line before their one-night stand (*G*, 265). However, Mitchell having expressed an interest in Buddhism, and having stated that the protagonists of *Cloud Atlas* were intended to be the same soul reincarnated, as signified by 'the motif of the comet-shaped birthmark' (Gilbert, 2010). The way *Cloud Atlas* raises such estranging questions for the reader follows the pattern outlined by Suvin, whereby cognition involves not just recognition but reflection (Suvin, 1979: 10): in the plural universes of Mitchell's multi-generic, quasi-SF texts, the object under the microscope is not some reassuringly alien environment, but reality itself.

'Endless connections between different domains': Mitchell, the Contemporary World Order and the Future

Mitchell's worlds are multiple, and, more importantly, interconnected, both within and between novels.[13] This suggests a complex response to the contemporary world in which, following the end of the Cold War, 'globalization became the defining term' (Luckhurst, 2005: 220). Human interaction has been reconfigured by information capitalism, in which digital technologies 'act upon all domains of human activity, and make it possible to establish endless connections between different domains' (Castells, 2000: 78 cited in Luckhurst, 2005: 220–1). Such a world begs for novels, and especially for nova, of the sort created by David Mitchell. His fiction is plural, polyphonic and interconnected, but this is not just because of the formally driven need to move beyond the generic and structural boundaries set by past literary and SF conventions.[14] It is all these things because of the plural, polyphonic and interconnected world of the globalized twenty-first century.[15] This is not, of course, something simply to be celebrated. The demonstration of the persistence of the will to power in *Cloud Atlas* ought to militate against that.

Earlier, I argued that the Zookeeper was an example of the sort of artificial intelligence predicted by Vinge's theory of the singularity, which is 'a point where our old models must be discarded and a new reality rules' and which will lead to 'a great surprise and a greater unknown' (Vinge, 1993). The 'greater unknown' of the future could be what Mitchell's science fiction is orientated towards. Mitchell's polyphonic, decentred novels are a reflection of the realities of globalization and the networked world; but elements of them, specifically his use of SF nova, are also predictive. They anticipate a coming age that is beyond what we can imagine; not necessarily because of the machine singularity of Vinge's theory but because of any one of a number of already-emerging changes that we cannot articulate and can only tentatively sketch out in symbolic forms such as literature.

Thus, when the Zookeeper destroys the spirit *noncorpum* that calls itself the fallen angel (and which had once inhabited Mo Muntervary), *Ghostwritten* is not enacting a literal prediction of a future, but is creating an image which can stand metaphorically for several possibilities that are, in nascent form, already being realized: that machine intelligence may triumph over irrationalist notions of spirit or soul; that technology will kill its own parents (the Zookeeper kills not only the fallen angel but also its designers when it blows up the research station where the scientists are based – it may eventually kill the entire human race); that ethical or doctrinal battles previously enacted either textually or through warfare will be increasingly played out in virtual, technological space. Zachry's post-apocalyptic Hawaii, and the other SF worlds and devices in Mitchell, allude to a similar list of emerging possibilities; they are metaphors, tentative images of a future that, although present in embryo, cannot be apprehended yet in any other way.[16]

The difficulty in comprehending the future-in-the-present leads to what I have called present-future alienation. I have already touched upon how Mitchell's novels suggest that the contemporary world is an often estranging place, driven both by science and by narrative, so that the 'real' world shares similarities to SF. By articulating this, Mitchell's fictions advance beyond the project of earlier SF that aimed to estrange by refiguring 'our present as past and as history' (Jameson, 1991: 286). As characteristic of this fiction, Jameson cites Philip K. Dick's *Time Out of Joint* (1959) in which a seemingly realistic (but simultaneously idealized, cloyingly perfect) 1950s small-town setting proves in fact to be a simulacrum created in the 1990s. He argues that Dick artfully manipulates the speciously reassuring data of 'favourite television programs; mild flirtations with the housewife next door;

game shows and contests; ... short haircuts, early rock and roll, longer skirts and so on' (Jameson, 1991: 279) by presenting them as real, then revealing that they are fake. However, the novel then shows they *never were* real, only 'a list of stereotypes, of ideas of facts and historical realities' (Jameson, 1991: 279). Thus, each mimetic detail in *Time Out of Joint* never was a datum, only a simulacrum. This was Dick's estranging method for exposing data themselves as not physical objects or actual events but cultural constructs, legitimized through an ideologically based consensus.

In Mitchell, by contrast, the datum is exposed not as a simulacrum, but as a novum, to the extent that the line between the two is often blurred. This poses new problems for the reader because it intensifies the texts's critique of the current social and political order. Jameson's account of *Time Out of Joint* shows how 'the very structure of the novel articulates the position of Eisenhower America in the world itself and is thereby to be read as a kind of distorted form of cognitive mapping' (Jameson, 1991: 283). Mitchell's fictions update Dick's estranging strategies and thus force the reader into a new and exhilarating form of cognitive cartography, a re-territorialization of the plural, decentred, estranging present and the already emerging future that is reality in the early twenty-first century.

Notes

1 Both Ridley Scott's film and Philip K. Dick's novel are based on the protagonist's hunt for outlawed replicants, or androids, who are superficially indistinguishable from humans. *Blade Runner* set the aesthetic template for the cyberpunk writing of William Gibson and others. It 'was a stunning visual expression of the cyberpunk world ... Few sf films have been made with such minute attention to the creation of a near-future world, and to a darkly realistic one' (James, 1994: 196–7). See Baryon Tensor Posadas's essay in this collection for a more extended discussion of the connections between Mitchell's fiction and cyberpunk [Ed.].

2 For representations of the robot on video see Mejilla Hyde 'Actoid Repliee Q1' (2008) and Hiroshi Ishiguru 'Female Robot 'Humanlike'' (2007), both available on *YouTube*.

3 In discussion at the David Mitchell Conference, University of St Andrews, September 2009, Mitchell confirmed that he was reading Dick's *The Man*

in the High Castle (1962) during the composition of *number9dream*, and that he was influenced by Dick's ideas. Eiji Miyake reads Dick's SF masterpiece but marginalizes it as 'a weird novel' (*n9d*, 236). *The Man in the High Castle* may also have influenced *Cloud Atlas*, as both texts deal with the same underlying theme of 'the quintessential Western will to domination' (Freedman, 2000: 172).

4 Epic poetry is Suvin's exception to his rule that most verse is based on low-grade metaphors. In the epic, an extended image comes to inform a lengthy poem in such detail that it becomes analogous to an imaginary world in SF. In this respect, Mitchell's first three novels resemble decentred epics, driven by an overarching design that is nevertheless incomplete for the reader. They might thus be linked to the fractured epics of high modernism, notably James Joyce's *Ulysses* (1922) and T. S. Eliot's *The Waste Land* (1922).

5 Mitchell's fourth novel, the autobiographical, realist *Black Swan Green* (2006), avoids nova entirely, but does acknowledge the influence of science fiction on the protagonist, Jason Taylor, who cites 'Isaac Asimov. Ursula Le Guin. John Wyndham' as his literary 'teachers' (*BSG*, 203). Mitchell has admitted that 'my teenage reading diet was rich in colourfully jacketed science fiction' (Mitchell, 2010: 6). Jason reads William Golding's futuristic fantasy *Lord of the Flies* (1954) to his English class (*BSG*, 262–3); *Lord of the Flies* was required reading for Mitchell's generation at O-level. Mitchell's fifth novel, *The Thousand Autumns of Jacob de Zoet* (2010), is free of SF content, except that one character, Doctor Marinus, is intended to be a *noncorpum* who will reappear in Mitchell's next two planned books 'via a *Ghostwritten*-like process of soul transference' (Wood, 2010: 32). Mitchell's next planned book will include both historical fiction and SF, as it is a collection of short stories set between 1969 and 2039 (Wood, 2010: 32).

6 Shippey's theory of the datum is close to that of Roland Barthes in 'The Reality Effect' (1986/1989). Barthes was concerned not with details that gave information about plot or character, but with seemingly incidental or irrelevant objects. It is these that signify the category of the real, and so 'the *reality effect* is produced, the basis of that unavowed verisimilitude which forms the aesthetic of all the standard works of modernity' (Barthes, 1986/1989: 148).

7 Other texts that mix historical fiction, realism and science fiction to which Mitchell's might interestingly be compared and contrasted include: Kurt

Vonnegut's *Slaughterhouse-Five* (1969), which combines the protagonist's experience of World War II with his kidnap by aliens; John Fowles's *A Maggot* (1985), whose eighteenth-century protagonists encounter space travellers in a starship; and, Peter Ackroyd's *First Light* (1989).

8   Adam Roberts discusses the power of SF to reinforce national values and to represent national concerns. He explains how the rise of American power during the Cold War period led 'both to SF texts that articulated imperial anxiety, for instance, *Invasion of the Body Snatchers* (1956), [a film whose body-invading aliens were a McCarthyite metaphor for covert Communists] but also to works (such as the ongoing *Star Trek* series) that are all about exploring the new frontier, transferring the colonization of the American continent directly onto the galaxy' (Roberts, 2006: 50).

9   Despite this, 'An Orison of Sonmi~451' does signify its considerable intertextual debt to earlier SF. There are parallels between the regimented dystopias of George Orwell's *Nineteen Eighty-Four* (1949), Aldous Huxley's *Brave New World* (1932), Yevgeny Zamyatin's *We* (1924) and Sonmi's universe. During her ascension into sentience, Sonmi even mentions that she has read Orwell and Huxley (*CA*, 220). Like SF writers, Mitchell is here building on a genre canon, or what has been called in SF circles the 'mega-text', the corpus of celebrated SF texts that the writer is expected to know and the competent SF reader certainly will know (Luckhurst, 2005: 7). 'Architectural features from pioneering SF classics such as Aldous Huxley's *Brave New World*, Yevgeny Zamyatin's *We* and *The Machine Stops* by EM Forster ... are present [in Sonmi's world], with rich dollops of *Blade Runner*' (Mitchell, 2010: 6).

10   There is a strong parallel between 'An Orison of Sonmi~451' and Kazuo Ishiguro's *Never Let Me Go* (2005), another recent dystopian text centred on a female clone whose body is to be harvested after a life of work. Ishiguro's novel poses similar cognitive challenges to the reader. In a list which might apply equally to Sonmi, Bruce Robbins points out the fundamental problems posed by Ishiguro's protagonist: 'What kind of system does her routine belong to? Where is the seemingly endless file of workdays leading? We ourselves do not look any ultimate questions in the face, but we watch as the character looks away from them, and are thus made to feel the force both of these questions and of our own resistance to them' (Robbins, 2007: 293).

11   Asimov's Three Laws of Robotics are well known. In paraphrase, they are: do not injure human beings; obey human beings; protect your own

existence (Asimov, 1950/1996: 8). Asimov's *I, Robot* (1950/1996) and his other robot stories spend a lot of time working out the problems and contradictions within and between these laws. The Zookeeper's four laws are never listed, but appear to mean: it must be accountable for its actions (*G*, 387, 391); it 'must remain invisible to the visitors' (*G*, 421) meaning humans; it 'cannot wilfully deceive' (*G*, 390); and must prevent humans from destroying themselves (*G*, 409).

12 Mitchell's language is part of the defamiliarizing process here. Zachry speaks in a dialect that Mitchell renders with plenty of apostrophes to indicate pronunciation. It is stuffed with neologisms that Mitchell derived partly from his reading of Russell Hoban's post-apocalyptic SF novel *Riddley Walker* (1980). The title of Zachry's section is conspicuously contracted: 'Sloosha's Crossin' an' Ev'rythin' After' (*CA*, 247). Zachry's exotic slang includes the affirmative 'yay' (*CA*, 250 and *passim*); clothes are 'clothesies' (*CA*, 249); and he finds an extremely distressing sight 'Heartbuggahin' (*CA*, 311). By contrast, Sonmi's pronunciation appears standard but the spelling of her dialect is altered to reflect a corporatized language close to text-speak: exhorted is 'xhorted' (*CA*, 190) and experience and experiment receive the same dropped 'e' (*CA*, 191); a shoe is known as a 'nike' (*CA*, 200) and a watch a 'rolex' (*CA*, 197). In each case, the novum of the orison is presented in a world whose language is itself a novum.

13 Mitchell is well known for making his novels connect through shared characters. For example, the Mongolian assassin Suhbataar from *Ghostwritten* reappears in *number9dream*; Neal Brose, the crooked banker from *Ghostwritten*, plays a minor part as a child in *Black Swan Green*; characters who straddle the worlds of *Ghostwritten* and *Cloud Atlas* include the crime novelist Luisa Rey and the publisher Timothy Cavendish; Eva van Crommelynck, Frobisher's beloved in *Cloud Atlas*, returns as a much older woman in *Black Swan Green*; Con Twomey, the Irish carpenter in *The Thousand Autumns of Jacob de Zoet*, is a distant ancestor of Mo Muntervary from *Ghostwritten*.

14 Luckhurst (2005: 239) argues that there is at present a 'widely shared perception that genre boundaries are shifting or even dissolving', and that 'some literary fiction, too, has edged into the science-fictional, despite the routine ignorance of genre writing that defines literary establishments in Britain and America' (Luckhurst, 2005: 241). He cites Mitchell as one of a number of recent novelists 'that fit this strange, interstitial space' of

generic hybridity, which itself presents an instance of 'uncanny return' (Luckhurst, 2005: 243) to the times of H. G. Wells, when for instance, Gothic fiction, utopian narratives and social satires were intermixed.

15 'Globalization, of course, is not one thing, and the multiple processes that we recognize as globalization are not unified or univocal' (Hardt and Negri, 2001: xv). The term has been defined as 'the removal of barriers to free trade and the closer integration of national economies' (Stiglitz, 2002: ix) but is also acknowledged to be 'political, technological and cultural, as well as economic' (Giddens, 1999: 10). Globalization 'involves more intensive interaction across wider space and in shorter time than before, in other words the experience of a shrinking world' (Nederveen Pieterse, 2004: 8).

16 Mitchell has revealed that he is pessimistic about the future, and that Sonmi's and Zachry's worlds respectively reveal his 'more optimistic' and 'less optimistic' estimates of what it may be like. The better estimate is still 'alarming' (Gilbert, 2010). 'Yes, I've destroyed the world twice and Tokyo once ... What if the oil runs out in 30 years? We won't be in a care home yet. This interests me very much at the moment, as a writer and a dad' (Nicol, 2010: 9).

Works Cited

Asimov, Isaac (1950/1996) *I, Robot*. London: Harper Collins.

Barthes, Roland (1986/1989) 'The Reality Effect', in *The Rustle of Language*, trans. Richard Howard, pp. 141-8. Berkeley and Los Angeles: University of California Press.

Baudrillard, Jean (1994) *Simulacra and Simulation*, trans. Sheila Faria Glaser. Ann Arbor: University of Michigan Press.

Castells, Manuel (2000) *The Rise of the Network Society*. Oxford: Blackwell.

Christensen, Bill (2005) 'New Robot Looks Strikingly Human', *Live Science*, 28 June, URL (consulted July 2009): http://www.livescience.com/technology/050628_real_robot.html

Delany, Samuel (1994) *Silent Interviews: On Language, Race, Sex, Science Fiction and Some Comics*. Hanover, PA and London: Welseyan University Press.

Dick, Philip K. (1995) 'The Android and the Human', in Lawrence Sutin (ed.) *The Shifting Realities of Philip K. Dick: Selected Literary and Philosophical Writings*, pp. 183–210. New York: Vintage.

Freedman, Carl (2000) *Critical Theory and Science Fiction*. Middletown, CT: Wesleyan University Press.

Giddens, Anthony (1999) *Runaway World: How Globalisation is Reshaping Our Lives*. London: Profile.

Gilbert, Harriett (2010) 'David Mitchell', BBC World Bookclub, 4 June, URL (consulted August 2010): http://www.bbc.co.uk/worldservice/arts/2010/06/100604_wbc_david_mitchell.shtml

Gribbin, John (1991) *In Search of Schrodinger's Cat: Quantum Physics and Reality*. London: Black Swan.

Griffiths, Philip (2004) '"On the Fringe of Becoming" – David Mitchell's *Ghostwritten*', in Stefan Glomb and Stefan Horlarcher (eds) *Beyond Extremes: Repräsentation und Reflexion von Moderniesierungsprozessen im zeitgenossichen britischen roman*, pp. 79-99. Tübingen: Gunter Narr Verlag.

Hardt, Michael and Negri, Antonio (2001) *Empire*. Cambridge, MA and London: Harvard University Press.

Hyde, Mejilla (2008) 'Actoid Repliee Q1', *YouTube*, 4 July, URL (consulted June 2010): http://www.youtube.com/watch?v=TiqcSRtXFF0

Ishiguru, Hiroshi (2007) 'Female Robot 'Humanlike'', *YouTube*, 28 April, URL (consulted June 2010): http://www.youtube.com/watch?v=MY8-sJS0W1I

James, Edward (1994) *Science Fiction in the Twentieth Century*. Oxford: Oxford University Press.

Jameson, Fredric (1991) *Postmodernism, Or, The Cultural Logic of Late Capitalism*. London: Verso.

Luckhurst, Roger (2005) *Science Fiction*. Cambridge: Polity Press.

Lyotard, Jean-François (1984) *The Postmodern Condition: A Report on Knowledge*, trans. Geoffrey Bennington and Brian Massumi. Manchester: Manchester University Press.

Mitchell, David (2010), 'Week Three: David Mitchell on Writing *Cloud Atlas*', *Guardian* (12 June): 6.

Nederveen Pieterse, Jan (2004) *Globalization and Culture: Global Mélange*. Lanham: Rowman & Littlefield.

Nicol, Patricia (2010) 'An Imagination that Runs Wild', *Sunday Times Culture Supplement*, 18 April, pp. 8-9.

Robbins, Bruce (2007) 'Cruelty is Bad: Banality and Proximity in *Never Let Me Go*', *Novel* 40(3): 289-302.

Roberts, Adam (2006) *Science Fiction*. Abingdon: Routledge.

Shippey, Tom (2005) 'Hard Reading: The Challenges of Science Fiction', in David Seed (ed.) *A Companion to Science Fiction*, pp. 11–26. Oxford: Blackwell.

Stiglitz, Joseph E. (2002) *Globalization and Its Discontents*. London: Penguin.

Suvin, Darko (1979) *Metamorphoses of Science Fiction: On the Poetics and History of a Literary Genre*. New Haven, CT and London: Yale University Press.

Suvin, Darko (1988) *Positions and Presuppositions in Science Fiction*. Kent, OH: Kent State University Press.

Vinge, Vernor (1993) 'The Coming Technological Singularity', March, URL (consulted July 2009): http://mindstalk.net/vinge/vinge-sing.html

Wood, Ed (2010) 'The Magical Worlds of David Mitchell', *Books Quarterly* 36: 26–32.

Zukav, Gary (1991) *The Dancing Wu Li Masters: An Overview of the New Physics*. London: Rider.

Notes on Contributors

Peter Childs is Professor of Modern English Literature at the University of Gloucestershire, UK. He has published widely on twentieth-century literature. His books include *Contemporary Novelists: British Fiction Since 1970* (2004), *The Fiction of Ian McEwan* (2005) and *Julian Barnes* (2011).

Sarah Dillon is Lecturer in Contemporary Fiction at the University of St Andrews, UK. She is the author of *The Palimpsest: Literature, Criticism, Theory* (2007) and has published articles and chapters on a range of writers including Jacques Derrida, Elizabeth Bowen, H.D., Maggie Gee and David Mitchell. Sarah is currently writing *Infidelity*, a study of infidelity in contemporary philosophy, literature and film.

Nicholas Dunlop is Lecturer in English Literature and Film at the University of Birmingham, UK. His research focuses on postcolonial theory and literatures of the Pacific, contemporary fiction and cinema and postmodernity. He has published a number of articles on the works of Peter Carey, Janette Turner Hospital and David Malouf, is on the editorial board of the literary journal *Antipodes* and is currently writing a book-length study of representations of education in science fiction.

Caroline Edwards is Tutor in English Literature at the University of Surrey. Her doctoral research, 'Fictions of the Not Yet: Time and the Contemporary British Novel', explores the representation of time and utopia in a range of late twentieth- and early twenty-first-century British fiction. She has co-edited *Mortality, Dying and Death: Global Interdisciplinary Perspectives* (Oxford: Inter-Disciplinary Press, 2008) and the special issue 'Collective Subjects, Emancipatory Cultures and Political Transformation', in *Subjectivity* (2011). Caroline has also written articles for *Textual Practice* and *Contemporary Literature* and has published reviews and interviews in *Radical Philosophy, Historical*

Materialism, the *Routledge Annotated Bibliography of English Studies* and the *New Statesman*.

James Green completed a doctoral thesis at the University of Gloucestershire on 'Flows, Routes and Networks: The Global Dynamics of Lawrence Norfolk, Hari Kunzru and David Mitchell'. He has also published 'Mapping the Guyanese Dream-Space: The Landscape of Wilson Harris's Guyana Quartet' in the *Journal of Postcolonial Writing* (2007).

Courtney Hopf is a doctoral candidate at the University of California, Davis, USA. She currently resides in London as a Junior Visiting Research Fellow at the University of Westminster's Institute for Modern and Contemporary Culture. Her research focuses on narrative theory, with an emphasis on collaboratively-authored texts from the twentieth and twenty-first centuries.

Hélène Machinal is full professor at the University of Bretagne Occidentale in Brest, France, where she teaches English literature. She is attached to HCTI/CEIMA, EA 4249 (http://www.univ-brest.fr/ceima/equipe%20cadres.htm). Her research focuses on the gothic, detective fiction and speculative fiction during the second half of the nineteenth century. She wrote a book on Conan Doyle published in 2004. She is the author of articles on nineteenth-century authors such as Doyle, Stoker, Stevenson, Machen and Collins and she has also recently studied the modes of resurgence of the mythical figures of the detective, the vampire and the mad scientist in contemporary British literature. Her more recent research includes articles on David Mitchell, Patrick McGrath, Kazuo Ishiguro and Will Self.

Will McMorran is a Senior Lecturer in French and Comparative Literature at Queen Mary University of London, UK. He has published widely on early modern European fiction and on its afterlife in contemporary culture. He is currently writing a book on the fiction of the Marquis de Sade.

Baryon Tensor Posadas completed his PhD in East Asian Studies at the University of Toronto, Canada. His dissertation examines the figure of the doppelgänger in Japanese films and fictions as it intersects with discourses of visuality, psychoanalysis, and colonial modernity. His most recent publication is 'Rampo's Repetitions: The Doppelganger in Edogawa Rampo and Tsukamoto Shin'ya', in *Japan Forum* (2009).

Kathryn Simpson is Senior Lecturer in English Literature at the School of Education, University of Birmingham, UK. Her research focuses primarily on modernist women's writing and she has published on Virginia Woolf (including *Gifts, Markets and Economies of Desire in Virginia Woolf* [Palgrave, 2008]), H.D. and Katherine Mansfield. Her research interests also include contemporary writers, such as Jeanette Winterson, Sarah Waters and David Mitchell. She is reviews editor for the new journal, *Katherine Mansfield Studies: The Journal of the Katherine Mansfield Society*.

William Stephenson is Senior Lecturer in English at the University of Chester, UK, specializing in utopianism, science fiction, literary theory and the literature of addiction. He has published two books, *John Fowles's The French Lieutenant's Woman* (Continuum, 2007) and *John Fowles* (Northcote, 2003), as well as essays on J. G. Ballard, Bret Easton Ellis, John Fowles, Alex Garland, William Golding, James Joyce and Irvine Welsh. He has a book chapter and journal article forthcoming on Iain M. Banks and Hunter S. Thompson. He is currently working on a book entitled *Gonzo Republic: Hunter S. Thompson's America* (Continuum, 2012).

Index